— We're thankful for your
part in the making
of our history.

enjoy,
Chris
Bob

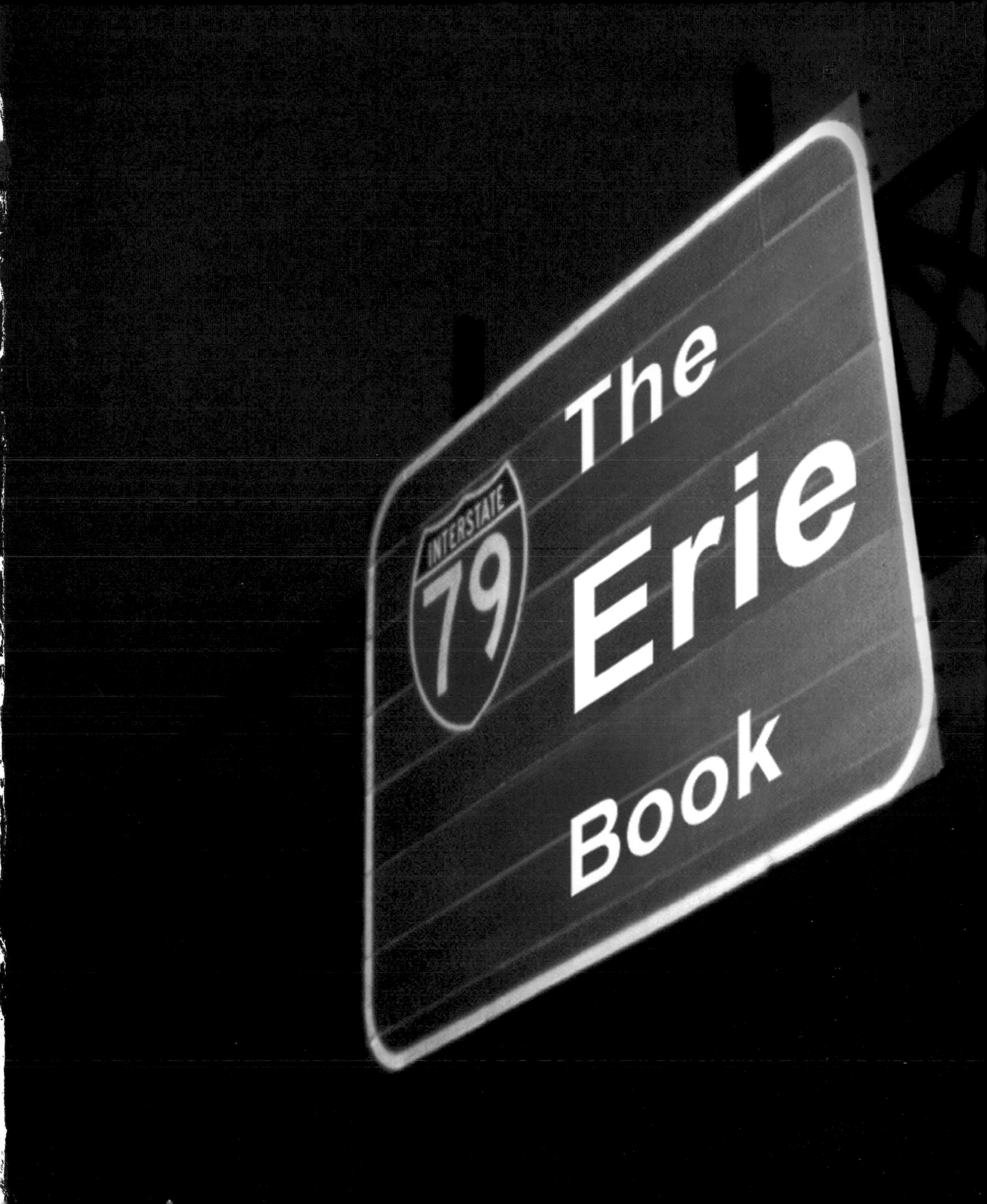
INTERSTATE
79
The
Erie
Book

John Horstman

# The Erie Book

## Community Profiles Edition

Created By

# Matthew D. Walker
## publishing

# PORTRAIT
# OF A CITY

**Matthew D. Walker**
Editor / Publisher

lost. Immigrants came to Erie from around the world to change their lives, build ethnic neighborhoods, and weave their stories into the fabric of the American quilt.

What Erieite doesn't know the success story of Oliver Hazard Perry leading a bunch of Yanks out of Presque Isle Bay to challenge the world's largest navy? But, let's not forget that it was the *Lawrence*, not *Niagara*, that started the day as Perry's flagship and that the Commodore's battle strategy did not exactly run as planned. Things changed. One can easily imagine the twenty-seven year old Perry (no doubt feeling a bit like David going to spar with Goliath) sailing to war, pacing the deck....reviewing his strategy....trimming the sails.....all the while never losing sight of where the wind was blowing, seeing every change as a golden opportunity.

Once again, the winds of change are with us. Not surprisingly, now is an appropriate time to pull out

The only thing that doesn't change is change itself. Today, these words ring true in Erie more than ever. Erie, as this book documents, is no stranger to change. The community's history is packed with change. From its birth as a military outpost, through its formative years as a bustling shipping and railroad port, to a strong industrial manufacturing economy, change prevailed. Fortunes were made and

## SUPPORT LOCAL: *The Community Profiles Edition*

If no characteristic is more defining of a community than its businesses, what book on a city is complete without information about them? After all, they are the very lifeblood of a town. Without them it's time to pack up and move on. This edition of The Erie Book features information on colleges, hospitals, manufacturers, restaurants, financial institutions, retailers, attorneys, doctors, hotels, even an auctioneer. They are the businesses that make Erie work. They provide a reason to get up on Monday morning and they dole out the paychecks on Friday. They define how we dress, what we eat, how we are educated, what we drive, even where we are born and buried. The businesses in this book support Erie. Support them back. Buy a house from the woman on page 234. Buy a car from the men on page 124. Listen to the stations on page 253. Support local music, art, dance, theater, sports, and businesses everywhere all the time.

the charts and mark our place in history. Things are changing. There are so many great things happening around town. Thanks to a shared vision and the dedication of many community leaders, the face of Erie's bayfront is being completely rejuvenated. Summit Township which not long ago was farmland has become a retail mecca. Education is thriving. All the while, the region's greatest resources, Lake Erie and Presque Isle, haven't gone anywhere. Then again, some things never change.

If the old adage, *"a picture is worth a thousand words"* is true, then surely the hundreds of images in this book speak volumes. Put together they form a more revealing image of where Erie is today. That is what the purpose of this book is: *To document this moment in time, for us now, and for those in the future.*

This book is a snapshot of our community at the dawn of the 21st century - with a glance off the stern to see where we've been - and perhaps a guess at what the waters ahead will bring. While the winds of change beckon, Erie stands at the ready, remembering the simple and effective command Perry gave that morning.

On behalf of Erie, Mayor Richard F. Filippi accepts an Outstanding Achievement award which was given by the U.S. Conference of Mayors for the City Livability Awards Program. It was presented by Pennsylvania Governor Ed Rendell at Celebrate Erie.

# ALSO AVAILABLE

## Presque Isle State Park
### A Scenic Tour of The Peninsula

**By Matthew Walker**
**Foreword By Tom Ridge**

This is the only book of its kind on Presque Isle State Park. Incorporating images from 55 top regional artists, photography and painting abound in this educational volume. Presque Isle, one of America's most popular state parks, has unique natural features which are made evident throughout. Text ranges from one-line captions to short essays.

- Finished Size 9 x12
- Hardcover with Dust Jacket
- 112 Pages - 100lbs. Coated Paper
- Breathtaking Artwork
- Full Color Maps
- Presque Isle History
- Science and Nature Studies
- Over 200 Full Color Images

PRESQUE ISLE
State Park

A Scenic Tour of the Peninsula

Matthew Walker
*foreword by* Gov. Tom Ridge

Louis Colussi

Ed Bernik

# Lores & Legends
## of old Erieland

### 1. Stuck in Erie
Many U.S. presidents have visited Erie, but none had such a memorable stay as William H. Taft. Rumor has it that during one of Taft's frequent visits to The Strong Mansion, he got stuck in the bathtub. As the story goes, the hefty president, weighing in at over 300 pounds had to be helped from the tub by the fire department.

### 2. Bubble Bubble Toil and Trouble
When the body of General "Mad" Anthony Wayne was to be moved from his original Erie grave to a family plot in Chester County, a local doctor cut and boiled the flesh from his bones to facilitate the transportation. The flesh was then reburied in the grave, and the bones taken by carriage to their new gravesite.

### 3. Go if You Dare, But Watch Your Neck
Axe Murder Hollow, off of Thomas Road in Millcreek Township has long been a favorite "haunt" of local teens. It is there that a farmer Is said to have hacked his wife and family to death with an axe.

### 4. Hey Big Spender
After finding oil on his farm, "Coal Oil Johnny" carried out an outlandish spending spree. He was once reported to buy a hotel on the spot when its manager complained that Johnny's party was too loud.

### 5. Smartie Artie
Mathematician, Artemis Martin, was distinguished in the world of academia for his self-published newsletter, *Mathematical Visitor*. He lived quietly in Erie as a humble gardener.

### 6. Erie's Big Shot
Erieite James Gibbons was the first Yankee soldier to fire a shot for the north in the Civil War at Fort Sumter on April 12, 1861. Serving under Captain Doubleday, Gibbons pulled the lanyard of Doubleday's gun when his commander yelled, "Fire!" The rest is history.

### 7. Dig This
In order to clear all of the tree stumps, while building early Erie roads, a city ordinance required that each man spend Saturday mornings digging up tree stumps. Another law dictated that anyone guilty of public drunkeness was required to dig up three stumps from the streets. A section of Erie was known as "Stumptown".

**John Buffington**

## PUBLISHER • EDITOR • DESIGNER
Matthew D. Walker

## ADDITIONAL WRITERS
Doug Campbell
Ellen Cohen
Jule Gardner
Dev Jana
Ben Johnson
Gary Joseph
Eric LaPrice
Christine McCammon Palattella
Aimee Nicolia
Scott Wesman

*with essays by*
Robert H. Allshouse
Mary Amthor
Suzanne Dandrea Sitzler
Rupert Stadtmiller
Erik Walker

## PHOTOGRAPHERS
Art Becker
Ed Bernik
Doug Campbell
Alan Chaffee
Ronald Cocke
Bob Hagle
John Horstman
Dev Jana
Denise Keim
Rick Klein
Eric LaPrice
Rob Ruby
Sam Stull

Ed Bernik

## WHO IS THIS BOOK FOR?

### ▸ FOR THE ERIEITE
Whether you have lived in Erie for your entire life or grew up in Erie and moved away, you will enjoy this book. These pages are filled with people and places that you are familiar with, plus more than a few that may be new to you. Erie natives and Erie expatriates alike will enjoy this book as a gift.

### ▸ FOR THE ERIE VISITOR
This book is also written for the person who is new to Erie. With basic information such as location and weather, you will learn the "ins and outs" of the City. If you are visiting the area for the first time or if you have a friend or relative out of town that you would like to show Erie to, this book makes a great tourguide.

### ▸ FOR BUSINESSES
As an information and networking guide, this book will help you make new business contacts in Erie County. Businesses may also use this book as a sales and marketing tool to promote the region to their clients.

### ▸ FOR THE FUTURE
If you are lucky, someone in the distant past – way back at the turn of the millennium – saved a copy of this book for future generations (like you) to enjoy. This book is a brief image of the "state-of-the-city" in the early 2000s. I imagine some things have changed.

## NO BOUNDARIES

It should be noted that this book is not called **The Erie City Book**. Why? Because, anyone who is from Erie knows that while the City of Erie boundary lines are at Pittsburgh Avenue, West Grandview Blvd., etc., not including Millcreek, Summit Township, Harborcreek, and other close boroughs would be silly. They are all integral to the identity of the community.

This is also not called **The Erie County Book**. Simply because the focus is much more on the Erie metropolitan area than anywhere else. But rest assured that other areas of the County have not been ignored. Enjoy looking through this book and come up with your own boundaries if you'd like.

Roy Ahlgren

**All books are a collaboration of efforts – this book is certainly no exception. Gratitude and acknowledgements are due to all of those who helped to put the pieces of this puzzle together. I am in their debt. Thank you. I have no doubt overlooked some names and I appreciate your understanding. Thank you twice as much.**

Most who contributed writing, design, editing, photography, and original artwork are listed on the credits page. All of them were patient, creative, encouraging, and helpful. Needless to say, this book would not have been possible without them. **Jacki Spiegel** was particularly instrumental for this Community Profiles Edition in the face of insurmountable odds and deadlines; patiently faxing, photocopying, calling, coordinating, and reminding. Going above and beyond to help someone else's vision, **Dev Jana** helped with nearly every aspect of this book and **John Horstman** was quick to lend a hand at any moment's notice. They are all encouraging, creative, and good friends. Thanks. **Rupert** and **Marilynn Stadtmiller** both helped with proofreading, writing, editing and constructive criticism - all well received. Periodically, design comments and assistance came from **Shelle Barron**, **Otis James**, **Mike Kraus MAK Design**, and **Mike Smith**. The **Erie County Historical Society and Museums** staff was particularly helpful in finding the right images to unlock Erie's past. **Annita Andrick** is due particular thanks for sharing her patience and knowledge. Other members of the ECHS&M staff including **Stephany Taylor** and **Melinda Meyer** continue to be very helpful to me. My friend **John Buffington** has flown me over Erie in his Cub several times to get a different perspective. Thanks for landing safely, John. **Anita Smith** at The Gannon Archives found some useful historic images. **Jennifer** and **John Laird** shared maps of old Erieland. **Steve Brown** and **Digital Alchemy**, were particularly helpful in production and patient in seeing this go to print. Also **Bud** and **Pete** at **Green Tree Press** in Erie should be acknowledged for their expert advice. **Bill Pysh**, **Mark Weber**, **John Mir**, **Buddy Stark**, **Jeff Kidder**, **Tom Camillo**, and **Tom DiBello** all read and commented on text. Additional help and inspiration came in various forms from **The Berean Bible Church**, **Blasco Memorial Library** staff, **Erie Times News, The news photographers of WSEE, Nancy Blakely, Michael Boetger, Patty Brown, Dan Berke, Almi Clerkin, Emily Conoway, Heather Dana, Lucia Dombrowski, Judy Husted, John Hyatt, Amy Kuzzola-Kern, Michael Lavery, John Leemhuis, Stacey Manz, Kathy Merski, Mariam Mir, One World Tribe, Kasha Otulakowski, Paul Perowicz, Don Prischak, David Pysh, Ron Raimondi, Sandra Brydon Smith, Doug Reider, Loring Sumner, Mick Stepnoski, Elly Vahey, David VanAmburg, John Vanco, Jim Welle, Casey Wells, Jim Coviello** & **Sally Walker**, **Aimee** & **Ray Nicolia**, **Bob** & **Gloria Walker**, **Erik Walker**. (last and most) **Rebecca Elizabeth Downing**.

"Erie: a name that has great share in American glory;
may this town ever enjoy a proportionate share in
American Prosperity and Happiness."
- General La Fayette

Erie is located in the northeastern United States in the Commonwealth of Pennsylvania.

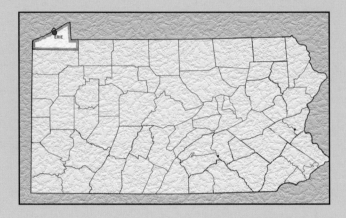

The city of Erie is located in Erie County which is Pennsylvania's northwestern most county. Erie County makes up 514,484.1965 acres (803.88 square miles) of northwestern Pennsylvania.

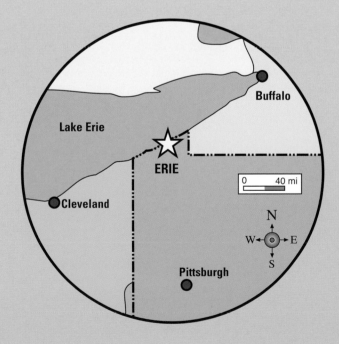

Major American cities which are close to Erie include Pittsburgh, Pennsylvania (125 miles south), Buffalo, New York (106 miles northeast), and Cleveland, Ohio (99 miles west).

## A CITY ON THE BAY

Erie is the only city in Pennsylvania located on two major bodies of water: Lake Erie and Presque Isle Bay. Much of the shoreline borders Presque Isle Bay which gives Erie the nickname "The Bay City". Shown above is the Bicentennial Tower, at the foot of State Street which divides the city east and west.

## GETTING THERE

Major arteries which run into the city include I-90 from the east and west, and I-79 from the south.

**Photos: John Buffington**

23

# ERIE COUNTY

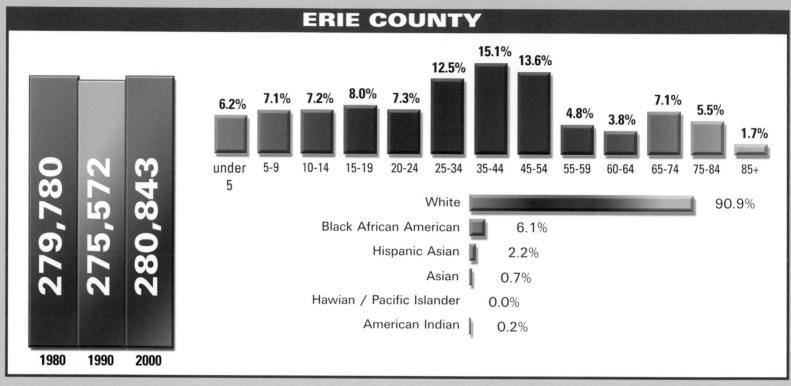

279,780    275,572    280,843

1980    1990    2000

| under 5 | 5-9 | 10-14 | 15-19 | 20-24 | 25-34 | 35-44 | 45-54 | 55-59 | 60-64 | 65-74 | 75-84 | 85+ |
|---|---|---|---|---|---|---|---|---|---|---|---|---|
| 6.2% | 7.1% | 7.2% | 8.0% | 7.3% | 12.5% | 15.1% | 13.6% | 4.8% | 3.8% | 7.1% | 5.5% | 1.7% |

White — 90.9%
Black African American — 6.1%
Hispanic Asian — 2.2%
Asian — 0.7%
Hawian / Pacific Islander — 0.0%
American Indian — 0.2%

# CITY OF ERIE

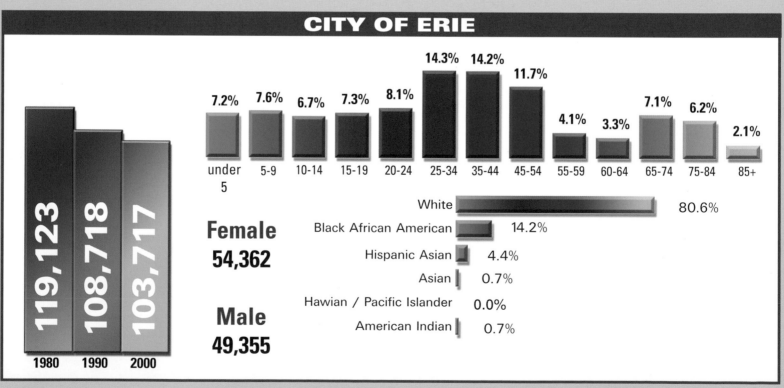

119,123    108,718    103,717

1980    1990    2000

| under 5 | 5-9 | 10-14 | 15-19 | 20-24 | 25-34 | 35-44 | 45-54 | 55-59 | 60-64 | 65-74 | 75-84 | 85+ |
|---|---|---|---|---|---|---|---|---|---|---|---|---|
| 7.2% | 7.6% | 6.7% | 7.3% | 8.1% | 14.3% | 14.2% | 11.7% | 4.1% | 3.3% | 7.1% | 6.2% | 2.1% |

**Female 54,362**

**Male 49,355**

White — 80.6%
Black African American — 14.2%
Hispanic Asian — 4.4%
Asian — 0.7%
Hawian / Pacific Islander — 0.0%
American Indian — 0.7%

Source: U.S. 2000 Census Data

24

# ERIE COUNTY POPULATION 1980 - 2000

| | 1980 | 1990 | 2000 | CHANGE |
|---|---|---|---|---|
| Pennsylvania | 1,863,895 | 11,881,646 | 12,281,054 | 3.5 % |
| Erie County | 279,780 | 275,572 | 280,843 | .4 % |
| Albion Borough | 1,818 | 1,575 | 1,607 | -11.6 % |
| Amity Township | 1,098 | 1,034 | 1,140 | 3.8 % |
| Concord Township | 1,434 | 1,384 | 1,361 | -5.1 % |
| Conneaut Township[1] | 1,893 | 1,938 | 3,908 | 106% |
| Corry City | 7,149 | 7,216 | 6,834 | 4.4 % |
| Cranesville Borough | 703 | 598 | 600 | - 14.7 % |
| Edinboro Borough | 6,324 | 7,736 | 6,950 | 9.9 % |
| Elgin Borough | 235 | 229 | 236 | .4 % |
| Elk Creek Township | 1,775 | 1,738 | 1,800 | 1.4 % |
| Erie City | 119,123 | 108,718 | 103,717 | -12.9 % |
| Fairview Borough[2] | 1,855 | 1,988 | 0 | NA |
| Fairview Township[2] | 7,518 | 7,839 | 10,140 | 8.2 % |
| Franklin Township | 1,301 | 1,429 | 1,609 | 23.7 % |
| Girard Borough | 2,615 | 2,879 | 3,164 | 21.0 % |
| Girard Township | 4,306 | 4,722 | 5,133 | 19.2 % |
| Greene Township | 5,238 | 4,959 | 4,768 | -9.0% |
| Greenfield Township | 1,677 | 1,770 | 1,909 | 13.8% |
| Harborcreek Township | 14,644 | 15,108 | 15,178 | 3.6% |
| Lake City Borough | 2,384 | 2,519 | 2,811 | 17.9 % |
| Lawrece Park Township | 4,548 | 4,310 | 4,048 | -11.7 % |
| LeBoeuf Township | 1,500 | 1,521 | 1,680 | 12.0 % |
| McKean Borough | 465 | 418 | 389 | 16.3 % |
| McKean Township | 4,047 | 4,503 | 4,619 | 14.1% |
| Mill Village Borough | 427 | 429 | 412 | -3.5 % |
| Millcreek Township | 44,303 | 46,820 | 52,129 | 17.7 % |
| North East Borough | 4,568 | 4,617 | 4,601 | .7 % |
| North East Township | 5,750 | 6,283 | 7,702 | 33.9 % |
| Platea Borough | 492 | 467 | 474 | - 3.7 % |
| Springfield Township | 3,395 | 3,218 | 3,378 | -0.5 % |
| Summit Township | 5,381 | 5,284 | 5,529 | 2.8 % |
| Union Township | 1,779 | 1,735 | 1,663 | -6.5% |
| Union City Borough | 3,623 | 3,537 | 3,463 | -4.4 % |
| Venango Township | 2,089 | 2,235 | 2,227 | 9.0 % |
| Washington Township | 3,567 | 4,102 | 4,526 | 26.9 % |
| Waterford Borough | 1,568 | 1,492 | 1,449 | -7.6% |
| Waterford Township | 2,874 | 3,402 | 3,878 | 34.9 % |
| Wattsburg Borough | 513 | 486 | 378 | -26.3 % |
| Wayne Township | 1,767 | 1,679 | 1,766 | - 0.1 % |
| Wesleyville Borough | 3,998 | 3,655 | 3,617 | -9.5 % |

1- Conneaut Township 2000 population includes approximately 1,885 persons at the Albion State Correctional Institution
2- Fairview Borough was consolidated with Fairview Township in 1998

Source: U.S. 2000 Census Data

Population & Demographics

BOB HAGLE

**SETH AND HANNAH REED SPENT THEIR FIRST NIGHT IN THE REGION CAMPED ON PRESQUE ISLE.**

# Birth of a City

## Erie's Early History
## 1615–1895

**BY ERIK WALKER**

*Almost twenty years to the day after fighting the British at the Battle of Bunker Hill, Colonel Seth Reed dragged his small sailboat up onto the sands of Presqu' Isle. His wife and two children had bravely accompanied him to this frontier – a place so removed from the cultured cities of Europe and the burgeoning settlements of America's eastern states that it could rightly be called the edge of the known world.*

*That evening the family slept by a small fire, no doubt in fear that hostile Indians could erupt from the forest at any moment. Ironically, just across the bay on a bluff which would later become Parade Street in Erie, Pennsylvania, a few American soldiers looked out and, seeing the fire, concluded that some Indians must be hunkering down on the peninsula readying for a brutal attack. The soldiers rowed out in the morning to investigate, and one can easily guess how relieved both parties must have been to discover each other.*

*Thus arrived the first "official" settlers to Erie, Pennsylvania on July 1, 1795. In many ways, though, these first settlers were simply playing their role in a story that had begun hundreds of years earlier....*

RICH NATURAL RESOURCES, INCLUDING TIMBER AND WATER, MADE THE REGION QUITE DESIRABLE.

JOHN HORSTMAN

# A Wilderness in Dispute

Erie is, of course, named for the Eriez Indians who lived along the southern shore of the lake that now bears their name and used the immediate locale as favored hunting and fishing grounds. Little is known of the Eriez, since they had no written language and only brief encounters with Europeans. In 1615, Joseph LeCaron lead a group of French missionaries into the area, but he met with little success in converting the natives to the Catholic faith. Eleven years later, the Jesuits tried their luck by sending Father D'Allyon to visit the Eriez villages, but he could do no better. With the exception of scant written records of these missionaries, the little we know of the Eriez has been revealed only through archeological excavation and oral history.

Tradition holds that this indigenous tribe was led by Queen Yagowanea, a North American Athena of sorts, who was renowned far and wide for her wisdom and fairness. When disputes arose amongst the Eriez– or even between other tribes – she was called upon to mediate and dispense her wisdom. Her people were fierce warriors, but they preferred instead to cultivate their status as a "neutral nation", acting as a buffer between the Iroquois alliance to the east and the Wyandots and Hurons to the west. Legend has it that when Yagowanea took sides in a dispute involving the murder of a Mississaguan Indian, the Seneca Nation became so enraged that they took up arms against the Eriez and eventually exterminated the noble tribe. While the historical veracity of this tale is questioned by modern scholars, it is undoubtedly true that the Senecas had virtually displaced the Eriez by 1654. Though the Senecas claimed title to the land, they did not occupy it. In reality, the land reverted to wilderness for the next one hundred years, slowly erasing footprints and village-sites of the previous inhabitants.

## TWO WORLD POWERS COLLIDE AT PRESQU' ISLE

The strategic geographical importance of Northwestern Pennsylvania was recognized early on by both the French Canadians and the British colonists. By the 1750's, the two great European powers were embroiled in a virtual world war, and one small but significant facet of the conflict centered around land claims to the Great Lakes and the Mississippi River Valley. During the previous century, a myriad of French explorers had mapped these lands and claimed them for France. Yet the official charters that created the British colonies on the Eastern seaboard typically used language like "from sea to sea", giving England claim to these very same lands. The wilderness of northwestern Pennsylvania would figure prominently in the resolution of this inherent dispute.

The French acted first in 1753 when Canadian Governor Duquesne dispatched an expedition under Sieur de Marin with explicit instructions to build three forts to protect the portage between Lake Erie and the Ohio River drainage. Previous expeditions had shown that the French could proceed up the St. Lawrence into the Great Lakes, and that by "portaging" (carrying their canoes and equipment over land) from what is now Barcelona, New York to Lake Chautauqua, they could access a waterway that would eventually drain into the Mississippi. This portage was literally the keystone between the St. Lawrence and the Mississippi – an all important link in the chain between the French cities of Montreal and New Orleans. Fortification of the route was imperative.

Just as Marin arrived at the site of the original portage, he received a communication from the Governor, urging him to travel further down

**GEORGE WASHINGTON**

**CHIEF PONTIAC**

the lake shore to a site that an unnamed "famous voyageur" had assured him would be an ideal harbor "where there is the best hunting, fishing, fertile land, immense meadows to feed and raise cattle, where Indian corn grows with unequalled abundance so that it need only be sown." That place, of course, was Presqu' Isle. Marin proceeded as directed, and, by August 1753, he could report to the Governor that a fort at Presqu' Isle had been completed, that a road to Lake LeBoeuf (Waterford) had been constructed, and that a fort at Le Boeuf was under way.

The Governor of Virginia, Robert Dinwiddie, heard about the French expedition and, seeing it as an intrusion into lands rightfully belonging to England, resolved to send a formal message to the interlopers to cease and desist. He chose for his official messenger a twenty-one year old surveyor named George Washington, who set out on Halloween with a small group of men and battled through early mountain snowstorms to arrive at Fort LeBoeuf on December 11, 1753. Washington was well received by the commander of the fort as he delivered Dinwiddie's letter. The French politely thanked him but issued a written response indicating that they intended to fulfill their orders and stay. When Washington returned to Virginia, he published his journals of the account of this, his first public commission. The journals were widely distributed throughout England and the Colonies, thrusting Washington into the public consciousness. The rest, as they say, is history.

As promised, the British spent the next six years (1753-59), endeavoring to attack and ultimately seize many of the forts constructed by the French. In 1759 the French were forced to abandon Fort Presqu' Isle, burning it to the ground as they left. The following year the British rebuilt the fort on the same site, seeming to claim this new frontier as their own. But they had not reckoned on the Indians.

## THE INDIANS RETALIATE

In 1763, the persuasive leader of the Ottawa Nation, Chief Pontiac, masterfully assembled an enormous coalition of Indian tribes including the Six Nations of the Iroquois. In one sweeping offensive, they simultaneously attacked British forts throughout the Great Lakes and the Ohio Valley. On June 15, Presqu' Isle fell, and LeBoeuf followed just two days later. The immediate area reverted to Indian control.

The British eventually quelled the uprising and retook many of the forts that had fallen; but troubles with the insurgent colonists on the Eastern seaboard turned British attention away from rebuilding anything in the region of Presque Isle. For the next three decades, while the East was enveloped in outrage, rebellion and, ultimately, war, the area was strangely quiet again and devoid of any European settlement.

BEACON LIGHT

VIEW OF PRESQUE ISLE BAY,

ERIE CITY & HAR...

ERIE CITY PENNA.

Published by Everts, Ensign & Everts,
716 Filbert St. Phila

BEACON BEACH

*Goist, Del. Warren, O.*

# Setting the Stage for Settlement

After the necessary distractions of the Revolutionary War, Americans again began looking to the West to satiate their hunger for land. Both the United States government and the Pennsylvania legislature sought to encourage this expansion, but the omnipresent specter of Anglo-American settlers being scalped by hostile natives was keeping most folks on the Eastern side of the Appalachians. The various governments sought to combat this fear in three distinct ways: first of all, they recognized that they needed to use the military to make the area secure for settlement; secondly, they needed to begin the process of surveying, and distributing land and physically laying out cities; finally, they reasoned, actual settlers would begin the process of moving westward, settling land, and putting down roots.

## MAD ANTHONY WAYNE

Historians today debate the degree to which reports of Indian raids on frontier settlements were exaggerated in frequency and brutality. However, one can safely say that the perception of danger was widespread, and, in a very real sense, was suppressing the willingness of families to move westward.  At the same time, the nascent sense of what would later be called "manifest destiny" was already setting up an inevitable conflict with the Indians who simply wanted to keep their homelands.  Through the prism of history, we now universally regard this as a tragedy; at the time, though, it was equally universally regarded as a threat.

To combat the threat, the newly-created Federal Government enlisted the help of General "Mad" Anthony Wayne, a Revolutionary sidekick to George Washington, to spearhead an ultimately successful series of military expeditions against the Northwest Indians.  The campaign, which began in 1792, was fought throughout the Ohio Valley, culminating in the Indians' defeat at the Battle of Fallen Timbers in August of 1794.  The treaty of Greenville, signed the following year, ceded vast lands north of the Ohio River to the United States.  Mad Anthony had finally made the area safe for settlement.

General Wayne left an even more indelible mark on Erie, Pennsylvania when he chanced to die at Fort Presque Isle on December 15, 1796 while quartered there.  Honoring his dying request, he was buried beneath the flagstaff on a knoll overlooking Erie's bay.  Thirteen years later, his son decided to move the body to the family burial plot in Radnor, Pennsylvania.  The body was exhumed and found to be in a remarkable state of preservation– making it much too heavy (and ripe) to withstand cart travel across the state.  In a gruesome moment that would become the stuff of legends, it was decided to boil the body in a great vat to render the flesh from the bones which were taken to Radnor; the flesh was reinterred beneath the flagstaff; and the debate continues to this day as to where the ghost of Mad Anthony Wayne resides.

## THE ERIE TRIANGLE

During the time that Wayne was fighting the Indians, the Pennsylvania legislature had begun to prime the pump for settlement by setting up a "Donation District" in Northwestern Pennsylvania that would be used to pay Revolutionary soldiers for their service with grants of land.  In reality though, land speculators, including the newly-formed Pennsylvania Population Company, wasted no time in gobbling up these parcels at bargain prices, temporarily thwarting the government's goal of populating this frontier with able-bodied veterans.

It was always obvious to the Pennsylvania legislature that a port on the Great Lakes would be an enormous strategic benefit.  The problem was that New York, Connecticut, and Massachusetts all

**GENERAL "MAD" ANTHONY WAYNE**

**THE ERIE TRIANGLE**

**EARLY SETTLERS MADE USE OF THE LAND'S RESOURCES FOR MANY PURPOSES.**

claimed what was called the "Erie Triangle". Ultimately, the Federal Government interceded, the various states withdrew their claims to the land, and, in 1792 the state of Pennsylvania bought the land for $151,640.25. Officials immediately appointed Thomas Rees to survey the land. For two years, he tried to fulfill his commission but was repeatedly repelled by tomahawk-wielding Indians.

By 1794, as Mad Anthony Wayne was busy defeating the Indians at the Battle of Fallen Timbers, Rees was joined by fellow surveyors Andrew Ellicott and General William Irvine under the protection of the Allegheny Brigade of the State Militia. The following year, Rees was finally able to begin surveying and selling land while Ellicott and Irvine began laying out the town of Erie.

## LAYING OUT A TOWN

An Act of the Pennsylvania legislature provided that Erie be laid out in three districts, each roughly one mile square. The districts ran from the bay front to 12th Street, with the first district between Parade and Chestnut, the second between Chestnut and Cranberry, and the third between Cranberry and West Streets. Each district was to include a park for public use; they can be recognized today as Perry Square, Gridley Park, and Frontier Park. The east-west roads were to be numbered and layed out at twenty rods (330 ft) apart. The north-south roads to the west of State Street would be named after trees. Those to the east would be named after nationalities.

Land was reserved on the Peninsula and at the harbor front for the Federal Government to erect forts and construct harbor facilities. The remaining land was surveyed in lots no larger than 1/3 acre, with "out-lots" of up to 5 acres in the area between 12th and 26th Streets.

## THE SETTLERS ARRIVE

Like a trickle, and then a tide, hardy pioneers began to cross the mountains and make their way to this wilderness outpost. The first to "officially" put down roots were Seth Reed with his wife and two children. Another early settler was surveyor Rees, who so fell in love with the place that he opted to stay. But it was his successor as agent for the Pennsylvania Population Company, Judah Colt, who was most instrumental in turning Erie into a true settlement. He surveyed and sold land, built roads, and set up a thriving provisioning business, selling everything from muskets to seed corn.

Settlers continued to come, secure in the promise that with an ax, a horse, and some hard work, they could cash in on the dream of real land wealth in this Western frontier. By the dawn of the nineteenth century there were eighty-one souls living in Erie, ready to capitalize on the town's location as a safe harbor and a critical point on the portage between the Great Lakes and the Ohio River Valley.

# The Work of a Town

Early on it was clear that Erie's position between the Ohio River drainage and the Great Lakes would make it an essential shipping and transportation center. The first trade to be economically significant was the salt trade. Salt, important enough to be considered the veritable currency of the day, was delivered in barrels by small boats coming down Lake Erie from Buffalo. At Erie, they were offloaded by teamsters, who began the arduous task of hauling them to Waterford. The road to Waterford was little better than the footpath that had been constructed by French troops in 1753, and the teamsters' ox-driven carts were often hopelessly bogged down in mud. The portage to travel the fifteen mile road typically took four days.

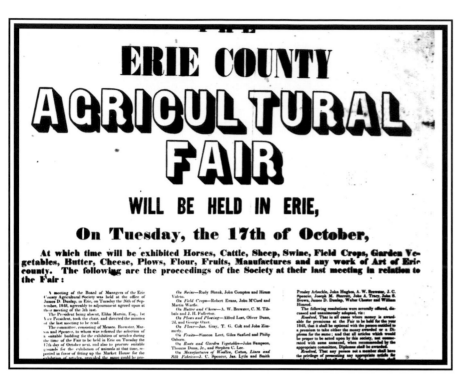

From Waterford, the salt boats continued down the Allegheny to Pittsburgh and points along the Ohio. The teamsters often returned to Erie laden with beef, pork, whiskey, flour, and grain headed for the Great Lakes communities. The salt trade sprouted many additional industries, including shipbuilding. The first commercial vessel to be built in Erie was the *Washington*, constructed near Four-Mile Creek and launched in 1798. The following year, Rufus Reed (the son of the first settler and tavern owner Seth Reed) built the *Good Intent* – a ship destined to sink seven years later but not before launching Reed into a shipping empire that would last well into the next century while making him fabulously wealthy.

Erie was not just a way station between other cities though; in fact, many homegrown industries sprung up to become the town's first exporters. One of the first was the sawmill built by Thomas Foster. In short order, streams throughout Erie County were powering sawmills that helped to harvest old-growth timber to be supplied to the shipbuilders of the Great Lakes. Much of the lumber was also used to build the houses of the burgeoning population of Erie.

The vast majority of early settlers were subsistence farmers and homesteaders who eked a living out of the ground. Like the Eriez Indians a century earlier, these farmers found the land ideally suited for growing corn and grains – and, in many instances, the flour from these grains was exported from Erie County.

Support industries fared extremely well during this era, and by 1810 the young town was populated with 400 stalwarts including blacksmiths, carpenters, brickmakers, tavernkeepers and provisioners.

**THE AGE OF STEAM**

The War of 1812 brought a rowdy bunch of soldiers, sailors and shipbuilders to Erie to assist in the construction of Admiral Perry's fleet. They brought to Erie a cosmopolitan feel, with sailors hailing from many-a-port'o'call, including a large number of freed slaves. Their expert work in constructing a fleet and in defeating the British Navy helped put little Erie on the map as a leading shipbuilding center. In fact, Erie was so widely regarded as the gateway to the west that the famous French dignitary Lafayette visited the town of 1000 people in 1825.

In 1826, Erie led the way into to Age of Steam by launching the *William Penn*, a massive 200 ton steamboat to ply the waters of Lake Erie on behalf of Rufus Reed's "Lake Erie Steamboat Line". Reed's company would become known throughout the Great Lakes as one of the foremost shipping lines.

At the time, Erie did not have sufficient harbor facilities to support the greater size and demands of steamships. The city government on several occasions endeavored to begin construction of a "public dock", but the plans never came to fruition. Reed took matters into his own hands and constructed a private shipping dock at the foot of Sassafras. For years, all ships coming into the bay were required to come to this dock.

In 1833, Hinckley, Jarvis, and Company constructed the first foundry in Erie, smelting iron ore for use regionally. For the next century, Erie would be at the forefront of the iron and steel industry, manufacturing stoves, furnaces, cooking implements, and machinery. Not surprisingly, the iron industry met the shipping industry early on in Erie when the *USS Michigan* (later named the *Wolverine*) was constructed in 1843, making it the first iron hull on the Great Lakes.

Twenty years before the onset of the Civil War, an all-important political rally held in Erie helped to cement the city's reputation as a foundry town. As Democratic President Martin Van Buren squared off against Whig challenger William Henry Harrison, competing rallies were scheduled in Erie. Supporters came from far and wide for the Frontier Convention, with an astounding 80,000 visitors to the city of less than 3500 people. The Presque Isle Foundry took advantage of the large crowds to showcase the iron plows and stoves that they were manufacturing; and the visitors eagerly bought every unit and placed orders for new merchandise. Harrison eventually won the election, only to die soon after of pneumonia contracted at his inauguration. But his vice-president and successor, John Tyler, made sure to reward Erie by giving Presque Isle Foundry a massive government contract to manufacture heavy artillery shot.

## THE AGE OF CANALS

In 1825, New York State completed the Erie Canal (which did not come to Erie, Pennsylvania) making it possible to travel from Buffalo to Albany entirely by water. Pennsylvanians looking north readily latched onto the idea of duplicating the feat by connecting Harrisburg to Pittsburgh, and, ultimately, to Erie, with a canal system.  The project was begun immediately, but by 1839 had stalled outside of New Castle.

The start of the construction on the canal did, however, light a fire under Erie's government to begin construction of a public dock.  They reasoned correctly that the increase in boat traffic would require world class facilities to accommodate trade.  In 1833, carpenter John Justice was hired by the town to construct a dock, which ended up being a 1500 foot extension of State Street to a water depth of twelve feet.  The dock, dubbed "Steamship Landing", included seawalls from the Reed Dock at the foot of Sassafras over to the French Street landing.

With or without the canal, the dock had an immediate effect on commerce in the city, and steamships along the Great Lakes made the

**A VESSEL MOVING THROUGH THE CHANNEL BETWEEN LAKE ERIE AND PRESQUE ISLE BAY.**

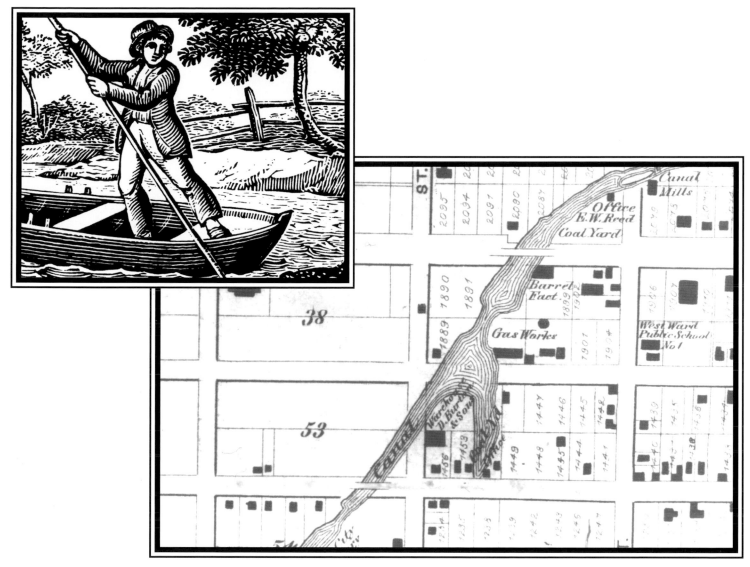

**ALTHOUGH THE ERIE CANAL DID NOT COME TO ERIE, THE ERIE EXTENSION CANAL DID.**

harbor a regular stop on their routes. By 1842, the state had all but abandoned the idea of completing the canal system. Wealthy Erieites, including the Reed family, agreed to complete the canal in exchange for ownership of the already constructed sections. The state readily conceded, and the "Erie Extension" was completed by 1844. On a cold December day of that year, the *Queen of the West* arrived with much fanfare, becoming the first canal boat to complete the journey to the foot of Sassafras.

The optimism of that December day was quickly supplanted, however, by the emerging reality that the future of transportation lay not in canals, but in the mighty railroads. The state had spent millions of dollars and two decades completing the canal, but, by the 1850's, the system was already in disrepair and was auctioned off to the Pennsylvania Railroad Company.

## FISHING

From the time of the earliest settlement in Erie, fishing was an important source of sustenance and commerce. Expert Native American fishermen plied the waters of Presque Isle Bay and Lake Erie with hook-and-line, angling for the bountiful herring and whitefish that they eagerly traded with the first settlers.

Historians trace the beginnings of commercial fishing in Erie to the turn of the nineteenth century when a free black man named McKinney learned the techniques of the Indians and became the young town's first fishmonger, selling his catch from a pier on the bayfront. When he died in 1815 (he poetically choked on a fishbone) his son-in-law "Bass" Fleming took over the business and expanded it.

In the period between 1830 and 1850, several local fishermen began to set out nets, quietly becoming the first large scale commercial fishermen in Erie. Their hauls were reportedly spectacular, with large whitefish and salmon filling the nets. Fishing from small cat-rigged sailboats, they occasionally pulled in a monster sturgeon, straining both the sails and the fragile nets.

The lake sturgeon, a fish reaching an astonishing length of six feet, was originally thought to be a nuisance fish. In short order, though, fishermen began to extract the roe, which could be salted and shipped to Europe and sold as the delicacy: caviar. Thousands of these magnificent fish were thus processed, and since their flesh was considered to be inedible, their huge carcasses were buried on the peninsula. It wasn't until several decades later that tastes changed sufficiently to create a market for smoked sturgeon, thereby ensuring the species eventual decline.

By the turn of the century, there were more than fifty fishing boats operating from Pennsylvania's shoreline, bringing in about 15 million pounds of fish each year. Erie was widely considered to be the freshwater fishing capital of the world with over 500 men directly employed in the enterprise, and perhaps twice as many in spin-off industries like boatbuilding, shipping, and outfitting.

A visitor to the busy docks at that time could have witnessed the fishermen unloading vast hauls of lake herring, whitefish, sturgeon, and blue pike and would have scarcely imagined that in fifty short years the industry (and the very fish themselves) would be nearly extinct. Overfishing, pollution, and regulations ultimately conspired to make the profession economically challenging. As of this writing, there is one remaining commercial boat fishing from the Pennsylvania shore of Lake Erie.

**BASS FLEMING WAS ONE OF ERIE'S FIRST COMMERCIAL FISHERMEN**

**THE "WAR OR OF THE GAUGES" HAD A GREAT ECONOMIC EFFECT ON DEVELOPMENT OF THE CITY.**

## THE WAR OF THE GAUGES

If canal building in Erie proved to be somewhat of a boondoggle, then Erie's entrance into the Age of Rail was nothing short of a comedy of errors. Problems began when local railroad companies built track from Erie to the New York state line using the largest width (or "gauge") available: six feet. Unfortunately, track coming in from New York and Ohio, was a more standard 4'10". It would seem to be obvious that the track through Erie County ought to have been the same gauge.

Erieites didn't see it that way though. Instead, they found the situation ideal because for so long they had viewed themselves as teamsters and freight handlers. Westward bound freight and passengers would have to be offloaded at the New York line, put onto local trains, and hauled to Ohio where the process would be reversed. Folks from outside Erie, though didn't see things that way, prompting former Erie resident Horace Greeley to write in the New York Herald "Let Erie be avoided until grass grows in her streets" – a plea thankfully less memorable than his notable quote: "Go west young man."

NEWSPAPER ADVERTISEMENT CALLING FOR SUPPORT.

Things came to a head in 1854 and 1855 when the railroads began to change the track size. Furious Erie residents responded by tearing up track and, in several cases, tearing down railroad bridges. People quickly took sides, and, as the railroads put down new track the opposition was often right behind them tearing it up. Vandalism, violence, and boycotts were the order of the day, making Erie the ridicule of much of the rest of the nation.

Eventually, cooler heads prevailed, and Erie began using the more common track gauge. Over the next century, the city was served by five major rail lines. As was the case throughout the rest of the country, rail became the favored form of transportation for both cargo and passengers.

## THE INDUSTRIAL REVOLUTION

At a point precisely in the middle of the nineteenth century, in 1851, Erie was finally chartered a city. The date is an interesting point of demarcation, for one can look at the first half of the century and see a town inextricably tied to shipping while the second half of the century would reveal a city seeking its fortunes in manufacturing. In many ways, of course, this was simply a duplication of what was happening in cities around the country (indeed, the world), but Erieites could take a certain pride in their seamless, successful transition to a manufacturing economy.

Erie was aided greatly by its proximity to the coal fields of Pennsylvania and the Great Lakes region in general. In addition, it enjoyed the growth of a hardworking immigrant population and the entrepreneurship of several leading citizens. The primary industry in Erie was metalworking, and by 1890 fully one in six residents (population: 40,000) were employed in this capacity. The multitude of iron and brass works produced engines, boilers, malleable castings, stoves, and heavy machinery.

The immigrants brought with them a variety of skills, which led to the creation of successful industries. For example, the city became a leading producer of pipe organs and pianos, due in large part to the musicality and craftsmanship of several German residents. The Koehler Brewing Company used old-world techniques to make its famous beer, which it sold far and wide.

By 1895, when Erie celebrated its 100th birthday, one could walk down its paved streets and sidewalks knowing that he or she was in one of our country's most thriving cities: a place where virtually any modern convenience could be made or purchased; a place where a multitude of nationalities coexisted en route to the American Dream; a place immensely prepared for the dawn of a new century. And a place quite unlike the foreboding shoreline that Colonel Seth Reed landed upon just one century before. ❖

**BY THE LATE 1800's, ERIE'S WORK FORCE HAD EVOLVED FROM FARMERS AND FISHERMEN TO SKILLED FACTORY WORKERS.**

# Erie's Ethnic Family

## BY RUPERT STADTMILLER

Although English and Scottish settlers like the Reeds, Judah Colt and Thomas Rees were the first settlers in Erie, the years between 1840 and 1850 produced a large wave of German immigrants. Until the turn of the nineteenth century, German influence was immense in Erie. Germans socialized at clubs like the Erie Maennerchor and the Siebenburger. Erie street signs were printed in German and English. Germans settled mainly in what was South Erie bounded by 18th, 26th, Parade to Cherry. Some had come before the Civil War. Most, however, came during the great German migration of the 1870's.

In those years there was also an Irish neighborhood from Myrtle to Cherry below the Erie Cemetery. Every part of town had different accents. The two big churches were St. John Lutheran and St. Joseph Catholic. German Baptist, Simpson Methodist and a small Chestnut Street Presbyterian church were built in the area.

Erie writer Cliff Taylor claimed that the German people ran most of the grocery stores, meat markets, bars, bakeries and, of course, breweries. It was wicked to drink whiskey in those days but not bad to drink beer. At this time, those of German ancestry also controlled most of the politics of the town.

There must have been some Roman Catholic settlers in Erie around the 1830's because there is a record that Father Phelan in 1827 came here from Butler, Pennsylvania and celebrated mass in the Dickson Tavern. The first permanent German settler was Wolfgang Erhart, a harness maker who came here from Baden, Germany in 1832. Catholic immigrants came from the Palatine and other parts of Germany and the Rhine. The first Roman Catholic Church, St. Mary, was founded in 1837. Father Ivo Levitz, O.F.M. was installed as the first pastor, and the services were in German.

The Great Irish Potato Famine occurred in 1845 and 1846. This calamity forced hundreds of thousands of Irishmen to emigrate to America, and many of them reached Erie. With this increase in the Roman Catholic population, new churches were organized and built; St. Patrick was the second Erie church and St. Joseph the third. Bishop Tobias Mullen had St. Peter Cathedral built debt-free for $273, 567.35.

The first anti-slavery society was formed in 1836. Among its leading members was William Himrod. He established a Sunday School for "colored people" and served as a "station agent" on the underground railroad, harboring slaves in his home at 2nd and French Street until they could be conveyed safely to Canada. Organizations like Booker T. Washington Center aided the black community, especially after World War II.

In the summer of 1864, an Italian musician, named Raeffle Braccinni, came to Erie with a carnival. He took an afternoon off, and decided to go fishing on Presque Isle Bay. The young man fell in love with the city and decided to make his home here, the first record of an immigrant from Italy establishing a residence in Erie. In 1895, there were 300 Italian people living in Erie. Today there are 25,000. Much of the history of the Italian people in Erie centers around St Paul Church, which was organized by its first Pastor, Father Becherini. In 1908, Father Louis Marino was assigned to the parish.

IMMIGRANTS FROM AROUND THE WORLD came to Erie and layed the foundation for an all-American city. At various times Irish, Blacks, Italians, Poles, Jews, and others, have strengthened the mix.

Politically, Italian mayors have dominated recent Erie politics. Mayors Louis Tullio, Joyce Savocchio and Rick Filippi have brought honor and prestige to the Italian Community.

Russian immigration can be divided in to three waves, beginning in 1870 with many settling in the Northeast, mainly New York and Pennsylvania. In Erie, Russians worked on the docks as stevedores. Later, they found work at the Hammermill Paper Works or at General Electric. The Neighborhood House, located at the foot of German Street, was built by the First Presbyterian Church. This facility became the center of social activities for the Russian community.

and continuous lines of Jewish families in Erie. The number of Jews in Erie in the 1850's was sufficient enough for the Anshe Hesed Society to be established.

In his thesis, "The Ethnic Factor In Erie Politics," Dr. William Garvey points out that the ethnic groups in Erie are the cause of extreme, political vigor. The Polish community in the city is a prime example of that vitality. The first wave came to Erie in the 1840's and 1850's in an attempt to gain political freedom. These people were educated professionals who blended well in to the community. In later migrations (1890 - 1920) more Poles came to Erie to join Erie's work force. Polish people were the last group of European immigrants to enter the cycle of ethnic politics in Erie. This factor forced the Polish community to be more close-knit and supportive of themselves through churches and social clubs, such as the Polish Falcons and Polish National Alliance. This community has been the strongest voting block in Erie.

Erie's ethnic groups have strong family ties. Denise Robison, a respected political figure in Erie, stated succinctly, "the most perfect form of social relationships is the family. Family ties are precious." Thus, while Erie is growing and changing, its residents continue to focus on their traditional values of family and friendship; they are forever small-town folks in that regard.

TODAY'S NEW ARRIVALS come to Erie from places like Russia, Africa, Bosnia, Albania, Iraq, Mexico, and Asia. For many, The American dream is still alive. Shown above, dancing at Latino's Restaurant on Parade Street.

From 1860 until 1862, Bernard Baker was a "clothier". His son Isaac continued the business. Beginning with Bernard's arrival in 1850, the Baker family, in six generations, represents one of the oldest

❖

Photos 40–41 : Denise Keim

OLGA ZAYSTEV (left and center) WORKS AT THE INTERNATIONAL INSTITUTE. THE LORYA FAMILY (right) IN FRONT OF THEIR EAST-SIDE HOME.

# A TALE OF TWO WOMEN

**M**any people take their freedom for granted, but not Yolanda Lorya. Before arriving in Erie with her family in 1996, Yolanda suffered through a religious war in her native Sudan, the plight of being a refugee, the death of her husband who was in exile, and a war-related aviation accident that left her severely burned and hospitalized for three years. Yolanda and her family were able to come to Erie thanks to the efforts of her oldest son, Albert, who applied for asylum in the United States after graduating from high school. Albert lived alone in Erie before bringing his family here, and describes that period without friends or family as being extremely difficult. Thankfully, however, the Lorya family has seen years of struggle and hardship turn into good fortune. Albert recently graduated from Penn State Behrend with a degree in plastics engineering, and after five years in the United States, the entire family is undergoing the process of becoming American citizens. One of the major organizations which helps to make this transition easier is the International Institute of Erie.

Located at 517 East 26th street, the Institute helps thousand of refugees and immigrants build new lives by assisting them with everything from answering questions about American culture to filling out impor-

tant immigrant paperwork. Olga Zaystev has a unique perspective on the organization, both as an employee of the Institute and as a Russian immigrant. Olga arrived here with her family in the late 1980s, a strange turn of events for a girl raised in a culture taught to fear and distrust the United States. While growing up in the former Soviet Union, Olga says she never dreamed she would come to America and remembers, "It was difficult to have an opinion of Americans at the time". Raised on the other front of the cold war, Zaystev points out, "Soviet propaganda taught us that American capitalists were the bad guys, but at the same time the media images of the United States made it look like a paradise."

On a not so humorous note, Olga and her family, who were Christians, suffered brutal religious persecution in the Soviet Union. "To be considered a spy meant only that you have a bible," says Olga. Arbitrary prison sentences of twenty-five years to life were not uncommon for Christians, not to mention interrogations, beatings, and threats from the K.G.B. Today, Olga calls North East home. When asked how she keeps herself busy, she retorts, "Eight hours of work, six children, and a husband. It's not hard to stay busy." Sounds like Olga has become a typical American woman.

## PAUL M. LOREI PHOTOGRAPHY

When you hear certain names in Erie, your mind instantly thinks of their business. In Erie, Braendel means painting. Hallman means Chevrolet. And Lorei, of course, means photography. In fact, if you grew up in Erie, odds are good that one or two of your school pictures were taken by a Lorei. Both Paul Lorei Sr. and his brother, John, had quite a business in the 60s and 70s. But when Paul Sr. wasn't busy taking photographs, he was building a family with his wife, Barbara. They had ten children. Son number four, Paul Michael Lorei, has taken to his father's trade but in a different way. He has developed into an excellent family, beach and portrait photographer.

Lorei's office and studio are located in the Jostens building near the Mall where brother Mark practices - you guessed it - photography. Paul's focus is on custom portraits of families, children and weddings, with a flair for the artistic. When you want a portrait that's a little nicer, that's as innovative as it is beautiful, Paul is your choice. With over eighteen years of experience, Lorei says "The best part of this is when we create a stunning portrait and the client loves it so much he or she is moved almost to tears. I say to myself, 'What else would I rather be doing?'"

**PAUL M. LOREI PHOTOGRAPHY**
**5940 SPIRES DRIVE**
**ERIE, PENNSYLVANIA 16509**
**814 868-0888**
**WWW.LOREI.COM**

# 5 *Generations* of *Serving Erie*

## The Story of Burton Funeral Home

Rob Ruhy

Peter J. Burton and Karen Burton Horstman, President and C.F.O. respectively, stand in front of a historic horse-drawn funeral carriage that sits in their 10th and Cherry location. Burton is Erie's premier funeral home.

**B**efore there was much of anything in Erie, there was Burton Funeral Home and, in a way, the story of Erie is the story of the Burton family. Its history dates back to 1811, when David Burton came to Lake Erie to help build Oliver Hazard Perry's famous fleet for the War of 1812. The family settled in the burgeoning community and, in 1876, A.P. Burton - one of David's 10 children — established the first Burton Funeral Home. "They were in the carriage business and had many of them," said current president, Peter Burton. Eventually, the family established

its business and home in what became the heart of the Gannon University neighborhood, 352 W. Eighth St. The Burton family later donated the home to the American Lung Association of Erie, which long hung a plaque there proclaiming the building "The Old Burton Homestead."

Gradually, the family expanded, adding funeral homes and specialized services throughout the Erie County. Today, the family's four funeral homes - in downtown Erie, east Erie, Millcreek, and Girard - are led by Peter Burton and his sister, Karen Burton

**The Burton Family** has been an integral part of Erie since the days of Oliver Hazard Perry. Above, a horse-drawn hearse at The Erie Cemetery in the early 1900s.

Horstman, the fifth generation. Their mission remains largely like the one established by their father, G. David Burton, his father, Donald C. Burton, and the Burtons who have come before: To offer quality funeral services to families from all walks of life, all financial circumstances and all religions, according to their individual wishes.

But the Burton name today is about more than history. It's also about options. For those thinking of cremation, the Burtons, since 1980, operate one of only three crematoriums in Erie County and the only one connected to an established funeral home. They've also added Whispering Pines Cremation Garden, a beautiful, thoughtful place of rest and contemplation located on the grounds of their Wintergreen Funeral Home, 2500 Norcross Road across from Wintergreen Gorge Cemetery. The family can also design cemetery memorials and other markers at their locations of Ericson Memorials, 2117 Chestnut St., West 26th Street and Powell Avenue, and

4940 Koehler Road.

Erie families who trust Burton have come to know the family's more modern traditions. They were the first Erie funeral home to offer pre-planning services. In addition, the family and staff are trained to help families fill out insurance forms, plan estates and understand the stages they'll go through in the loss of someone loved.

For more than 127 years, the Burtons have been taking care of local families in their time of grief. The Burton family - like the community its five generations have lived and worked in - has grown and changed, realizing its future is built on the foundation of its past.

**BURTON FUNERAL HOMES AND CREMATORY INC.**
**G. DAVID BURTON, SUPERVISOR**
**602 WEST 10TH STREET**
**ERIE, PENNSYLVANIA 16502**
**814 454-4551**
**WWW.BURTONFUNERALHOMES.COM**
**WITH 3 ADDITIONAL AFFILIATED LOCATIONS**

East Erie - 2500 Norcross Road

Burton Funeral Homes has four locations to conveniently serve the Erie community.

Downtown - 602 West 10th Street

West Erie - 3816 West Lake Road

Girard - 525 Main Street East

John Horstman

# *War*

BY ROBERT H. ALLSHOUSE

**A**lthough the American nation was forged by revolution and the frontier was secured by fighting Indian tribes as settlers pushed westward, war was considered a major departure from the norm. In Erie, the same mentality held true although events were to dictate activities of the citizenry shortly after its initial settlement in 1795.

The **Treaty of Paris** of September 20, 1783, which ended the **American Revolution**, and the **Articles of Confederation,** drawn up afterwards, did not solve all the problems. It was **The Constitution** of 1789 which formally established the United States and gave the new nation a central government which could deal with foreign and domestic issues. The nation's freedom had to be preserved, but fear of a standing army led Congress to pass a militia law in 1792 that maintained the concept of the citizen soldier.

With the British and Spanish committed to keeping the Americans within the treaty boundaries of 1783, there was the potential for friction since Britain did not abandon all the posts she held along the Northern Frontier because the United States failed to recover debts owed to loyalists. The British continued to hold posts at

**OLIVER HAZARD PERRY came to Erie to build a fleet that would successfully challenge the world's largest navy.**

Oswego and Niagara on Lake Ontario; Miami and Detroit at the western end of Lake Erie; and Michilimackinac on the island guarding the straits between Lakes Huron and Michigan until 1796.

Another potential threat came from the military alliance signed with France during the American Revolution. The outbreak of the **French Revolution** in 1789 led to war between France and Great Britain, and, by 1812, it touched the United States. Britain and France pursued policies making it more difficult for the United States to remain neutral as they aggressively stopped and searched American vessels. The tensions increased, and relations with those nations deteriorated to the point that Congress declared war against Great Britain on June 18, 1812, and narrowly failed, by only two votes, to pass a similar declaration against France.

America's "Second War of Independence" would involve Erie directly. **Daniel Dobbins**, a native of Cumberland County, came to Erie in 1796. He earned a good reputation as ship captain, and in 1809 went into partnership with **Rufus Reed**, purchasing and rebuilding the schooner, **Salina**. Dobbins was at Ft. Michilimackinac when the British took the fort. Dobbins and Salina were seized although he and the other civilians were paroled on rather lenient terms. When he went to Detroit, he was again captured and paroled.

Dobbins returned to Erie (according to one account, he stole a canoe and paddled across to Sandusky). Upon telling his story to **General David Meade**, who commanded over 2,000 Pennsylvania militia encamped at Waterford, he was told to report his findings to officials in Washington. Dobbins talked with members of Congress, the Cabinet, and **President James Madison**; he was given orders to "proceed without delay to **Presque Isle**, on Lake Erie and there contract... for building four gunboats...."

Erie, with fewer than sixty buildings and five hundred people, had the timber and a safe harbor for building the ships but lacked the skilled shipwrights, blacksmiths and materials necessary for building a fleet. Nearly three hundred workers along with critical supplies were brought from Pittsburgh, New York and Washington. Dobbins' experience with rebuilding Salina allowed him to undertake the project. In January and February, 1813, **Commodore Isaac Chauncey**, commander of the naval forces on the Great Lakes, instructed Dobbins to add two 300-ton brigs to the ship order. **Scorpion**, **Porcupine** and **Tigress** were built at **Lee's Run**, between Peach and Sassafras Streets, and the brigs, **Niagara** and **Lawrence**, along with the fourth ship, **Ariel**, were built at the mouth of **Cascade Creek** to the west.

Twenty-seven year old **Oliver Hazard Perry** arrived in Erie to take command of the fleet still under construction on March 26, 1813. He and Dobbins continued to expedite construction, so that by the end of July the fleet was ready to sail. However, getting the ships into the lake was proving troublesome. Fortunately, the British commander, **Captain Robert Heriot Barclay**, took his ships off patrol on July 31st and returned to Buffalo. Perry offloaded all heavy gear and tackle, and made use of devices known as "camels" to float the larger ships across the shallow sand bar which had denied the British entrance to the harbor. After refitting the ships and mounting the cannon, Perry sailed from Erie on August 11th to **Put-in Bay**, South Bass Island, Ohio. There he prepared for the upcoming battle.

On September 10, 1813, the British fleet, which had sailed the day before from Fort Malden, Ontario, near the mouth of the Detroit River, engaged Perry at noon. With six ships displacing a total of 766 tons vs. the American squadron of nine ships of 889 tons, the British were at a disadvantage. However, that tonnage was balanced by their advantage in firepower; sixty-three guns to the Americans' fifty-one. In the initial two hours, Perry's flagship **Lawrence** took terrible punishment, and Perry was obliged to transfer his command to **Niagara**. He cut the British line and delivered broadsides to turn the course of battle. His message to **General William Henry Harrison** was succinct: *"We have met the enemy and they are ours."*

**The Battle of Lake Erie** was among the few bright

COL. STRONG VINCENT was promoted to Brigadier General by Abraham Lincoln for leadership at Little Round Top.

lights in a war that has been called the "Battle of the Bunglers". The Treaty of Ghent of 1814 reestablished relations to their pre-war status.

The **Black Hawk War** and the continuing push against Indian tribes further west had little impact upon the community. Not until the **Civil War** was Erie called upon to make major sacrifices. **Colonel John W. McLane** originally formed the **83rd Pennsylvania Infantry Regiment** for three months' service. It had been disbanded by the time of the **First Battle of Manassas** and was reassembled after McLane's second call to arms. Almost one thousand men, including "nearly 300 of the old regiment", responded. The 83rd played an important role during the campaigns

SARAH REED was known for her nursing and humanitarian work during the Civil War.

suffered mortal wounds. Before his death he was promoted to the rank of Brigadier General by **President Lincoln**.

Not all war efforts were on the battlefield. As more hospital trains came through Erie, **Sarah A. Reed** helped organize efforts to provide nursing care and sustenance to the wounded. She was to go on to other humanitarian work after the war, as were members of the **Women's Relief Corps**, which was very active during the conflict. After the war, the **USS Michigan**, an "Iron Barkentine" launched in 1843, continued to operate out of Erie, patrolling the Great Lakes. The side-wheel top sail schooner-at-war was considered great duty as she was laid up during

in the first two years of the war and ranked second of all Union regiments in the number of battle deaths. As the war dragged on, the **111th** and the **145th Regiments** were formed.

It was at **Gettysburg** that the 83rd and its commander, **Col. Strong Vincent**, achieved immortality. Vincent, who took over the regiment after the death of General McLane at **Gaine's Mills, Virginia**, marched his troops to Little Round Top, a rocky hill overlooking the Devil's Den on the left flank of the Union line. Vincent and his troops reached the top just in time to withstand a furious assault from Confederate troops led by **Lt. Gen. James Longstreet**. The Confederate efforts were thwarted, and the line held. Strong Vincent

*courtesy of Edna Huntington*

USS MICHIGAN which served as a Union Navy recruiting vessel was later renamed USS Wolverine.

the winter months. Erie was affectionately named the "Mother-in-Law of the Navy" because so many officers married Erie women. A distant cousin of Strong Vincent, **Harriet Vincent**, married one such officer, **Charles V. Gridley**, who commanded the **USS Olympia**, Admiral Dewey's flagship, in the Spanish-American War. At the **Battle of Manila**, Dewey gave the order: *"You may fire when ready, Gridley."*

On April 27th, 1898, two days after the Congressional resolution declaring war upon Spain, Company A and Company C of the **Fifteenth Regiment**, United States Volunteers, of the National Guard of Pennsylvania marched up State Street to the tune of *"There's a Hot Time in the Old Town Tonight."* Although neither unit saw action, they suffered several casualties, including **Pvt. Etsel French** of Company C who "died of a stomach-ache."

Although **World War I** broke out in August, 1914, it made little impact upon Erieites until the United States declared war on April 6, 1917. Ten days later, the crew of the **USS Wolverine,** (Michigan was renamed in 1905, as state names now were reserved for battleships) which had been ordered to report to the **Philadelphia Naval**

**Yard**, marched up State Street to take the train. These members of the **Pennsylvania Naval Militia** were stationed around the world. Company G of the 112th Regiment of the Pennsylvania National Guard was not to follow until September,

As the drama of World War Two unfolded, Erie papers like "The Dispatch" carried the news while Erie boys, like Louis Rossoni, took up arms to defend the Nation. Below, the "Greatest Generation" celebrates American victory in a parade down State Street.

# ▲HONORING HEROES

SACRIFICE AND COURAGE are honore[d] memorial which can be found at the [...] Street and Glenwood Park Avenue .

departing for Camp Hancock, Georgia, and becoming part of the 28th or **"Keystone" Division**. Company G was in combat on the Western Front for well over a month (including the second **Battle of the Marne** and **Chateau Thierry**) when a surprise German attack on August 26th decimated it, with 122 out of 134 men killed, wounded or taken prisoner. Approximately 3,000 Erie County draftees also were called by local draft boards to serve through the newly inaugurated **Selective Service**. A large number were sent to Camp Lee, Virginia and joined the 80th or **"Blue**

**Ridge" Division**. Many were assigned to the **313th** and **315th Machine Gun Battalions**. They went into action September 1st and remained in combat until the end of the **Meuse Argonne Offensive** on November 9th. Their thirty-eight combat deaths brought the total for Erie County to 154.

On the Home Front, War Bonds and United States War Savings Stamps were sold; the **American Red Cross** conducted Tag Days; "war gardens" sprang up in vacant lots and back yards; and women entered the work force to support the war effort as factory workers.

and the **Army Nurses Corps**. The Civilian Defense Volunteer Office listed 718 men and one woman (2nd Lt. **Clare Celestine Riley**, killed in action in North Africa, June 29, 1943) who were killed or died in service.

By early 1941, the **Roosevelt** Administration switched to a limited preparation for war. The National Guard was mobilized under federal command, and Erie's **112th Regiment** of the **28th Division** began training in February, 1941. The 28th was held in reserve in England awaiting the results of D-Day and landed at St. Lo, France, in July, 1944, after Cherbourg was captured.

The 28th lived up to its heritage. It was among the first American units to march into Paris; it helped with the liberation of Luxembourg; and it repulsed German counter-attacks at the Hurtgen Forest (suffering 6,184 casualties) and in the **Battle of the Bulge**. For those efforts it received the **Presidential Unit Citation**, a rare honor; and a nickname, the *"Bloody Bucket"*, bestowed because of its sacrifices and the keystone shape on its insignia. Pushing to the Rhine, the Division crossed Remagen Bridge on March 7, 1945 and fought through Germany until **V-E Day** (May 7th), ending its campaign near Frankfurt.

Unit valor was matched by personal bravery. The most famous war hero to come from Erie was **Col. Philip G. Cochran**, who became a lead character in two newspaper comic strips drawn by his friend from Ohio State University, **Milt Caniff**. **Col. Flip Corkin** from *Terry and the Pirates* and **Gen. Philerie** in *Steve Canyon* both were modeled on Cochran, who demonstrated a unique approach to campaigning. In North Africa and Burma, his successes burnished his reputation. Countless others served with the Navy, Marines and Army Corps in the Pacific as well as the Coast Guard and Merchant Marine in the Atlantic.

**WORLD WAR II MEMORIAL**

COMMITTEE

JOHN C. FERGUSON — CHAIRMAN
WILLIAM J. GREGG — VICE CHAIRMAN
DONALD E. GRUMBLATT — TREASURER

ADVISORS

ARTHUR W. BALDWIN — JOHN M. VAUGHN
DESSIE R. FORD — THOMAS W. KENNEDY
CARL J. ANDERSON, III — THOMAS E. HAGEN

PARTICIPATING CONTRACTORS

WHIPPLE CONSTRUCTION, FRANK E. WHIPPLE
GEIGER & SONS MONUMENTS - MIKE GEIGER
ZIMCOAT SPECIALTY FLOORING - COMPASS
DAHLKEMPER LANDSCAPERS,
DANIEL J. DAHLKEMPER - ARCHITECT & CONTRACTOR
UKASIK ELECTRIC,
CARL UKASIK - ELECTRICAL CONTRACTOR
WILLIAM J. PUSTELAK MASONRY,
WM. J. PUSTELAK - MASONRY CONTRACTOR

MATERIALS DONATED BY

A. DUCHINI, INC. — A. ANTHONY & SONS
ERIE CONCRETE & STEEL — GEIGER & SONS MEMORIALS
CITY OF ERIE - BUREAU OF WATER — CITY OF ERIE GARAGE PERSONNEL
SERV-ALL CONCRETE, INC.

LAND DONATED BY - ERIE SCHOOL DISTRICT
PLAQUE DONATED BY - LAKE SHORE INDUSTRIES - LEO BRUNO

The "War to end all wars" failed at the conference table at **Versailles**, in what **John Maynard Keynes** called a "carthaginian peace". Thus, World War I was but a prelude to **World War II**. With the Japanese attack on **Pearl Harbor**, December 7, 1941, Erie - like the rest of the nation - was again at war. Ten per cent (13,941) of the city population was called to serve. A total of 26,105 men and women served from Erie County. Included in that total were 598 women volunteers who joined the **WACS** (Army), **WAVES** (Navy), **SPARS** (Coast Guard), **WAF** (Air Force)

**FLY BOY** Col. Phil Cochran earned pop culture icon status in WW II. Seen here in a poster designed in Erie for support on the home front.

*courtesy Maritime Museum*

Guard and Merchant Marine in the Atlantic.

Service was not limited to the military. In Erie, the war effort was given backbone by the number of industries producing parts and weapons. Thousands of women in the county helped boost war production. Their efforts were magnified by volunteer groups and social agencies involved in doing war work. Volunteers staffed draft boards; collected funds and scrap metal; served as fire guards, messengers and nurses aides; established Civil Defense and First Aid stations; organized speakers bureaus and relief committees; and oversaw victory gardens, rationing and price controls.

The end of the war brought no real sense of peace, however. **The Cold War**, which began in 1946, heated up with the **Korean War**, officially called a "Police Action." The Erie Battalion of the 28th Division marched again to Union Station. After training at **Camp Atterbury, Indiana**, the division was sent to Germany for the duration of the conflict. Other Erie men volunteered or were drafted to serve in Korea – sixty-six of whom were killed.

The Cold War spawned another conflict in Asia. In French Indochina, a colonial war in **Vietnam** had escalated into a "war of national liberation" and was spreading to **Laos** and **Cambodia**. A conference at Geneva produced a settlement that resulted in two Vietnams: North and South. The subsequent failure of the Geneva Accords led the United States into one of the most unpopular wars in the history of the Republic. Several thousand men and women served in Vietnam from Erie County, including **Sgt. Tom Ridge**, who was later to serve twelve years in Congress and be elected to two terms as Governor of Pennsylvania. The names of fifty-seven Erie County men are inscribed on a memorial in the courtyard of the Erie County Court House as a remembrance of their ultimate sacrifice. Four more names of those missing in action are recorded in West Perry Square.

The American experience in Vietnam, the first of its kind in the history of the United States, led to major changes in American priorities. The draft was abolished, and an all-volunteer military establishment was inaugurated. The reconstituted American forces were deployed in **Grenada** and **Somalia** and comprised the largest assembly of military might in the **Persian Gulf War**.

The collapse of the Soviet Union in 1991 meant a new role for the American military establishment because the loss of central control in the USSR unleashed forces previously held in check. Erie County residents were called to serve in **Bosnia** and **Kosovo** after "ethnic cleansing" began in the former Yugoslavia. The Soviet breakdown was accelerated as weapons and strategic materials fell into the hands of terrorists.

Terrorism, which had always been considered something alien to the United States, took on an entirely new meaning on September 11, 2001. With simultaneous attacks on the World Trade Center, The Pentagon, and the crash of a highjacked airliner near Pittsburgh, war had come to the United States. Pennsylvania **Governor Tom Ridge** was called upon by President George W. Bush to take up the duties of the newly-created position of Director of Homeland Security.

For Erie County residents who were members of the Reserves and National Guard, homeland security after 9/11 meant a call to active duty. Members of the armed forces served in various capacities at home and abroad. Local residents (male and female) were deployed to Europe, Latin America, Africa, Asia, and the persian Gulf. Specific assignments in several transcaucasian republics of the former Soviet Union, as well as Afghanistan, India, and the Philippines added a new dimension to service by many of the Erie community who continued to serve well and honorably.

*Art Becker*

**TOM RIDGE** accepted heavy responsibility and great honor in becoming America's first Director of Homeland Security.

*John Horstman*

# Religion

BY MARY AMTHOR

As the world watched the horror unfold in the United States on September 11, 2001, Erie did one thing it does well - it prayed. While thousands of images of terror, destruction and pain were transmitted into the living rooms of America, the times of dozens of local prayer services scrolled across the bottom of Erie's television screens amid cancellation notices. This was not a knee-jerk reaction, but the obvious response of a city with a deep faith and long religious history.

Gazing upon Erie from the lofty third floor windows of the **Collegiate Academy** on State Street, one can easily count eight steeples reaching to the heavens from Erie's skyline. These are but a minute sampling of Erie's faith community. A glance in the phone book reveals over 300 listings for churches, synagogues, mosques, fellowships, and gatherings. The 2000 census lists the population of Erie County as 280,843, so there could be a place to worship for about every 900 residents in Erie County! Some worship sites have well over 1,000 worshippers at weekend services; for example, over 2,000 people attend services at the largest Catholic parish in the diocese, **St. George**.

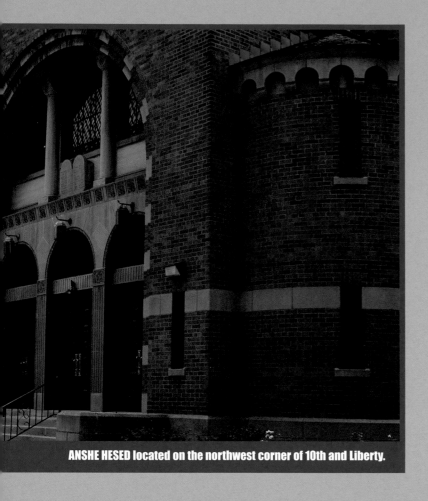

ANSHE HESED located on the northwest corner of 10th and Liberty.

Erie's deep religious roots clearly stem from its immigrant beginnings. For, as the immigrants who make up a colorful demographic quilt came to this country and to this city, they each brought with them a special brand of faith. Many immigrants established their own, mostly Christian churches, in the early 1800's. The Jewish community got its start in 1853 when Jewish residents formed the **Anshe Hesed Society** and the black community founded its first independent church after the Civil War in the 1860s: The **African Methodist Episcopal Church**. By the 1860's, Erie had about a dozen houses of worship. There are various claims to being the first organized church in Erie County. Some consider it to be

**Middlebrook Presbyterian Church**, which was founded in 1801, a dozen years before Commodore Oliver Hazard Perry's victory in the Battle of Lake Erie. The legend is that founding church member James Hunter told a group of young people to show up at the intended church site with axes and dinner. The building this enterprising congregation erected was, however, eventually to be humbled by the magnificent structures that started appearing in Erie during the next 150 years. In fact, various neighborhoods in Erie grew up around their churches. The early Italian community went to **St. Paul**, the Irish congregated at **St. Patrick**, the Poles prayed at **St. Stanislaus**, and many Germans gathered at **St. John Lutheran Church**. A look at one lower East side neighborhood reveals six churches in three blocks. There was, indeed, a church on almost every corner!

As the new millennium gets underway, actions speak louder than buildings when it comes to the faith community in Erie. The list of religious organizations, clubs, and groups in the city is a long one, so long, in fact, that the **Erie Times-News** dedicates a section to religious life each Saturday - the **Faith** section. The paper covers local and national religious news, music, books, videos, and movies, and offers both a religious activity directory and calendar.

Erie is a strong Catholic community with Catholics making up an estimated 36 percent of county population in 2001, according to **Walt Spiller**, Director of Planning at the **Erie Roman Catholic Diocese**. Spiller estimates that there were around 101,000 Catholics in Erie in 2001. These figures are a three-year average. Other estimates have put the Catholic population in Erie County as low as 30 percent of the population. Erie is the seat of the diocese, which has undoubtedly impacted the city in many ways.

Lutheran and other Protestant churches make up the next largest groups in Erie County, but the conservative, evangelical and non-denominational churches have experienced rapid growth. **First Assembly of God** on Oliver Road is one of the fastest growing denominations. It is a vibrant community with this unofficial motto: *"Walk the walk, don't just talk the talk"*. And, indeed, its 3,000 parishioners take their spiritual lives to work and play with them; for example, the community recently rallied around high school senior **Lindsay Fuhrman** when she needed a heart transplant. Fuhrman had been waiting for weeks at the **Cleveland Clinic** for a donor heart and when one finally arrived at midnight on July 23, 2001, at least forty people made the middle-of-the-night drive to give Lindsay a spiritual send off into surgery. Her father, **Mark Fuhrman**, says that those relationships with the people from the church, both in prayer and in action, kept Lindsay connected – and alive. The community puts on an **Easter Passion** play as well as Easter and Christmas music shows that draw 6,000-8,000 people per production.

Anyone who has spent a July in Erie has heard of the **Greek Festival** and headed to West Lake Road and the **Assumption Greek Orthodox Church** for authentic Greek food, music and a good dose of culture. The church dates back to 1917 when it was founded to meet the spiritual needs of a small Greek immigrant community. Today the Greek community prays in a beautiful Byzantine church. Followers of Eastern Orthodox faiths gather in six Erie County churches. The center of the Russian Orthodox community is the **Old Orthodox Church of the Nativity** on East Front Street, whose shining golden dome can be seen from many parts of the city and the bay. These churches follow regional patriarchs

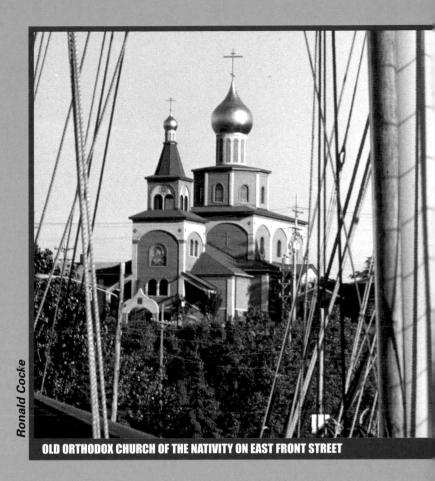

Ronald Cocke

**OLD ORTHODOX CHURCH OF THE NATIVITY ON EAST FRONT STREET**

instead of the Pope and are very traditional.

Religious life is paramount to the African-American community here, which numbers around 14,000, according to **Bishop Brock** of the non-denominational **Victory Christian Center of Erie, Inc.** Brock points out that not only is the church the center of African American life, but that the preacher is often a spiritual and a political leader. Any politician, African American or not, who is courting the vote of the group must start by announcing his or her candidacy from the pulpit.

Erie's Jewish community numbered in the thousands before WWll, but has since dropped below 1,000. Until the 1960s, Erie Jewish residents were mainly merchants whose stores lined the streets of downtown Erie. Two key factors have changed the demographics: many of the Jewish children who go off to college have not been returning home to take over family businesses, and those family businesses have given way to the many national chain stores that have moved in, according to Erie Times-News reader advocate, **Jeff Pinski**. The Jewish community is alive and well, says Pinski, but not what it used to be. Erie Jews can worship at **Brith Shalom Congregation**, a conservative congregation and Anshe Hesed, a reform congregation. The Jewish Community Council works to educate Erie and heighten awareness about Jewish customs and culture.

**Mary Al-Hasnawi** of the **International Institute**

estimates Erie's Muslim population at 1,500, most of whom are from Bosnia, Iraq, and Somalia. Both Sunni and Shi'ite Muslims have centers for prayer in Erie, although Al-Hasnawi says the more popular one is the **Islamic Cultural Center** on East 12th Street.

According to an Erie Times-News article by **Robin Cuneo**, about 33 percent of Erie County residents attend weekly services. It may not be an overwhelming number, but it is an active group and the presence of religion is Erie is clearly palpable. Many churches run educational institutions. The Erie Catholic Diocese supports **Gannon University** and **Cathedral Preparatory High School**, The **Sisters of St. Joseph** control **Villa Maria Academy** and the **Villa Center**, the **Sisters of Mercy**

## ▼ SIGNS OF THE TIMES

God Bless the Whole World
Erie Regional Peace and Justice Center
LAMAR
West 26th Street

10th and Sassafras
GOD BLESS AMERICA

8th and Parade
Grace of Calvary Baptist Church
SUNDAY SCHOOL 10:00 a.m.  WORSHIP SERVICE 11:00 a.m.-6:00 p.m.  WED. SERVICE 7:00 p.m.
THERE IS NO 2ND CHANCE BEYOND THE GRAVE. PREPARE TODAY! HEBREWS 9:27
"YE MUST BE BORN AGAIN"
Dr. George H. Alquist, Jr., Pastor
INDEPENDENT
806

24th and Peach
St. Joseph Church
Bread of Life Community
MASSES
Saturday 5:15 PM
Sunday 8 AM, 10 AM, 11:30 AM
Weekday Mass 7 AM
THERE IS ONLY ONE TRAGEDY - NOT TO BE A SAINT

founded **Mercyhurst Preparatory** and **Mercyhurst College**; and there are numerous parochial and private Christian preschools, kindergartens, elementary and middle schools. At this writing, Bishop Brock's church is also currently involved in building a Bible college on Pennsylvania Avenue. Administrators claim that these schools often produce well-educated students who become active members of their religious communities. Many churches also have established Sunday schools and religious education programs for the area's public school children.

There is not much doubt that, overall, Erie is a conservative community and its religious strengths are often difficult to separate from its moral make-up. For example, after months of protests, parading, and legal tangles, **Kandy's Dinner Theater**, a strip club on upper Peach Street, closed its doors. The final straw was a 1994 ordinance banning totally nude dancing. It was challenged all the way to the Supreme Court, which in March 2000, upheld Erie's right to force performers to cover up. Although the protests and legalities were based on moral outrage and not officially sponsored by any of the city's religious institutions, many of the protesters were churchgoers, and the topic was addressed from more than one pulpit. This is just one example of how Erie's religious community reaches beyond the confines of weekend pews to mold city life.

Councilman **Mario Bagnoni**, a veritable institution in city government since 1971, says the city does listen to churches when they come to City Council with an issue. He says there is a large community of deeply involved churchgoers here and that he finds the city to be deeply influenced by its religious base - something not to be ignored.

Action and controversy are not new words to Erie's **Benedictine Community**, which has made its own indelible mark on Erie life. Strolling to the entrance of the Neighborhood Arthouse, one sees the names of many prominent Erie citizens engraved on the walkway bricks. The Art House offers inner city children a safe, fun, and yes, religious place to go after school. Kids enjoy free lessons in the fine arts, physical arts, literacy and much more in the brightly decorated building at 10th and French Streets. But, whatever they do, they begin each afternoon with a gathering song.

Just a few blocks away, fellow Benedictines are getting ready to serve hot meals to long lines of waiting diners at the **Emmaus Soup Kitchen**. The Benedictines also provide day care centers, job training and work placement, summer camp

18th and Parade

WHERE WILL YOUR SOUL AND CONSCIENCE BE IN ETERNITY?
JOHN 3:16

21st and Ash

TRY GOD "His Way is Perfect..."
II Samuel 22:31 Psalm 18:30

*John Horstman*

73

and environmental programs. They are but one of the four extremely active religious orders who continue to help fight negative influences and build positive alternatives for Erie residents.

It's impossible to do justice to all of the different religious organizations permanently and positively affecting the people along the shores of Lake Erie. They range greatly in size, influence, and public profile. One of the more interesting religious groups is the **Carmelite Sisters**, who live a cloistered life. They spend their days and nights praying behind the walls of their humble home on East Gore Road. Many miracles have been attributed to the prayers of these remarkable women, who never venture beyond their front door.

A group of Erieites protests the construction of a medical office that would provide abortions in Erie. Local churches will frequently organize groups with the purpose of becoming involved with social issues.

**Hofmann's Church and Religious Goods** is a sprawling store on East 26th Street, near Parade. Since 1960, it has catered to an ecumenical crowd, selling everything from priestly garments to shelves full of Bibles, kids' videos, statues, rosaries, greeting cards and much more. President **Jacquie Hofmann** says the fact that Hofmann's can exist alongside other major religious stores, **Beacon Books**, **Gospel Book and Supply Center** and **Angel Loft**, in a community the size of Erie, is a statement in itself. She has noticed that shoppers are buying smaller and more personal articles, that personal faith seems to be taking on a greater significance. Religion is important to local residents, and so they invest in religious goods on an ongoing basis, says Hoffmann. It's not hard to see religious statues in the yards of folks while driving around the city, for example.

The personalized faith that Hoffmann is referring to is also a sign of the times - the current trend of personal spirituality and a re-examination of our national religious consciousness, particularly in the wake of the September 11 attacks. Erie County residents are among those helping books like **The Prayer of Jabez** to retain top spots on the New York Times bestseller list.

Perhaps one of the more encouraging trends in Erie's religious life is the focus on ecumenism and inter-faith activities. Some of the major prayer services on September 11, 2001, for example, included leaders from several different faiths and churches. Prayer groups are welcoming people of all faiths, East and West. **Monsignor Biebel** of **St. Peter Cathedral** says the goal is for churches not to do things separately that they can do together. The Monsignor is involved in **Inter Church Ministries**, which is a network of 130 churches in Erie County. One example is the efforts of many area churches to stymie attempts to set up an off-shore gambling boat. The plan was shelved after local churches drew up a white paper opposing the idea.

Religion has also become a part of Erie's mainstream media. General Manager **Joel Nataly** says that since October 1967, **WCTL** has been proclaiming the message of Jesus Christ to Erie. The goal of the station is to connect listeners to Jesus, other listeners and ministries through Christian music and programming. The radio station supports local churches by providing an outlet for information, sometimes free of charge, as public service announcements. WCTL is a non-profit organization, which raises more than half of its budget through its estimated 30,000 listeners. **Focus on Family** draws the biggest listening audience. Other churches produce Sunday morning services and an occasional special program, which Erieites can watch on three main local television stations.

**Pax Christi USA**, the national Catholic Peace movement, has its national headquarters in Erie, giving the city some national religious exposure. Pax Christi USA is part of Pax Christi International. The group has 14,000 members who all work towards removing all forms of vio-

*John Horstman*

SPREADING THE GOSPEL OF JESUS CHRIST over the Erie County airwaves.

lence from the world.

Many Americans have been taught not to tangle with religion or politics in conversation. In Erie, however, the topics are not always easy to avoid. The religious groups in the city are varied and many; they unleash strong feelings, and the level of involvement in religious related activities is high. As the writer of this essay and native of Erie County, I am proud to come from a community, which places its faith on such a visible and active pedestal. Indeed, the many faces of religion in Erie truly define the town, as its people continue to define their religions. It is an infinite process. †

Special thanks to Robin Cuneo, Kevin Cuneo, and Jeff Pinski of the Erie Times News, Annie Cafardi, Dr. Thomas Parthenakis, Mario Bagnoni, Monsignor Biebel, Mark Fuhrman, Jacquie Hoffmann, Bishop Dwayne Brock, Marilyn Amthor, Betsy Wiest, Walt Spiller, Sr. Mary Lou Kownacki OSB, Monsignor Richard Mayer, and Barb Nichols.

NATURE

Photo: Ed Bernik

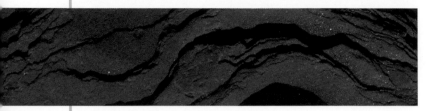

## GEOLOGIC FORMATION

Erie County is situated within two physiographic provinces: the Central Lowland (lake plain) which is characterized by low and generally flat appearances; and the Appalachian Plateau, which features higher elevations and rolling characteristics. Between the two provinces is an area known as the escarpment slope.

There are eight (8) classes of bedrock in Erie County; however, the county is dominated by: Northeast Shale, Girard Shale, the Chadakoin Formation, and the Venango Formation. These four (4) dominant classes of bedrock consist mostly of gray shale, siltstone, and fine-grained sandstone. The bedrock in Erie County dates back to the Upper Devonian geologic time period (350-400 million years ago). There are some smaller "younger" areas in the southern portions of Erie County, near the border with Crawford County, that date to the Lower Mississipian

geologic time period (310-350 million years ago). The Northeast Shale, the oldest exposed bedrock in the county lies in a band along Lake Erie and approaches a thickness of approximately 400 feet. The Girard shale ranges from 50 to 200 feet in thickness. The Chadakoin formation is about 300 feet thick, contains some marine fossils and is the most extensive bedrock in the county. The

Ed Bernik

Venango Formation approaches a thickness of nearly 250 feet and exhibits more of a bluish-gray color of sandstone.

Although the City of Erie relies on Lake Erie for drinking water, people living in the rural areas rely on groundwater wells. The groundwater yielded from the aquifer of the dominant classes of bedrock in Erie County is generally acceptable at an average yield of 4.5 gal/min, with the Chadakoin formation yielding the highest quality of water.

*top left photo:* Ed Bernik

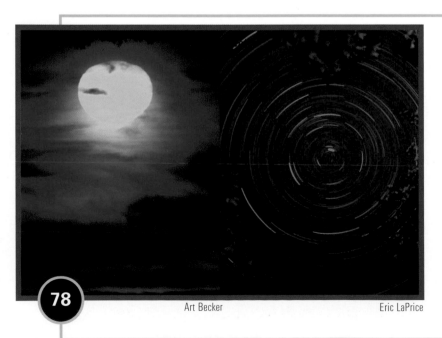

Art Becker                    Eric LaPrice

## CHANGING SKIES

The skies over Erie are always changing. Regional weather effects can create scarlet sunsets, grey mornings, or cobalt summer days. Night brings a wide array of stars, constellations, nebulas, and galaxies. Erie is far enough north that, on occasion, the Aurora Borealis, or Northern Lights, can be seen shimmering across the north sky. Astronomy in Erie has a strong following. In 1994, local astronomer **Tom Whiting**, President of **Erie County Mobile Observers**, discovered a group of stars he called "The Little Coat Hanger", located south of the last star in the handle of the Little Dipper. Nearly four years later, his discovery was featured in *Sky & Telescope Magazine*.

## WEATHER

There is a local expression that says, "If you do not like the weather in Erie, wait fifteen minutes". No doubt, the statement holds true in many instances as the weather in Erie quite often does change very significantly in short periods of time. However, one of the generally accepted realities about the sky in Erie is that it is overcast and there is a lot of rain.

The city does have the luxury of experiencing four distinct seasons, sometimes referred to as "almost winter", "winter", "still winter", and "construction". All jokes aside, the seasonal changes in Erie are truly dramatic. The winter skies are cold, barren and grey: quite often, arctic winds blow across the Lake and ravage the city, driving the temperatures down close to zero. The snow does eventually melt and gives way to blooming flowers and the warmer blue skies of spring. Tourists arrive with the hot temperatures, commonly in the 70's and 80's, to enjoy the Erie summers. A kaleidoscope of color marks the landscape as the trees change color and the cool nights of fall arrive.

Erie's familiarity with cold arctic-like conditions for nearly half of the year has made Erieites a hearty and rugged group of individuals who do not flinch at the thought of freezing temperatures or several feet of snow falling in one day.

## RECORDS

| | | |
|---|---|---|
| Hottest | 100°F | June 25, 1988 |
| Coldest | -18°F | Jan. 19, 1994 |
| Most Rain in Season | 61.7" | 1977 |
| Most Snow in Season | 144.9" | 2000 |

Art Becker

Did you know that the first documented use of the term **Indian Summer** - *a spell of summerlike weather late into Autumn* - came from Erie?

Ed Bernik

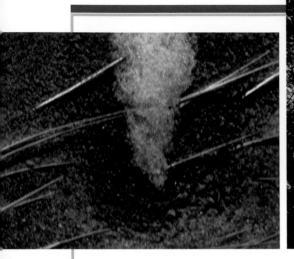

Ed Bernik, Ed Bernik

# NATURAL RESOURCES

## GAS

If one were to take a drive through the Erie County countryside, one may notice many private gas wells. Geologic surveys have indicated that approximately half of the eastern part of the county lies over deep fields of natural gas which is still a popular source of clean energy for cooking and heating.

## GRAPES

Concord grapes only grow successfully in a few places in the United States - one of which is Erie County just east of the city in a community known as North East. A narrow band of land along the lakeshore, only 3-5 miles wide, has been producing grapes for over 150 years. The Concord grapes are of such a high quality that the largest **Welch Foods, Inc.** Concord grape processing plant is located in Erie County as well as many independent wineries.

## TIMBER

Erie County has a diverse tree population, and the city streets themselves are lined with many trees. Maple, oak, beech, poplar, hickory, pine, and hemlock are all common to this area. Trees are still a valuable resource, important in construction, furniture making and the production of paper products.

## WATER

The City of Erie benefits greatly from its location on Lake Erie, which is a gigantic reservoir of fresh water. It is not uncommon in the summer to hear that other cities in Pennsylvania impose sprinkling bans and other water use restrictions due to low water supplies. Erie, however, with such an immense water supply, remains immune to such restrictions.

## SAND & GRAVEL

There are many sand and gravel pits located around Erie County. These pits provide much of the material used for construction in the Erie area. One of the more interesting gravel pits in the county is **Gravel Pit Park**, located on the eastern side of the county within the community of North East. Gravel Pit Park is a reclaimed section of a gravel pit that has been converted into a community park.

80 *Beata Stark*

Water is unquestionably Erie's greatest natural resource. Overlooking Lake Erie, the shallowest of the Great Lakes, and Presque Isle Bay, the City of Erie is the only Pennsylvania city with a seaport.

## LAND

There are four low rolling ridges in Erie County, all of which are parallel to Lake Erie. Between each of the ridges are generally level valley areas. The highest ridge, located 8-10 miles from the lakeshore, forms a watershed divide. A drop of water on the north side of the ridge will flow into Lake Erie and eventually out the St. Lawrence Seaway. A drop of water on the south side of the ridge will flow into the Allegheny River to the Mississippi River and eventually into the Gulf of Mexico. Except for the low ridges, Erie County is generally flat. The highest point in the county, 1795 feet above sea level, is at the top of a knoll, located in Venango Township, near the border with Greenfield Township and New York State. Except for the intense urban development in and around the City of Erie, the majority of the county consists of forested areas and farmlands. The most extensive soils in the county are part of the **Erie Series**, a deep, somewhat poorly drained upland soil, whose native vegetation consists of a beech-maple type of forest.

## LAKE ERIE

Imperative to the identity of the City of Erie, **Lake Erie**, the oldest of the Great Lakes, has been recognized as a vital resource since the days of the first Erie settlers. As part of the largest continuous mass of freshwater on Earth, the value of Lake Erie as a source of fresh drinking water is paramount. In

addition, Lake Erie has been known as the fresh water fishing capital of the world, the shipping gateway for America's westward expansion, a resource for Industrial Age manufacturing and a recreational playground. Lake Erie has and always will be a defining feature on the face of Erie. One unfortunate side effect from the industrial developments of the 19th and 20th centuries was a Lake Erie infamous for polluted waters. However, with stricter environmental regulations over the last thirty years, Lake Erie enters the 21st century boasting the cleanest water of the **Laurentian Great Lakes**. Swimming, fishing, boating and other recreational water activities dominate the lakefront.

# CREEKS

**T**here are many creeks and runs located within Erie County, far too many to discuss here in detail. Erie County streams flow both north and south from a watershed divide which runs diagonally across the county, roughly where Interstate 90 is located. Fishing is popular on the Erie County streams, especially those in the **Lake Erie Watershed**, i.e., those that flow north into Lake Erie. The streams contain a vast array of fish including: steelhead, bass, northern pike, muskie, walleye, brown trout, catfish and various panfish.

The "Big Daddy" or largest stream of the Lake Erie Watershed is **Elk Creek**. As such, it is the most popular Lake Erie tributary for fishing. The locally famous **"American Legion Hole"** is found on Elk Creek. One of the eeriest geologic formations, a long and very narrow outcropping of rock, called **"Devil's Backbone"**, is located on Little Elk Creek, south of where Little Elk meets Elk. However, to reach "Devil's Backbone", without traversing privately owned and posted lands, one must hike several miles through the stream itself, which belongs to the Commonwealth.

Another one of the large waters in the county is **French Creek** although it flows to the south and eventually empties into the Allegheny River. French Creek is a designated Pennsylvania Scenic River and boasts the greatest diversity of organisms of the Pennsylvania streams.

**Walnut Creek** is well known in the county for the **Project Waters**. Due to landowners posting nearly every inch of streamside property in the county and not allowing for public access, recreational opportunities on streams are severely restricted. The Project Waters is a series of man-made pools that were created by the **Pennsylvania Fish and Boat Commission** in 1999. The pools were built on Fish and Boat Commission property near the mouth of Walnut Creek for the purpose of providing accessible public fishing opportunities.

An incredible spectacle can be seen each fall on **Trout Run**, a stream located on the west side of the county, as the steelhead "make their run" back to their spawning grounds (there is a nursery on Trout Run). The mouth of the Creek is literally loaded with steelhead.

Eric LaPrice

## Significant Creeks & Streams of Erie County

| CREEK | CURRENT | |
| --- | --- | --- |
| Elk Creek | North | Home of "American Legion" Fishing Hole |
| Trout Run | North | Hotspot for Steelhead in Autumn |
| Walnut Creek | North | Contains project waters for Public Fishing |
| Four Mile Creek | North | |
| Twenty Mile Creek | North | Flows through Local Wine Country |
| French Creek | South | Largest Diversity of Organisms in Erie County Streams |
| Cussewago Creek | South | |

Sam Stull

## PRESQUE ISLE STATE PARK

It has been called "Our region's greatest natural wonder and most profound artistic inspiration." Named by French explorers, Presque Isle means "almost an island". Years of sand and sediment accumulation on top of a glacial moraine have created a peninsula, which, in turn, has created the best natural harbor on Lake Erie. Presque Isle has no bedrock foundation and is anything but static. It is in a constant state of flux, continually eroding, reforming and growing as new sediment is deposited. The peninsula has always been a defining mark on the face of the community.

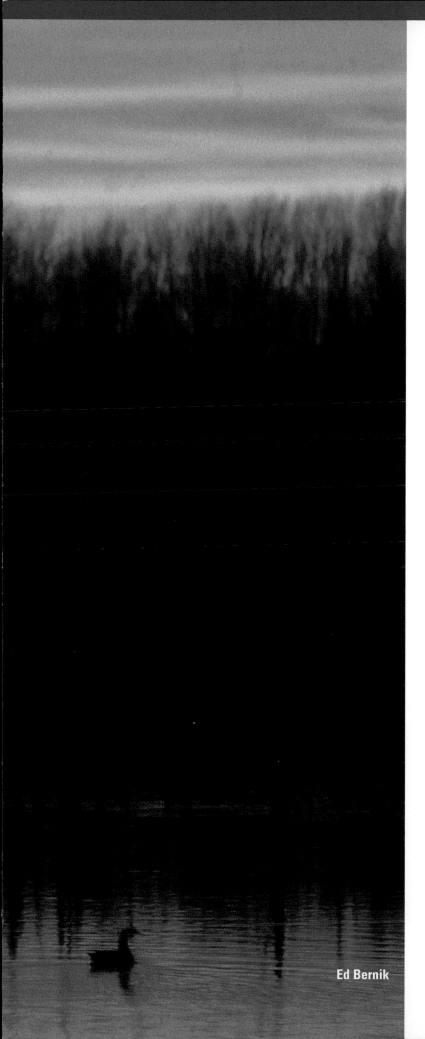

Ed Bernik

Paul Lorei

# Nature

**Presque Isle is the most popular State Park in the East.**

Designated a state park in 1921, Presque Isle is a popular relaxation and recreation spot that draws over four million visitors a year. Both tourists and Erieites frequent the Presque Isle peninsula throughout the year and are attracted by spectacular sunsets (as seen on the facing page) unique Birding opportunities and most often a day at the beach. Presque Isle is the backbone of the tourist industry of Erie and continues to be a major focus of the region's economic development.

85

Denise Keim

"One touch of nature makes the whole world kin"
–Shakespeare

# WILDLIFE

**Robin red-breast**, one of the most common birds in Pennsylvania, was abundant in the Penns Woods before they were cleared. This bird is found everywhere in Erie County and adapts quickly to the influence of man. It is just as comfortable in a manicured grass lawn as in the forest,: however, the Robin has not become dependent upon man.

Although there are many species of gulls, the most common are **herring gulls** and **ring-billed gulls**. There are two places where one is almost guaranteed to see these birds, Presque Isle State Park and along the waterfront areas of the City, especially Dobbins Landing at the foot of State Street.

Both the **red** and **grey fox** are found in Erie County, each reaching the size of a small dog (10-15 pounds). Both are shy and nocturnal, so the best chance of seeing either is usually around dawn or dusk. A unique characteristic about the grey fox is that it is the only member of the dog family with the ability to climb trees.

The **American Beech** is very common in Erie County. The bark of this tree is very smooth and light in color into old age.

A common dune plant that is found wherever there is sand along the coast, **Beach Grass** is a valuable sand binder. This is abundant on the sand dunes of Presque Isle State Park.

The **Eastern Hemlock** is a large and common conifer in Erie County. It is a rugged species that is long-lived and does not require exposure to direct sunlight. This hearty species is the official State Tree of Pennsylvania.

The **white tailed deer** is a very common game animal in Erie County. Every year, hunters take to the woods in an attempt to harvest a trophy-sized deer. Others prefer to shoot the deer with cameras. Generosity is displayed every year with stories of the hunters donating large quantities of the highly-prized venison to the needy.

## MILL CREEK FLOOD

The "Flood of 1915" is unparalleled as the most devastating natural disaster in Erie history. During a storm on August 3, 1915, debris accumulating against a tree that had fallen across a culvert at 26th and State Streets began to act as a dam to the floodwaters rushing down Mill Creek. The water backed up and formed a lake in the area now occupied by Veterans Stadium. The water pressure in this lake, which was estimated to be 30 feet deep, caused the dam to break and a wall of water 30 feet high raced north through the city, devastating all properties on the banks of Mill Creek. 37 people were killed and hundreds were left homeless. Soon after the flood, the city raised the money to put Mill Creek underground. This massive underground tunnel is called the **Mill Creek Tube**. The entrance to the tube can be seen just east of Veterans Stadium.

## ERIE EXTENSION CANAL

The legendary Erie Canal was located in the State of New York, and never came to Erie. The success of the Erie Canal in New York prompted the Pennsylvania legislature to construct the Pennsylvania Canal. In what seemed more like an afterthought, the Erie Extension Canal was built to connect Pittsburgh to Erie. The Canal only lasted 27 years before being replaced by railroads, but it did contribute to the growth of Erie as a lakeport; and, the towns of Platea and Girard appeared due to canal activities.

WSEE

## ALBION TORNADOES

At approximately 5:05 PM on May 31, 1985, tragedy struck the placid little town of Albion area, located southwest of Erie. A sound as deafening as 1000 jet engines cut the silence as a massive tornado, classified on the Fujita scale as an F-4 (F-5 is the largest in terms of damage and terror) pulverized the downtown area. It was all over within minutes, but in the wake of destruction over 100 houses had been destroyed and 12 lives lost. A memorial plaque, located on State Street in downtown Albion, lists those killed in this, one of the worst natural disasters in Erie.

## FISHING

Fishing has always been important to Erie. For many years, the legendary **Blue Pike**, a subspecies of the walleye, was the cornerstone of the Erie fishing industry and was considered to be a better catch than yellow perch. Although the last successful spawning of the species was in 1954 and the species was declared extinct in 1983, periodic rumors about anglers catching suspect blue pike continue to surface. Luckily, a genetic blueprint of the Lake Erie blue pike has been developed by the United States Fish and Wildlife Service using trophy mounted specimens and specimens that have spent 20-30 years in freezers. There is now a blueprint to which suspects can be compared.

Eric LaPrice

## WOOLY MAMMOTH

In the early 1990's, scuba divers at **Lake Pleasant** observed some large and unusual objects underwater. **Dr. Jude Kirkpatrick**, Gannon University Professor of Archaelogy, identified the strange items as the remains of the most perfectly preserved wooly mammoth skeleton in the United States.

## PRESQUE ISLAND

The neck of the **Presque Isle Peninsula** is thin enough and the storm waves of Lake Erie are restless enough that the peninsula (whose name is French for *almost* an island) has, in fact, become separated from the mainland. At least four times since 1819 the neck has been broken. In past years, the shipping and fishing industries took advantage of this second channel into Presque Isle Bay.

COMMON GOOD

Photo: Denise Keim

Ed Bernik

**GOVERNMENT OFFICES** Three of Erie's major government office buildings are clockwise from top - The **City of Erie Municipal Building**, a.k.a City Hall, located just off of South Park Row at 626 State St., **The County Courthouse** on West 6th. and **The Federal Courthouse**, also located at 6th and State.

Doug Campbell

Doug Campbell

## COUNTY GOVERNMENT

Erie County government consists of a County Executive and seven council members, all of whom serve four-year elected terms. To prevent all members from running for office at the same time, elections are staggered. To ensure that the people of the county are accurately represented, every councilman represents a district based on population. While the County Executive can veto ordinances and resolutions, the council members can override that veto with a majority vote (four or more). The responsibilities of the county government are set forth in a charter, which prevents the body from infringing on the rights of other home-based forms of government, such as cities, municipalities, and boroughs.

## CITY GOVERNMENT

Erie City government, which has always been predominantly Democratic, consists of a mayor and seven council members. The council is headed by a presdent, and each member serves the entire city rather than a ward or a district. Elections are staggered to prevent all members running for election the same time. The council can override the mayor's veto if it has a majority vote (four or more). Both the mayor and council members serve four year elected terms.

Doug Campbell

## GOVERNMENT OFFICES

### CITY

Economic and Community Development
Building Inspection
Property and Maintenance
Electrical Inspection
Enterprise Zone
Grant Administration
Planning
Plumbing Inspection
Zoning Officer
Bureau of Fire
Bureau of Police
Public Works, Property, and Parks
Tax Office
Water Authority

John Horstman

### COUNTY

| | |
|---|---|
| Courthouse | Jury Coordinator |
| Adult Probation | Juvenile Probation |
| Assessment | Library-Public |
| Children Services | Licenses |
| Clerk of Courts | Mental Health / Mental Retardation |
| Clerk of Records | Microfilm Bureau |
| Controller | Operations |
| Cooperative Extension | Personnel |
| Coroner | Planning |
| Town Council | Prison |
| Court of Common Pleas | Probation & Parole |
| Credit Union | Protection from Abuse |
| Custody Conciliation | Prothonotary |
| Director of Administration | Public Defenders Office |
| District Attorney | Purchasing Bureau |
| Domestic Relations | Reassessment |
| Drug and Alcohol Abuse Program | Recorder of Deeds |
| E-911 Administrative Office | Registrar of Wills |
| Emergency Management Agency | Revenue |
| County Executive | Sheriff |
| Finance Director | Support Office |
| Health and Safety | Tax Claim Bureau |
| Housing Authority | Veterans Affairs |
| Human Relations Comission | Voter Registration |
| Human Services | Weights and Measures |
| Job Listings | Telecommunications Devices |

**CAUGHT ON CAMERA** City police nab a suspect during a burglary in progress.

## ERIE POLICE DEPARTMENT

The **Erie Police Department** currently has 206 officers in its force, with 20 to 23 officers on the street at any time. Officers on the street include patrol, canine, motorcycle, and bicycle units. On average, between 3 and 10 of these officers are either killed or injured every year while performing their duties. The Department is structured into four main divisions: the patrol division, the criminal investigation division, training and development and internal affairs. Each of these divisions is run by a deputy chief, all of whom report to the chief of police.

94

## ERIE FIRE DEPARTMENT

"To save lives and property, in that order, as quickly and safely as possible" is the mission for the firefighters of Erie County, whether they be volunteers or full time employees of the city. While fire departments in Pennsylvania the counties are generally volunteers, the Erie Fire Department is a "career" agency, which means all its members are paid employees, and its stations are manned 24 hours a day, seven days a week. But that distinction doesn't keep agencies from working together. Volunteers and career firefighters know that they can depend on one another in a partnership they refer to as "mutual aid".

The Erie Fire Department itself has six fire stations throughout the city, 176 firefighters, and about 30 vehicles (pumpers, aerial ladder trucks, and support vehicles). To help the department run effectively, the organization is very structured. In the city, 170 firefighters work on suppression, which refers to combating fires, and providing general life support and extrication from

*photo courtesy: WSEE*

accidents. Six firefighters work in prevention and inspection, which entails inspecting every commercial and industrial property in the city and conducting all fire investigations. The department is headed by a chief, an assistant chief, and 5 deputy chiefs. The chain of command continues, assigning every member of the department a place and role in the hierarchy. In 2001, the Erie Fire Department answered 5,676 calls, 3,150 of which were fire runs and 2,526 of which were EMS (emergency medical service) calls.

**ON CALL** Firemen at the 12th and Sassafras station go through long hours keeping their gear in the best shape possible, prepared for a call 24 hours a day, seven days a week.

*Denise Keim*

ENGINE CO. 3

ERIE FIRE DEPT.
EFD 3

## PENELEC

**T**he **Pennsylvania Electric Company** (Penelec), a **FirstEnergy Company** is proud to serve all of our customers in 32 counties across Pennsylvania, including Erie County, our largest metropolitan area.

In addition to Penelec, our FirstEnergy family of electric companies includes Penn Power in western Pennsylvania, Metropolitan Edison in eastern Pennsylvania, Jersey Central Power & Light in New Jersey, and the Ohio companies, Cleveland Electric, Ohio Edison and Toledo Edison.

Across 17,500 square miles in western, northern and central Pennsylvania, Penelec serves 586,000 customers, with over 100,000 right here in Erie county. Penelec is headquartered on Evans Road in Erie, and is home to 152 of our 929 employees.

The Company is committed to a long-standing partnership with Erie customers, community, and civic organizations. Penelec continues to be a proud supporter of Celebrate Erie, the Arts Council of Erie, The Erie Regional Chamber and Growth Partnership, The American Red Cross and many other educational and community service organizations across Erie County and our entire service territory.

Penelec's employees are widely recognized for their volunteer efforts in our communities, giving their time and talents to organizations such as Harvest for Hunger, the United Way, as well as sporting, youth and community service groups.

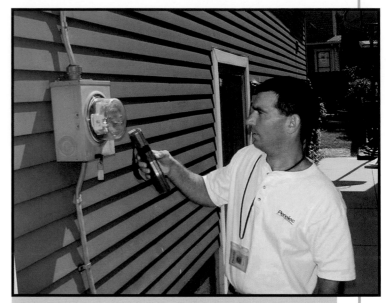

**PENELEC** brings electric power to over 100,000 customers in the Erie Area. Their employees are known in the community for volunteering for many local organizations.

Photos Courtesy: Penelec

*Denise Keim*

## STREETS DEPARTMENT

The **Department of Public Works, Bureau of Streets,** is responsible for all street operations: snow and ice removal, limb and leaf removal, cleaning, pothole patching, and street paving. The agency, located at 2001 French St., has 50 employees and uses approximately 55 vehicles to do its job. More than 320 miles of linear road fall under the agency's care. In a year, work on these streets include 10 miles of paving, 320 miles of snow plowing and over 80 miles of salt spreading.

*Denise Keim*

## CITY REFUSE DISPOSAL

In the city, demolishing commercial and residual waste is a responsibility of the **Refuse and Disposal Bureau**. Much of it goes to **Lake View Landfill**, located at 851 Robison Road in Summit Township, which is responsible for its safe handling and disposal. Lake View is the primary waste disposal site for Erie County and has, not surprisingly, become one of the highest geographical points in the County. With 20 employees and 25 vehicles, the agency annually handles more than 500,000 tons of garbage.

*John Buffington*

**97**

## PARKS

The **Department of Public Works, Property & Parks** is responsible for the maintenance of city parks and playgrounds, capital improvement, recycling programs and streetlights. More than 70 different areas fall under the responsibility of

this department. including 21 playgrounds with a 22nd pending, 3 golf courses, and 46 parks (21 with playgrounds, 13 undeveloped, and 12 special use). The special use parks typically include popular features: baseball and softball fields.

M. Walker

Doug Campbell

## GLENWOOD PARK

With 126.8 acres of land, Glenwood Park is the largest and one of the most used parks in Erie. The park, running parallel to Glenwood Park Ave., includes a golf course, a picnic area, and a playground (adjacent to the zoo).

Denise Keim

## FRONTIER PARK

Shown above, Frontier occupies 32.3 acres of land just north of 8th Street and west of the Bayfront Parkway. It includes a playground, six tennis courts, cross country/biking trails, bridges, a stream, and an amphitheater gazebo. The park is home to a number of Erie events, including the annual **Erie Art Museum Blues & Jazz Festival**. While Frontier remains the property of the public, **L.E.A.F.** (Lake Erie Arboretum at Frontier Park), a recently formed group, has concentrated on beautification by planting 250 varieties of trees, building an amphitheatre, and placing many sponsored benches and structures throughout the park.

Denise Keim

City of Erie Parks and

*Denise Keim*

*Denise Keim*

## PARKS

### WESTSIDE

| | |
|---|---|
| Baldwin Park | West 25th & Berst Avenue |
| Barbara Nitkiewicz Park | West 3rd & Cascade |
| Bayview Park | West 2nd between Cherry & Walnut |
| Brabender Park | West 21st & Baur Avenue |
| Chestnut Street Launch Ramp | Bayfront at Chestnut Street |
| Cloverdale Park | West 27th & Harvard Blvd |
| Columbus Park | West 16th & Poplar |
| Frontier Park | West 6th & Seminole Drive |
| Garden Park | West 36th & Norman Way |
| Glenwood Park | Glenwood Park Avenue & West 38th Street |
| Gridley Park | Park Avenue & Liberty |
| Griswold Park | Peach Street at West 14th Street |
| C. Francis Hagerty Park | West 32nd & Schaper Avenue |
| Lakeside Park | Front/ Peach Streets to Sassafras |
| Martin Luther King Jr. Park | West 4th Street near Chestnut |
| Myrtle Street Playground | Myrtle Street at West 19th |
| Pebble Lake Playground | Washington Avenue & Cold Springs Drive |
| Perry Square Park | State Street at West 6th Street |
| Ravine Park | Bayfront and foot of Kahkwa Blvd |
| Reservoir Park | West Grandview Blvd & Wood Street |
| Victory Park | Lincoln Avenue at West 13th Street |
| Washington Park | West 24th & Raspberry Street |
| Woodland Park | Woodland Drive & Kahkwa Blvd |

### EASTSIDE

| | |
|---|---|
| Burton Park | East 38th & Burton Avenue |
| Chautauqua Park | Lakeside Drive & Chautauqua Blvd |
| Cranch Park | Lakeside Drive & Cranch Avenue |
| Euclid Park | Lakeside Drive & Euclid Avenue |
| Franklin Park | East 7th & Marne Street |
| Garden Heights Playground | East 40th & Brewer Avenue |
| Hillside Park & Sunset Blvd | East 41st between Old French & Sunset Blvd |
| Joseph Walczak, Sr. Park | East 45th & Alan Drive |
| Kosciusko Park | East 12th & Wayne Street |
| Lake Park | Lakeside Park & Lake Avenue |
| Land Lighthouse Park | Foot of Lighthouse Street |
| McCarty Playground | East 2nd & Pennsylvania Avenue |
| McClelland Park | 26th & McClelland Streets |
| McKinley Park | East 21st & East Avenue |
| Nate Levy/ Jaycee Park | 200 block of East 3rd Street |
| Perry Square East | State Street and North Park Row |
| Pulaski Park East | 10th and Hess Avenue |
| Rodger Young Park | Buffalo Road & Downing Avenue |
| Roessler Park | East 15th & Reed Street |
| Roma Park | Zimmerman Road at East 35th Street |
| Wallace Street Playground | Front & Wallace Street |
| Wayne Park | East 6th & East Avenue |
| 19th & Wayne | 19th & Wayne Street |
| John G. Carney Park | Woodland Avenue East of Cameron |

A statue of Commodore Oliver Hazard Perry stands guard over a public park, named in his honor, in the center of the city. The statue was erected in 1985 to commemorate the 200th birthday of Perry who became one of Erie's favorite sons by defeating an entire British fleet during the battle of Lake Erie.

100

**Ed Bernik**

## PORT AUTHORITY

The **Erie Western Pennsylvania Port Authority** is a corporate and political body with a mission to promote and balance water-related industry and recreation on **Presque Isle Bay** and adjacent waters for the citizens of Pennsylvania. The Port Authority has legislatively mandated powers that allow it to acquire property, construct facilities, enter into agreements and generate new private investment. The organization is also responsible for the safe and ecologically-friendly use of the Bay.

Bob Hagle

John Horstman

**Main Postal Facility at 38th and Zimmerman**

## POST OFFICE

The Erie District Office of the **United States Postal Service** processes more than 3.7 million pieces of mail daily and over one billion pieces annually. Most Erieites don't realize that the Erie District Office is also responsible for 22 counties in Pennsylvania, covering 17,337 square miles. That volume translates to approximately 3,900 employees with 1,147 city routes and 600 rural ones at 481 different post offices and 18 different stations and branches. The main processing facility is located at west 38th and Zimmerman Road in the city.

John Buffington

## COAST GUARD

The **U.S. Coast Guard** is another important force on the shores of Lake Erie. The city, and more specifically, **Presque Isle Peninsula**, is home to a **U.S. Coast Guard Station**, located at the southeastern tip of the Peninsula, next to the channel between Lake Erie and Presque Isle Bay.

**101**

## EARLY PARKS

An act of Pennsylvania legislature designated Erie to be laid out in three 1 mile square districts, running from the Bayfront to 12th St. Each district included a park (**Perry Square**, **Gridley Park**, and **Frontier Park**). **Glenwood Park**, shown above in its early years, was not added until later in city history.

## THE ERIE STONE

All street planning and construction owe their origins to one stone - **"The Erie Stone"**. Three inches thick, 48" long, and 16" wide, the stone was set in the southeast corner of Parade and Front streets in 1795 by **General William Irvine** and **Major Andrew Scott**, State Commissioners, with a corps of surveyors and a protective military escort. All measurements for streets in Erie were computed from this landmark.

## CAPITOL

On August 25th, 1849, **President Zachary Taylor** had an "acute attack of bilious trouble" while traveling through Cambridge Springs, PA. He was promptly transported to the Reed house in Erie, where he spent 10 days recovering while the city served as the nation's capitol.

## INTER-CITY TRAVEL

Starting in 1906, Erieites could travel to Cleveland or Buffalo via trolleys known as "inter-urbans," so called because they traveled between cities.

## MAYOR TULLIO

Without doubt, **Lou Tullio** is one of the best known figures in the history of Erie politics. He was mayor for an unprecedented six terms. Tullio spent his early career as a coach at Gannon University.

## OLD FIREFIGHTERS

Erie has a long tradition of firefighters. The first fire station in Erie was built in 1873 at West 5th and Chestnut Streets. The site now serves as a museum.

103

EDUCATION

Photo: Art Becker

John Horstman

School Board members oversee both in-school and after school activities for city students.

## ADMINISTRATION

The **Erie School Board** oversees the schools that educate the nearly 12,800 students in the city. The students themselves come from diverse economic and ethnic backgrounds - the collective student body speaks 26 languages other than English, and roughly 43% of the students are minority students. To provide learning and growth opportunities for students, the School Board directs several programs, including an Academic Sports League that gives scholarships to deserving students, a delinquency prevention program that operates after school, on weekends, and over the summer, a vocational education program that teaches marketable education skills, and many other programs that foster intellectual and emotional growth. For Erie's 1,601 member school staff, the Board provides programs, such as the instructional technologies program which encourages the use of computers that help make teaching and learning easier in the classroom.

## ERIE COUNTY SCHOOL DISTRICTS

1. Corry Area School District
2. Fairview School District
3. Fort LeBoeuf School District
4. General McLane School District
5. Girard School District
6. Harborcreek School District
7. Millcreek Township School District
8. North East School District
9. Wattsburg Area School District
10. Northwestern School District
11. Union City Area School District
12. Iroquois School District

## CITY OF ERIE PUBLIC SCHOOLS

### ELEMENTARY SCHOOLS
1. Burton
2. Grover Cleveland
3. JoAnna Connell
4. Diehl
5. Edison
6. Emerson-Gridley
7. Pfeiffer-Burleigh
8. Glenwood
9. Harding
10. Irving
11. Jefferson
12. Lincoln
13. McKinley
14. Perry

### MIDDLE SCHOOLS
1. Wilson
2. Wayne
3. Roosevelt

### HIGH SCHOOLS
1. Central
2. Northwest Collegiate Academy
3. East
4. Strong Vincent

*Denise Keim*

## GERTRUDE BARBER CENTER

**F**ounded in 1952, the humble beginnings of the Gertrude Barber Center gave way to world-wide respect as a special education innovator. **Gertrude Barber** was serving as Assistant Superintendent in the Erie School District when she realized that Erie did not have adequate special education or support for many of its students. Often these students had to be sent far from home to get the services they needed. She organized a program for these students and ran it out of a single room in the local **YWCA**. A curriculum had to be constructed as one did not exist yet. Word quickly spread and curriculums were added. In fact, Gertrude Barber Center has added a new service or opened a new facility every year since its inception. Now, the Gertrude Barber Center serves over 2,600 people in Erie, the Pittsburgh area, Corry, Girard, and other areas. The Barber Center employs over 1,300 staff members.

## HOME SCHOOLING

**5**50 households in Erie County educate their kids themselves. Lack of religious education and prohibitive costs of private education are two of the reasons that in Pennsylvania, one in every 100 schoolchildren is homeschooled. **The Erie County Home Schoolers Association** issues diplomas. To assure compliance with national benchmarks, standardized tests are given in grades 3, 5, and 8.

*Sandy Hughes*

*Art Becker*

## DAYCARE AND ELEMENTARY

**T**here are more than 50 daycare facilities dedicated to socializing and preparing young children for formal education. Erie County has more than 40,000 children between the ages of 5 and 14. Approximately 25% of elementary and middle school students in Erie County attend private schools.

**107**

## ADDITIONAL LEARNING OPPORTUNITIES

Certainly learning does not need to stop at a high school or collegiate level. The Erie region offers many opportunities to expand one's knowledge through a wide variety of resources. While there are classes all over town, some of the following institutions are well known and respected.

### THE ERIE ART MUSEUM (page 134)

### THE ERIE COUNTY HISTORICAL SOCIETY AND MUSEUMS

If you are interested in Erie's rich historical heritage, look no further than the **ECHS&M.** The non-profit organization oversees three sites which include: The **Erie County History Center** & **Cashier's House** (400 block between State and French), **Watson-Curtze Mansion** (West 6th Street), and **The Battles Museums of Rural Life** in Girard. The group collectively showcases traveling and permanent collections relevant to Erie's colorful past, provides genealogical information and publishes **The Journal of Erie Studies**. Also at the 6th Street site is The **Erie Planetarium,** which features science experiments and Planetarium shows.

### THE ERIE MARITIME MUSEUM

**The Erie Maritime Museum** is home to the **U.S. Brig Niagara**, a reconstruction of one of the vessels used by **Commodore Oliver Hazard Perry** to defeat the British in the War of 1812. The museum offers tours of the Niagara when it is in port. Excellent multi-media presentations offer insight into Erie's maritime history. If you have not visited this museum yet, put down this book and go today. You'll be impressed with the quality of the

*Denise Keim*

The **Raymond M. Blasco Memorial Library** is more than just books. Beyond its more than 1/2 million volumes, the new facility attracts record numbers of visitors with CDs, videotapes, children's toys, genealogical information, and Internet access.

exhibits and with the city's maritime story.

### THE ERIE PUBLIC LIBRARY

Located at 160 East Front Street near Dobbin's Landing, the main branch of the Erie library is named for **Raymond M. Blasco**, a local physician whose generous donations helped build the new library. In addition to the Blasco Library, the Erie County Library System has several other branches, as well as traveling bookmobile services.

### expERIEnce CHILDREN'S MUSEUM

In the 400 block of French Street, the Children's Museum offers interactive presentations that teach kids in an entertaining way. Though the Children's Museum targets kids between the ages of 2 and 12, the museum is an experience for the whole family.

### NEIGHBORHOOD ARTHOUSE (page 133)

## HIGH SCHOOLS

**E**rie County has more than 20,000 high-school-aged children. The majority attend one of 18 public or 3 parochial high schools. There are also a number of families who choose to send their children to private schools or school them at home.

*photos courtesy from top :* McDowell, East High School, Ed Bernik

### ERIE AREA HIGH SCHOOLS

#### PUBLIC HIGH SCHOOLS
1. Central High School
2. Corry Area High School
3. East High School
4. Fairview High School
5. Fort LeBoeuf High School
6. General McLane High School
7. Girard High School
8. Harborcreek High School
9. Iroquois High School
10. McDowell High School
11. North Coast High School
12. North East High School
13. Northwestern High School
14. Northwest PA Collegiate Academy
15. Seneca High School
16. Strong Vincent High School
17. Union City High School

#### PAROCHIAL HIGH SCHOOLS
1. Cathedral Preparatory School
2. Mercyhurst Preparatory School
3. Villa Maria Academy

#### PRIVATE HIGH SCHOOLS
1. Bethel Christian Academy
2. Community Country Day School
3. Girard Alliance Christian Academy

*photo courtesy :* Mercyhurst Prep

Rob Ruby

# Catholic Schools

Have Faith in Education! Catholic schools offer a rich opportunity to learn and grow in a setting inspired by spiritual development and academic growth. With more than 150 years of history in the Diocese of Erie, Catholic schools enjoy a unique tradition of quality, value-centered education in a Christian atmosphere. Opportunities for a Catholic education abound within the 13 counties of northwestern Pennsylvania that make up the Diocese of Erie.

Catholic elementary schools prepare students to meet the challenges of high school and beyond, focusing on the needs of the individual student.

Catholic high schools are college preparatory; millions of dollars in scholarships are awarded annually to college-bound seniors in diocesan schools. Challenging academic programs, safety and discipline within the school environment and a wide variety of sports and extracurricular programs provide a well-rounded education for the mind, body and soul.

A Catholic education is one of the best ways to pass on your faith - a continuation of the teaching mission of the Church. The professionals within the Catholic school setting are committed to sound educational practices, responding to the needs of both student and parent. The dedication of its faculty, the teaching of values, and the safe, caring, environment are among the qualities parents enjoy about a Catholic school.

Photo Courtesy: Cathedral Prep

# Cathedral Preparatory School

Developing the whole man in spirit, mind, and body is the mission of Cathedral Preparatory School, founded in Erie in 1921 by Bishop John Mark Gannon. Cathedral Prep boasts a long tradition of excellence in the spiritual and educational development of young men. The students, faculty, staff and administration commit to promoting an environment that is positive, supportive and Christ-like, while fostering a relationship of mutual respect with the community.

A well-recognized history of success in the placement of its graduates into colleges and positions of leadership makes Cathedral Prep a cornerstone in the success of their students. Cathedral Prep alumni have become some of the area's most successful leaders: chief executive officers, engineers, attorneys, judges, priests, surgeons and the Secretary of Homeland Security. "Share the Vision," a multi-million dollar renovation project, will allow Prep to modernize facilities... incorporate cutting-edge technology throughout the school (wireless internet access and tablet PC program)...and upgrade the learning environment for the classrooms.

The focus of Cathedral Prep's academic program is fortified by both accelerated courses and the Advanced Placement Program which offer college credit options. Cathedral Prep has a cooperative agreement with Gannon University enabling students to earn college credits at a fraction of the cost... these credits can be transferred to colleges and universities across the nation. Over 97% of Cathedral Prep graduates are accepted and enroll in a college, university, or service academy.

Looking to the future, Cathedral Prep stays on the cutting edge of technologies, including a tablet P.C. program, the latest software, computer hardware, and wireless internet access available to all students. This gives students the necessary tools to perform to the best of their abilities in an ever-changing world.

Photos Courtesy: Mercyhurst Prep

# Mercyhurst Preparatory

Mercyhurst Preparatory School is a private Catholic co-educational high school  founded in 1926 and operated by the Sisters of Mercy.

The school has a tradition of innovation, offering challenging programs that better prepare students to face this ever-changing global world.  In 1985 MPS became the second Catholic school in the United States and the fourth Pennsylvania school to be accepted into the prestigious International Baccalaureate Program.  It is the only school in Western Pennsylvania to offer this challenging curriculum.

IB challenges students to become excellent critical thinkers and problem solvers.  Recipients of the IB diploma can earn automatic admission and advanced standing at some of the most selective colleges and universities in North America.  Some institutions grant a full year's credit to diploma graduates.

In 1993 and again in 1998, The United States Department of Education awarded MPS its highest honor, the Blue Ribbon School of Excellence Award.

Another unique offering is the Seniors at Mercyhurst (SAM) program, allowing advanced students to enroll at Mercyhurst College for college credit hours.

Mercyhurst Prep was the first school in the Erie area to commit to excellence in arts education.  The school boasts nearly 50 course offerings in the performing and visual arts, with nine full-time teaching professionals.

Campus Ministry and volunteer programs provide over 34,000 annual service hours to the community.  The effects of this generous spirit reach people all over the world.

The school offers a full athletic program for both boys and girls, including 40 varsity, junior varsity, and intramural teams in fifteen different sports,  with Erie's only high school competing crew team.

Through the leadership of the Sisters of Mercy, the school continues its commitment to prepare students from all religious and ethnic backgrounds for a successful, productive, and compassionate life in an ever-changing and interdependent world.

# Villa Maria Academy

In Erie, the corner of 8th and Liberty has long been a city landmark. In 1892, a large red brick building, which encompassed a whole city block and was surrounded by quaint black iron pickets, opened its doors to Erie city children. Villa Maria Academy and Villa Maria Elementary began this chapter in Erie education history at this 8th and Liberty Street foundation, ably guided by the Sisters of St. Joseph of Northwestern PA.

In those early days, students often boarded at the school, as did our notable local figure Dr. Gertrude Barber, the founder of the Barber Center. Whether by trolley or on foot, young students from all over the city came to study piano and music at the Villa Conservatory. Readin', writin', and 'rithmetic were finished with fashionable studies like china painting and needlepoint. Originally the Academy opened to both boys and girls, but gradually became an all-girls school until 1987, when again the Academy became coeducational.

In the 1960s, the Academy moved to its current home, 2403 West 8th, on the Villa Maria Campus, with sister school Villa Maria Elementary. Today, Villa Maria Academy, known as one of the finest coeducational secondary private schools in the Erie area, offers excellence in academic college preparatory programs, as well as excellence in Fine Arts, Performance Arts, and Athletics. VMA fields 21 team sports for males and females. This smaller school community welcomes and nurtures students in a family atmosphere, with many growth opportunities in Fine and Graphic Arts, Performance Arts, and Athletics.

Times and curriculums change. Villa Maria, though, still stands as a leader in the Erie area for exceptional education that creates leaders for life. Villa Maria Academy and campus sister school Villa Maria Elementary celebrate over 100 years of educating students of all faiths and diversities to become leaders of tomorrow.

By taking a holistic approach LECOM students are taught to treat the patient - body, mind and spirit.

**ON THE FAST TRACK,** LECOM students can earn a Doctor of Pharmacy degree in just 3 years.

## LAKE ERIE COLLEGE OF OSTEOPATHIC MEDICINE

Our world is changing faster than at any other time in human history. Every day, amazing

discoveries in technology, science and medicine help millions around the globe. We are indeed living better, longer and healthier lives than ever before. With a focus on preventive care, **LECOM**, the **Lake Erie College of Osteopathic Medicine**, is training tomorrow's doctors and pharmacists to successfully face the healthcare challenges of a new era.

Since opening day in August 1993, the mission of LECOM has been to provide a strong foundation of medical knowledge in a program that also cultivates character, compassion, dependability and professionalism. By developing clinical skills and a holistic approach to medicine, the students learn to care for the whole person - body, mind, and spirit.

LECOM is one of only twenty osteopathic medical colleges in the entire U.S. It is the only school with a focus on three specific methods of learning: lecture and discussion, small-group problem-based learning, and independent study.

The school is growing by leaps and bounds and stays on top of current trends. For example, to meet the demand for pharmacists, in 2002 LECOM opened a school of Pharmacy that enables students to earn a Doctor of Pharmacy degree in just 3 years. This school has a planned enrollment of 320 students. From an inaugural graduating class of 37 students to a present-day enrollment of nearly 800, the college continues to grow, with plans to open a branch site in Florida in 2004. The Florida branch of LECOM will have a planned enrollment of 600 students, which will make LECOM the largest medical school in America.

The school is proud to be part of the Erie community and thankful for the support that they have received for over a decade.

**115**

**Edinboro University of Pennsylvania** is one of the 14 universities in Pennsylvania's State System of Higher Education.

## EDINBORO UNIVERSITY OF PENNSYLVANIA

**W**ith more than 46,000 graduates all over the world, Edinboro University boasts a 146-year history of preparing students for their futures. From choosing a college major to lifetime career assistance, Edinboro University provides a variety of services to help students discover themselves and their futures.

The main campus in Edinboro consists of 43 buildings on 585 acres, with a five-acre lake and plenty of wooded areas. Edinboro University in Erie - The Porreco Center consists of 12 buildings and offers classes during the day, evening and on weekends for the convenience of the students.

The Meadville Access Center, located 20 miles south of Edinboro, offers classes and information on programs and activities.

### Faculty

An atmosphere of mutual respect and genuine caring among students and faculty members is part of the Edinboro experience. Students benefit from faculty who get to know them and care about them inside and outside the classroom. The faculty is diverse in ethnic, cultural and racial backgrounds, and more than two-thirds have doctoral degrees or the highest degree in their field.

### Academics

Edinboro University offers more than 100 associate, bachelor's and master's degrees in 24 academic departments,

### Financial Aid

More than $46 million in student financial aid is available to Edinboro University students each year through a variety of grants (federal aid, Pennsylvania aid, OIG for Ohio students, and assistance from Edinboro University). In addition, an extensive scholarship program has been established (from which more than 500 scholarships are awarded each year), and approximately 900 student jobs are available on campus.

### Facilities

From research to technology, Edinboro is a campus that meets your needs. The seven-story library has more than 480,000 bound volumes and 1.3 million microform units, with access to a collection of ebooks. Six residence halls house approximately 2,500 students, and each room is wired for digital-satellite cable-television services, high-speed data connections, and telephone connection, making the campus one of the most advanced technological environments of any university in the nation.

Explore the universe at the planetarium and solar observatory, study the characteristics of DNA in one of the modern science labs, or experience the technology of the new millennium in a robotics lab. A reading clinic, speech and hearing clinic, math clinic, and writing center all provide valuable hands-on experience for Edinboro students.

### Athletics

The Fighting Scots compete in 14 intercollegiate sports: men's basketball, cross country, football, swimming, track and wrestling; and women's basketball, cross country, indoor track, soccer, softball, swimming, track and volleyball.

**Edinboro University of Pennsylvania provides a quality education at an affordable cost through full-time professional faculty members in an environment that is caring, attractive, safe and secure."**

- Dr. Frank G. Pogue, President

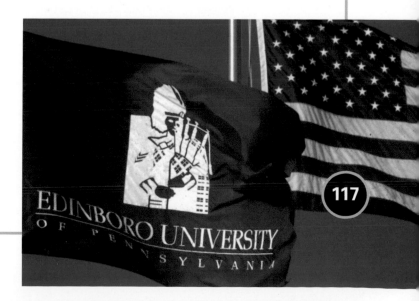

## ERIE BUSINESS CENTER

**S**tep into any business, law or medical office in Erie and the surrounding counties and, chances are, you will find an Erie Business Center graduate at work.

EBC is a private, two-year college that has the distinction of being the longest-established career training institution in the Erie area. The school's director, **Donna Perino**, estimates that up to 80 percent of the businesses in the area employ at least one EBC graduate.

The school, which has campuses in downtown Erie and New Castle, Pennsylvania, offers two-year associate in specialized business (ASB) degrees and one-year diploma programs. In 2003-2004, students could work toward any of 12 ASB degree programs in a business, computer, secretarial or specialty career; or toward one of 11 different diploma programs.

In the school's most recent reporting period, more than nine out of ten EBC graduates had found jobs in their fields. The school consistently records job placement rates above 90 percent. EBC relies on advisory boards of area professionals as well as student internship programs to tailor its studies to the needs of employers.

EBC graduates are employed throughout the Erie area.

"We talk to employers," Mrs. Perino says, "and we adapt and enhance our programs to match their needs. Students here take the courses that will enable them to hit the ground running in a range of career fields."

Under the guidance of **Charles P. McGeary Jr.**, president and chairman of the board, and his wife, **Hope A. McGeary**, who serves as vice president and board secretary, enrollment at the school continues to grow and the focus remains very much on the future. In 2003-2004, enrollment was up almost 25 percent with 330 full-time and 150 part-time students. Students range from new high school graduates to adults retraining for new careers by choice or by necessity because of job loss.

"It is such a pleasure to teach people who want to be here, who want to learn," says Mrs. Perino, who came to EBC from private industry and taught at the school for six years before becoming the director. "These are people who want to make a difference in their lives."

EBC offers a friendly, supportive environment for professional development and personal growth.

Today, the college has about 100 employees and a faculty of 10 full-time and more than 30 part-time instructors. The student-to-faculty ratio is 15 to 1.

At the direction of chief administrator **Sam McCaughtry**, EBC invested more than $1 million over the past five years to upgrade its computer equipment and software. The result is evident in advanced computer training labs, a high-speed information systems network and an on-campus help desk.

As an example of the school's personal, supportive approach to learning, Fridays at EBC are considered Advantage Days. There are no scheduled classes, so students can use the free days to do homework, study and complete other projects. EBC instructors are available on Advantage Days for make-up work,

Erie Business Center offers more than 20 different associate in specialized business degrees and diploma programs.

**Charles and Hope McGeary**

Photos: Rob Ruby

tutoring and other assistance. The school's computer labs and the campus library are also open.

Erie Business Center, which will mark its 120th anniversary next year, has been owned and headed by just two families. It was founded by **H.C. Clark** as **Clark's Business College** in 1884.

**Charles P. McGeary Sr.** later became owner and president of the school, renamed Erie Business College, and directed it until his death in 1953. His wife, **Chelsie S. McGeary**, subsequently served as president until her death in 1972. At that time, Charles P. McGeary Jr. assumed the role of director. Leadership of Erie Business Center by the McGeary family continues today.

## ALLEGHENY COLLEGE

Established in 1815, Allegheny College is a selective, liberal arts college of nearly 2,000 students in Meadville, Pa.

Campus visitors are impressed with Allegheny's beautiful, historic setting, but its academic programs are where the College shines brightest. Allegheny College produces scientists, artists, educators, and entrepreneurs of the highest caliber. Small classes and an array of experiential learning opportunities ensure that students and faculty work as colleagues on research and community-development educational projects.

Recognized as one of the nation's foremost colleges promoting applied learning, community involvement and leadership development, Allegheny College is committed to preparing students for a lifetime of personal and civic responsibility.

For more info on Allegheny College visit www.allegheny.edu or call 800-521-5293

## EARLY LIBRARY SYSTEM

Erie has come a long way since 1806 when Erie established its first library company. At that time, library companies raised around $200 and began purchasing books for Erie's population. It was not until 1895, that an effort was begun to bring an organized public library to Erie. In that year Pennsylvania passed the Pennsylvania Free Public Library Act, legislation that was proposed by the Erie School Board. By 1899, the **Erie County Public Library System** procured enough space on Perry Square and French Street and constructed a grand building in the Italian Renaissance style. The cost approached $150,000, $6,000 of which was donated by **Andrew Carnegie**.

## ERIE ACADEMY

**The Erie Academy** began operation on the southeast corner of Peach and 9th Streets in 1823. The first building was in a state of disarray when it was closed in 1874 and was renovated in 1878. Classes continued at the location until 1916, when the building was closed due to lack of enrollment. The Erie School District sold the building for approximately $250,000 and used the money to build the newer Academy High School at 28th and State streets.

## FIRST SCHOOL

Education in Erie had humble beginnings. Erie's first school was constructed in 1806 on a lot donated for the purpose by Daniel Dobbins. 100 dedicated Erie citizens raised the $30 needed to build the 18 x 22 foot rough-hewn log schoolhouse on the site at 7th and Holland Street. From the center of town at 4th and German, children followed a path through the woods to the school, then dubbed the **Presqu' Seminary**, which prospered until 1987.

*historical photos courtesy:* **Erie County Historical Society & Museums**

**Photo: Beata Stark**

## DAVE HALLMAN CHEVROLET

To several generations of Erieites, the name **Dave Hallman** has been synonymous with shiny new Chevy cars and trucks. Since opening their doors nearly thirty years ago, the Dave Hallman Chevrolet dealership has been a fixture of the Erie car market, matching thousands of brand new Corvettes, Impalas and Silverados with smiling happy customers. In fact, if you bought a new Chevy any time during the last 29 years in Erie, chances are you bought it from **Dave** or his son **David, Jr**.

And why wouldn't you? After all, Chevrolets run so deep in the Hallman family that it's a wonder they don't all have oil cruising through their veins. Consider this: when Grandaddy **Maynard Hallman** started his first Chevrolet deal-

Ed Bernik

**Longtime employee loyalty is a Hallman trademark. Above with the year they started, left to right: Lou Berti (1960), Carolyn Mahoney (1958) and John Wurst (1974).**

CONSERVE YOUR CAR! SAVE THE WHEELS THAT SERVE AMERICA!

LET CENTRAL CHEVROLET SERVICE YOUR CAR REGULARLY DURING 1943

Ed Bernik

Rob Ruby

**Dave Hallman with his son David Jr. in their State Street showroom. Hallman Chevrolet outsells other car dealers in Erie County month after month, year after year.**

ership in Rochester, NY, FDR was the President, the Great Depression was in full swing, and the brand new Chevy was a Master Coupe.

Since that time, the entire family has had a significant role in keeping Detroit working. Maynard went on to establish a dozen more dealerships as far south as Miami and west to Reno, Nevada. He also found time to raise five boys who worked in the business as well.

It's not surprising, then, the Hallmans are proud when talking about the high quality of these American-made vehicles. It's a diverse offering, indeed, ranging from the Cavalier - "perfect for the first-time buyer" to the Corvette - "still the best

sports car value on Planet Earth." Add in the vast array of trucks and vans and there's certain to be something ideal for any buyer.

Ask Dave Hallman what he is proudest of, though, and he doesn't hesitate to praise his 165 employees. "We have virtually no employee turnover - some people have been with us since the 1950s. That kind of loyalty creates a nurturing work environment that translates into top-notch service to our customers."

DAVE HALLMAN CHEVROLET
1925 STATE STREET
ERIE, PENNSYLVANIA 16501
814 452-6731

F8533E

Fly Erie

## ERIE INTERNATIONAL AIRPORT
## TOM RIDGE FIELD

**E**rie International Airport, Tom Ridge Field is a public use, primary commercial service facility owned and operated by the **Erie Municipal Airport Authority**. Situated in Erie County in northwestern Pennsylvania, the airport is less that 5 miles from major highways Interstate 79 and Interstate 90, allowing travelers easy access to most locations within the region.

The airport is the Erie region's gateway to the global community. Currently serving more than 265,000 passengers annually, with an expectation to increase passenger levels to 400,000 in the near future, this market represents a tremendous opportunity for growth.

To accommodate anticipated growth, the airport is making dramatic capital improvements including extending the runway by 1,900 sq. ft., substantial improvements to the terminal building, a new stand-alone air traffic control tower and the development of a multi-modal International Trade Center which will include a manufacturing and cargo facility.

Even as airport officials look toward the future, they continue to develop business relationships with new and existing airport tenants which include four major carriers: US Airways, Northwest, Delta/Comair and Continental. These major carriers connect to four major hubs and destinations to more than 1,100 locations world-wide.

To promote the various airport services, officials launched an aggressive marketing campaign appropriately entitled *"Fly Erie...More Reasons Now Than Ever."* The campaign encompasses the public relations effort associated with strategic development at the airport as well as a multi-media advertising campaign being funded by contributions from area businesses that recognize the impact of the airport to the regional economy.

**ERIE INTERNATIONAL AIRPORT**
**4411 WEST 12TH STREET**
**ERIE, PENNSYLVANIA 16505**
**814 833-4258**

Photos Courtesy: Erie International Airport

## NORTH COAST CHARTER

**N**eed to get somewhere in a hurry? Or are you a business traveler who seeks the best that Erie airlines have to offer?

Discover **North Coast Charter -** a local Erie aircraft charter company. North Coast Charter is located at the Erie International Airport, Tom Ridge Field.

North Coast Charter's first-class private flights and accommodations are renowned for their attention to safety and customer service. Flights within a 1200-mile radius can accommodate up to eight passengers. The company offers a secure traveling environment without the inconvenience of waiting in screening lines or enduring extensive personal searches. You will also be able to increase productivity by working, conducting business, and holding conversations during your flight. Other perks of flying with North Coast Air include free parking and complimentary snacks and beverages.

North Coast Charter's top priority is safe, secure, reliable service for their corporate and private customers. The service is available 24 hours a day, 7 days a week. Call today to book your next flight. Facility tours are happily provided and available by appointment.

NORTH COAST CHARTER
1609 ASBURY ROAD
ERIE, PENNSYLVANIA 16505
814 836-9220

**NORTH COAST CHARTER** is the solution for quick, safe and fun air travel.

The spacious and clean hangar bay at **NORTH COAST AIR** can efficiently accomodate your needs. Clients enjoy a full array of amenities.

## NORTH COAST AIR

**N**orth Coast Air is located at the Erie International Airport, Tom Ridge Field. The company is a leader in Fixed-Base Operator (FBO) service. North Coast Air ensures their customers from around the country can fly into Erie confident that, upon landing, they will receive exceptionally high quality, world-class customer and mechanical service and support.

This is accomplished by providing world-class amenities, including 24-hour on-call service, competitive air BP fuel prices, WSI weather briefing, maintenance, complimentary crew cars, courtesy van, reservation services for hotels, restaurants and events, rental cars, a comfortable lounge, ramp fees waived with fuel purchase, catering services, complimentary snacks, and location adjacent to US Customs. North Coast Air is the proud recipient of the Pennsylvania Fixed Base Operator of the Year award.

NORTH COAST AIR
4645 WEST 12TH STREET
ERIE, PENNSYLVANIA 16505
814 836-9220

Rob Ruby

## NORTH COAST FLIGHT SCHOOL

**H**ave you ever wondered what it would be like to fly? **North Coast Flight School** has your answer. You can experience first hand, how exhilarating, challenging and awesome it is to fly while they take you step by step through the process of becoming a private pilot.

North Coast Flight School also offers Instrument, Commercial, Multi-engine and CFI instruction. Whether you fly in one of their planes or your own, you are assured of safe and professional training that is always enjoyable.

Owner **Bonnie Moorhead** encourages, "Bring a camera! You won't believe how awesome things look from the air. Rides and tours can be tailored just for you. Be creative. North Coast pilots love to fly and would be happy to fly over your house, school, or wherever you'd like to go. The sunset over Presque Isle is amazing from the air." North Coast Cessna 172s can comfortably accommodate the pilot and up to three passengers. Bring your friends and let a North Coast FAA-certified commercial pilot guide you on an experience of a lifetime.

NORTH COAST FLIGHT SCHOOL
1605 ASBURY ROAD
ERIE, PENNSYLVANIA 16505
814 836-9220

## HARBOR CHANNEL

**A** seven-mile sand spit peninsula, **Presque Isle State Park** projects into Lake Erie, creating **Presque Isle Bay**. The channel that links Lake Erie and Presque Isle Bay, as well as federally designated harbor areas, is maintained by the Army Corps of Engineers. Arguably the best harbor on Lake Erie, Presque Isle Bay has much to offer. Pleasure boating, sport fishing, jet skiing and water skiing are among some of the favorites. At the head of the channel is North Pier Light. Painted in a distinctive black and white design, the light is also referred to as "The Harbor Light." The channel is a popular spot for fishing in the summer months.

John Buffington

## BAYFRONT PARKWAY

**U** ntil recent years, Interstate 79 ended at West 12th Street. The completion of the **Bayfront Parkway** in 1990 opened Erie's waterfront to citizens and visitors to northwestern Pennsylvania. Linking communities east and west, it also created new business interest along the bayfront.

In fact, the Parkway is a classic example of how transportation can drive economic investment in the form of new office buildings, residential construction, retail establishments, and recreational opportunities. The 35-mph speed limit means this road is a Parkway, not a highway.

John Buffington

John Buffington

## Union Station

Before the days of Fords and Chevrolets, the mode of transportation from town to town was on the rails. In Erie, the major stop was Union Station, a grand depot at 14th and Peach Streets. Folks saw their loved ones off with tearful good-byes and welcomed them home with joyful hugs. President Abraham Lincoln himself stopped at the train station twice - once on his way to the Oval Office, then again on his funeral train.

## THE FINAL FRONTIER

After being born in Erie, **Paul J. Weitz** went on to spend 28 days in space in 1973. At the time it was the longest time any human had spent in Earth Orbit. Weitz was also commander of the shuttle **Challenger** on its maiden voyage in 1983.

# Erie Firsts
### in Transportation

**1797**
First vessel built in Erie
*"The Washington"*

**1818**
First
Steamboat
Visit

**1849**
First
Locomotive
Visit

**1889**
First
Electric
Street Car

**1929**  First Bus

**131**

*unless noted, historical photos courtesy:* **Erie County Historical Society & Museums**

BUSINESS

Photo: Art Becker

## MAJOR EMPLOYERS

**G**eneral Electric and **Erie Insurance Group**, as well as many other nationally known names, are major employers in Erie County. It is a major industrial center, and approximately one third of all jobs are in manufacturing. **Bush Industries**, manufacturer of furniture, is home to approximately 1,500 employees. Other major manufacturers include **Spectrum Control**, **PHB Corporation**, **Steris Corporation** and **Lord Corporation.** Goods produced at these companies include electromagnetic filters and capacitors, die cast rubber and plastics products, hospital equipment, and aerospace and industrial products. **Plastek Industries** employs 1,600 people and, as a producer of precision molds and molded plastics, helps Erie to provide over ten percent of the nation's plastic injection molding. Four of the top fifty plastics companies in the nation are located here in Erie. The **Erie City** and **County Governments** employ 2,225 people and the **School District** another 1,350. Erie is also home to the **Gertrude Barber Center**, a world-renowned special education facility that employs 1,300 staff members.

Art Becker

**General Electric:** More than half of the diesel freight locomotives currently operating in North America are manufactured at the local GE Transportation Systems plant. The locomotives also operate in 75 countries worldwide.

## TOP 40 EMPLOYERS

1. General Electric Company
2. Erie Indemnity Company
3. Hamot Medical Center
4. Pennsylvania State Government
5. Saint Vincent Health Center
6. School District of The City of Erie
7. United States Government
8. Plastek Management Group Inc
9. Erie County Government
10. Millcreek Township Government
11. Dr. Gertrude A. Barber Center Inc
12. City of Erie Government
13. West Telemarketing
14. Edinboro University
15. Steris
16. Verizon
17. Lord Corporation
18. Wegmans Food Markets Inc
19. Wal-Mart Associates Inc
20. Snap-Tite Inc
21. Country Fair Inc
22. Gannon University
23. Career Concepts Services Inc
24. The Tamarkin Company (Giant Eagle)
25. Pennsylvania State University (Behrend)
26. Spectrum Control Inc
27. Pleasant Ridge Manor
28. YMCA
29. Penn Traffic Company (Quality Supermarkets)
30. Mercyhurst College
31. Parker White Metal Company Inc
31. Fast Food Enterprises  (Burger King)
32. Erie County Plastics
33. Clinical Pathology Institute Inc
34. Rent-Way Inc
35. Welch Foods Inc
36. Bush Industries
37. Carlisle Engineered Products
38. HCF Inc (nursing homes)
39. Modern Industries Inc
40. K-Mart of Pennsylvania

PA Dept of Labor & Industry , Center for Workforce Information 2002

# ECONOMIC DEVELOPMENT

Becca Martin

Retaining and creating family-sustaining jobs for our region is the goal of Erie County's economic development system. The Erie Regional Chamber & Growth Partnership is leading Erie County's progressive and dynamic approach to economic development - an approach that views any individual or company looking to make an investment in the community as our most important customer.

The Erie Regional & Growth Partnership was created by the business community to unify its voice and elevate its involvement in local economic development while maintaining and improving a menu of services. It is a bold step toward taking control of the region's immediate and long-term economic well-being.

As the gateway into Erie County's economic development system, the Erie Regional Chamber manages all business prospects with their strategic partners: the City of Erie, County of Erie, Economic Development Corporation of Erie County, and Corry Redevelopment Authority.

A central component of this customer-centered approach is the Business Calling Program, a state-sponsored, locally administered program committed to growing and maintaining businesses and jobs in Erie County. Economic Development Specialists at the Erie Regional Chamber conduct personal interviews with business leaders, develop action plans and connect businesses to the local, state or federal service providers who can address the specific needs of the businesses . The Economic Development Specialists serve as a concierge to nearly 1,000 businesses in Erie County.

In addition to its strategic location, Erie offers a variety of competitive advantages for business expansion and relocation, including a readily accessible, affordable workforce, plentiful and affordable utilities, a high-tech campus at Knowledge Park, a plastics technology cluster, and a Center of Excellence in E-Business, and a growing logistics and remote diagnostic cluster.

Pennsylvania's only Great Lake port offers strong transportation infrastructure, substantial technology opportunities, Foreign Trade Zones, and Keystone Opportunity Zones.

## INTERMODAL TRANSPORTATION CENTER

Located at the foot of Holland Street, the Intermodal Transportation Center is a joint project between the Erie Metropolitan Transit Authority and the Erie-Western Pennsylvania Port Authority. Completed in 2002, the Center is a hub for Erie's public transportation as well as home office to the Erie Port Authority, Erie Regional Chamber & Growth Partnership, Convention and Visitors Bureau, and a variety of other businesses.

135

## What makes you qualified to find the right people for the right jobs?

When I first started my career path after graduation, I had no real idea as to what I wanted to be. I was a swing shift manager at McDonalds, and an Assistant Manager in a Beauty Salon. I worked at a gas station, I did bookkeeping for an auto body shop, bank teller (my least favorite job) and a products and inventory assistant at Erie Press Systems. I worked for a software company doing payroll, receptionist work, as well as assisting people with software problems. While I was working at this job (not career), I realized as I was reading the want ads that having done so many different jobs, I would be great at placing people in a job. I saw an ad for a placement coordinator and went for it. I got the job and my career started. I have never looked back, and I know this was what I was meant to do.

## What makes your agency different?

What makes Advanced Placement Services, Inc. different from other staffing agencies is the level of professional customer service we offer. Each customer feels as if he or she is our only customer. We are working toward being a one-stop shop for our clients. We offer every opportunity to make staffing and human resources easier for our clients. We plan to offer testing and training opportunities that are state of the art and flexible for our clients' schedules.

## What made you go into business for yourself?

I decided to go into business for myself because I had a vision of how this industry should be run.

# Multi-Tasking

an interview with
## DENISE CHRISTIANSON

*Denise Christianson owns Advanced Placement Services, Inc., a full service staffing agency offering employment opportunities for clerical, professional, technical, and labor placements. They handle pre-screening, testing, background checking, reference checking and recruiting for local businesses. They began July 12, 1999.*

ADVANCED PLACEMENT SERVICES, INC.
1932 WEST 8TH STREET
ERIE, PENNSYLVANIA 16505
814 454-7305

136

I had worked for ten years for another staffing agency and realized I had a different perspective. My husband felt that I had what it takes to own my own business and run it successfully. With his support and guidance, I was able to make this a reality. He continues to support me with his strength, love, and broad shoulders.

When I finally decided to take the plunge, I worked with Gannon SBDC and the National City SBA loan department. We wrote a business plan and before I knew it, we had Advanced Placement Services, Inc. It was exciting and very scary, all in one. We grew beyond my one-year business plan within the first three months. We have just celebrated our fourth year in business and look forward to the years to come.

## Have you found it difficult to be a female business owner?

I had the fortunate opportunity this past year to be a part of the Athena Powerlink. This is a mentoring opportunity for women business owners. A panel of experts are assembled together to offer consulting and support based on business goals. For one year I had experts in legal, accounting, marketing, insurance, banking, and business issues at my disposal. It helped me to grow as a person and a business woman, as well as opening new opportunities and ideas for my business. This is a program that is valuable to any woman business owner.

## Do you have any advice for someone just starting out?

The advice I would offer others interested in starting a business would be to make sure the business they plan to start can offer a living. Research your competition and make sure that it can survive in

the area you plan to locate. Surround yourself with others who are wiser and willing to lend their advice and support. The most important advice is to make sure to make time for you.

## Where is the reward?

The reward comes when you have a company that is excited about the person we place and how this person will help them meet their goals, and the person placed is also excited about their future career path. The energy and excitement that comes from the marriage of the two is a great feeling. Helping people is what we do.

## What's next?

I want Advanced Placement Services, Inc. to be the first company to come to mind when anyone thinks of staffing assistance or jobs. I hope to start a medical staffing division. I want to become a franchise. To continue to partner with our customers and work as if we worked directly for them, and to continue to assure our customers that we are here to be part of their staffing solutions. We truly go the extra mile every time!

Christianson's West 8th Street office

137

# A Cut Above

an interview with
## DAVE THORNTON

*David Thornton is the owner of David Lee Designs, a furniture design and manufacturing firm specializing in wooden case goods, including beds, tables, armoires, cabinets, desks, nightstands, bookcases. Thornton started in 1990 (it became a formal business in 1992). He currently has 15 employees.*

DAVID LEE DESIGNS
107 CLAY STREET
NORTH EAST, PENNSYLVANIA 16428
814 725-4289

## How did you get started?

I do not have any formal training in design or woodworking. Like everyone else, I had shop class in high school. That's about it.

I suppose that I had an interest in the creative and artistic end of it. In the early 90s, I was doing carpentry work. Primarily built-in cabinetry, crown moulding, and things like that. For supplemental income I began to build small furniture pieces and sold them at arts and crafts shows, as well as from my workshop, and things evolved from there.

## How is the furniture sold?

Primarily through independent sales representatives, who call on furniture stores and interior designers. We have our own showroom in High Point, North Carolina at the International Home Furnishings Market.

## What makes your furniture special?

I would have to say style, design and finish. Most of the furniture is available in 24 finishes, which are occasionally updated as trends change. We do some customizing, which is very appealing to our interior design customers. We are always adding new pieces and collections.

## What are your business plans?

We have outgrown our current facility and are exploring various expansion options. New incoming orders have been exceeding our production capabilities by 15-20% each month.

## What do you attribute your success to?

A variety of things: good designs, a quality product, and a need in the market for our product. I also cannot do it all myself, so I have to commend the people that I work with everyday.

### Do you have any advice for someone just starting out?

Be aware. Be aware of your costs, your overhead, your prices, your competition and probably most of all your customers.

### What are your newest products?

We have just come out with a new line of furniture called The French Countryside Collection. The collection includes cabinets, bookshelves, hutches, pantries and sideboards with artwork. The pictures are printed on canvas and then laminated onto the wood. We then coordinate the colors on the pieces with the printed canvas artwork.

Photos Courtesy: David Lee, Portrait - Rob Ruby

## Loud and Clear

an interview with

### SONDRALEE ORENGIA

*Sondralee Orengia is the owner of Custom Audio, which sells and installs mid to high-end audio, video, car stereo, and home theater systems.*

CUSTOM AUDIO
4453 WEST 26TH STREET
ERIE, PENNSYLVANIA 16506
814 833-8383

140

## HOW DID YOU GET STARTED?

In 1983, my former partner Joe Villo and I began offering a service that was not available in the Erie marketplace, a mobile car stereo installation service. We installed for stereo shops that didn't offer installation to their customers. This allowed them to compete with the other stores that offered installation, and helped keep us in business! There was very little capital needed to start up the business. All that was needed were a few business cards, a pager, some tools and a vehicle.

Customers liked us and our service and requested that we begin selling equipment. Because we didn't want to compete with the stores that were sending us the business we decided to open up a store that only sold vehicle security and a small line of car stereos. Revenue was generated by continuing to install for many stores and catalog showrooms. The largest account was a chain of electronics stores called The Appliance Store. This enabled us to create more revenue to expand our inventory and product lines. No loans from the bank were ever needed. How fortunate was that?

## Where was your first store?

The first store was located at 1550 West 26th Street, in the old Montgomery Wards building. The showroom was sparsely stocked at first, but after a few years more space was needed, and the store was getting full. The location was very good. The neighborhoods surrounding Custom Audio supported it quite nicely. After 10 years in that location, it was time to move on. The only hurdle was finding the right piece of property for Custom Audio, and it was highly specialized.

A garage was required for installation, and good sized showroom along with a great location. Unfortunately, most of the properties that fit this model were old garages or auto body shops! Today Custom Audio is happily housed at 4453 West 26th Street, in the Hickory Plaza.

### What was different about your approach?

To give the customer a great product, offer exceptional service and be knowledgeable. This may sound simple, but I see so many businesses that miss the mark in these areas. They only think of the bottom line first and the customer second. I truly believe that any business is about building relationships with your customer, long term relationships, the money always comes later.

The other thing that makes Custom Audio different, is that we have carved out a niche in the marketplace. That niche is a store that sells audio equipment and the accessories that go along with it. We are committed to helping the customer make their audio system sound better, whether it be home or car audio. I am not interested in doing home security, central vacuuming, performance car parts, etc., I feel these are only ways to spread the company thin. To keep Custom Audio strong we must stick to our roots, which is audio!

### What advice would you have for someone going into business for themselves?

First and foremost, get into something you are passionate about. Your passion becomes infectious and spreads to your staff and to your customers. How can that possibly go wrong? Also, know what you are getting yourself into. Don't ever go into a business unless you've researched and studied it completely. Today, competition is fierce and you must know your competitor.

Another good piece of advice is to not worry about what your competitor is doing, be aware of it, but don't lose sleep over it. Any energy you expend worrying about your competition should be used constructively towards your own business. You will win in the end with this approach.

Photos: Rob Ruby

**141**

# Fresh Ingredients

*J. Honard and Marci Honard are co-owners of Calamari's Squid Row (see pg. 278), which is a popular eating and drinking establishment in downtown Erie. Calamari's was the first successful venue in Erie's entertainment district at 13th and State. Both of them have extensive experience in the hospitality industry. Jay talks about the business...*

**CALAMARI'S**
1317 STATE STREET
ERIE, PENNSYLVANIA 16501
814 459-4276

**142**

### How did you get started?

I had been in the restaurant business since 1986 when I worked at the Bel Aire. I went to New Orleans and worked for a national chain restaurant, eventually moved back to Erie and tended bar at a local downtown restaurant. From there I went on to work for a wine and spirits distributor out of Philadelphia. I was a regional sales representative. And finally I sold food wholesale for C.A. Curtze to restaurants, schools, and organizations. This taught me how to sell to people with a variety of budgets. Curtze really opened my eyes.

### Were you looking to buy your own restaurant?

Yes. I was looking to own a restaurant, but more than a restaurant, something that offered entertainment, food, and a great social atmosphere, let's say. I was out on my route and was calling on a new restaurant being constructed named Calamari's. I found out right away that the owner was planning on selling it after he opened.

### Did you change much about the place?

Initially, no. We just tried to market the food a little harder. We recognized that gradual change is better. With the other side of the coin you don't know what you are going to get. We tweaked it a little bit at a time. Adding more cooks in the kitchen and hiring more waitresses as we need them.

### What is the biggest challenge in being a restauranteur?

Definitely managing your people. The age range that we deal with is 18 to 28. A lot of college students - scheduling is very difficult. On a regular basis we have around 55 employees. The moment one employee doesn't show up, you have to cover immediately. Otherwise you might set yourself back. We have to market our business so that our employees can make money.

## What are the fun parts?

Working with Marci has been great. We complement each other. She is very organized. She is very good with administrative tasks. We picked this business because it is a social business. You can make people extremely happy with an opening of a beverage and a "Hello" or food that is so good that they can't wait to come back. We'll let people sample a taste of some soup that I just made and next thing you know we are selling gallons of it!

## What new things are in the works?

I added a banquet room that has been going great. The room has been very well received. We do a lot of wedding showers, big birthday parties, rehearsal dinners. We can serve any number of people. I have been catering since 1999 and have been doing weddings since last year.

## Anything new in the kitchen?

I recently expanded the kitchen. We added on a food preparation and catering area. I change the menu a lot. We are always adding new items, so by the time something is considered new, there is another new item in the works.

## Tell us about your bar business?

Let's put it this way - if you and I went down there around 10:00 tonight - we may not get in! *(with a laugh)* People know when the drink specials are, and let's say the joint is jumpin'. We are very grateful for the business that we have. There is a full gamut of activity starting when we open. There are certain specials for Happy Hour and other specials for different times of the evening."

## Why do people love Calamari's?

When people come to Calamari's, they know that they can get a lot of things. They can get a beer, a sandwich, or dinner. We have a clock that my friend Bill Bucceri made for us. It hangs above our bar and reads: Time to Get 'er Done. What that means is that any time of the day or evening that you are there, it is time to have fun. This is a place to relax and leave your worries at the door.

Photos: John Horstman

# What's in a Name?

an interview with
**BRYAN POL**

*Bryan Pol is the co-owner of Pol's Trucking. The company provides trucks for various industries, including pavement and construction. Pol's also provides landscaping supplies such as bark, mulch, topsoil, gravel, brick, and decorative stone. They service a 10 to 20 mile radius, mostly in Erie County.*

POL'S TRUCKING
813 EAST 18TH STREET
ERIE, PENNSYLVANIA 16503
814 454-0206

**144**

### How did you get started?

My father, Al Pol, worked at General Electric and owned a small rubbish trucking business as an extra source of income. In fact, I would ride with my father when I was young just to be with him. He taught me about the rubbish business. By the time I was 15 or 16, my father had had enough of the rubbish business and he was going to get me involved or move on to other things. As soon as I got a driver's license, I started working the rubbish route.

### So you got involved?

We owned two trucks at that time. I would work before school, park the dump truck in the Cathedral Prep parking lot, and go out again after school. I liked working long and hard. Our business was growing in all different directions, landscaping, snow plowing and even real estate rentals. No matter what it was, we did it. My father had the capital funds and, since I was young, I was aggressive, self-motivated, and had the drive. No matter what the weather was, if I told a customer that I would be there, I would be there.

Before I graduated from Cathedral Prep, we bought a facility and formed Pol's Trucking and Disposal, Inc. By the time I was 22, we had about 6 trucks and 4 or 5 employees. In the next 8 years we purchased another 4 small hauling companies to expand our business and area. We also formed Pol's Real Estate Partnership to take care of our growing real estate business. During this time we also sold off the landscaping and snow plowing business since we were fully involved with the rubbish waste disposal business, trucking, and real estate. In March 2000, we sold the disposal division to Waste Management, Inc. I was 29 years old with approximately 18 employees and we serviced 2 states.

## To what do you attribute your business success?

The bottom line is customer service. You have to take care of the customer. You only have one chance to service the customer and when you give your word to do something, you must do it to satisfy the customer. Abiding by your word is what makes your name and reputation.

## How important was your father's role?

My family is the key to my success but we are really a team. If it wasn't for him, I wouldn't be where I am and if it wasn't for me, he wouldn't be where he is. My dad has always been involved in the company. About 2 years before we sold our disposal division, he retired from General Electric. He can now spend all his time helping to grow the companies, particularly the Real Estate business.

## Do you have any advice for someone just starting a business?

The more energy you put in, the more rewards you'll get out. You are only as good as your word, so you had better do what you say that you are going to do. You have to have a lot of support from others such as employees, family and friends. You can't do everything on your own, so you must surround yourself with good people. Nothing will come easy; you have to work hard at it and make the right decisions every day. You must be aware of the financial health of the company so you can plan for the future.

## What's in the Pol name?

When people see the name Pol's, it is not just a name. No matter what we are doing or selling,

Al and Bryan Pol: "When we say something, it gets done!"

Photos: John Horstman

people know that when they call Pol's, they are going to get good service. That is the main thing. People know the name. When we say something, it gets done!

## What's in the future for Pol's?

The plan is to continue to provide exceptional service to our customers and potential customers. We are formulating plans now to purchase additional trucks to be able to serve our growing 'For Hire' trucking business. We are also exploring the possibility of expanding into other lines of business, but we can't comment at this time. If we stick with our underlying principles of providing exceptional service and continue to have the support of our great employees, we know that whatever we do, it will be a success.

## The Right Angle

an interview with

# TODD DAUBENSPECK

*Todd Daubenspeck is the owner of Daubenspeck Brothers which is a home remodeling company in Fairview. They build custom decks, patios rooms, roofing, and windows and doors. They have been in business since 2000.*

DAUBENSPECK BROTHERS
5739 WEST RIDGE ROAD
ERIE, PENNSYLVANIA 16506
814 835-0606

146

### Where did you find your interest in construction?

I had done some construction work even in my high school days. After graduating, I joined the Navy and became a seabee (Navy construction). I learned my skills in the Navy. I came back to Erie and graduated from college from Edinboro with a bachelors in history and an associates in business administration. I did side jobs while in college and continued with the seabees in the reserves.

### How did you get started in business for yourself?

I worked with a company in Atlanta, Champion Windows and Patio Rooms, the second largest remodeling company in the US. They had just opened the Atlanta market and at the time they had 14 markets. I started as an installer for them in Atlanta and became a manager for remodeling sunrooms. After years of working for someone else I realized there wasn't any further I could go. I wanted to be my own boss and have my own company. I felt like I was doing all the work and not reaping the benefits. I felt I gained enough experience to go out on my own.

### What experience did you gain there?

My experience of being with a larger company in a bigger city and working with people from different backgrounds has a lot to do with it. I took a lot of the positive traits of my former company and modeled mine from their example.

### Do you have a specialty?

We specialize in maintenance free decks. They are built with composite and vinyl materials.

# Entrepreneurs

## What is the most important aspect of your business?

We are very customer service oriented and meticulous. We do quality work and pride ourselves in our workmanship. You get what you pay for and we may not be the cheapest but it's more expensive to have quality people. Service is our top priority; our customers are treated like friends and family. We always keep them informed of what is going on with their job.

## What is the majority of your work?

We do all facets of remodeling. We do decks, sunrooms, roofing, siding, replacement windows and doors, and additions. We also do insurance work. Basement remodels. We go in to a basement and put in a bathroom, some bedrooms or maybe a play room. We've done some very elaborate decks.

## Have you done any elaborate jobs lately?

One of the biggest jobs we did this past summer was a deck overlooking the lake in North East. The location and size was unique, and the detail was done in a specific design. We worked with the homeowner and came up with the concept.

## What to you see in the future?

We are always looking at new products. At the rate of speed we've grown, we've almost doubled every year for the past three years. Our goal is to grow. Sometimes the amount of growth is uncontrollable. We concentrate on quality and customer service while maintaining the reputation we are known for.

Photos Courtesy: Daubenspeck Brothers, Portrait-Ed Bernik

**Better Baked Foods is world renowned as the <u>inventor</u> of French Bread Pizza.**

# Recipe for Success

## The Story of
## *Better Baked Foods*

By Suzanne Dandrea Sitzler

**B**ob Miller, co-founder of Better Baked Foods, Inc., will never be the kind of person who looks back on his life and says, "What did I accomplish"? His story is one that amazes people and it should! Bob Miller is one of those rare individuals who truly is a "self-made man."

His journey began in 1964 with $500 of borrowed money and a handshake. Bob and his partner, Bruce Underwood, leased a small plot of land from Bruce's father for $1 a year.

With nothing but some scrap wood, a used hot water tank, a $60 oven, and the help of a kindly carpenter, the **B & B Drive-In** became a reality on July 3, 1964. The original idea was a hot dog stand, but by opening day the menu had already grown to include a delicious, thick-crust square pizza using a recipe that Bob developed. (When asked about the unusual square shape, Bob admits the only pans they had were square!)

This experience laid the foundation for Bob's dream to start a company that he could build and grow. A company where he could help others develop to their maximum potential through challenge and encouragement of their own individual talents and abilities. He realized way back then that the excellence and value that a company delivered to its customers would be recognized and rewarded. In his words "We had to give first and get later."

149

Better Baked Foods' founder, Bob Miller, stands with his oldest son Chris, the company's C.E.O.

Today Better Baked Foods is world renowned as the inventor of French Bread Pizza and is the largest manufacturer of single-serve microwaveable French Bread Pizza in the world.

Bob and **Janet Miller** are the parents of seven successful children: **Kathy**, **Michele**, **Chris**, **Mark**, **Julie**, **Jeff** and **Rebecca**. Each of their children has worked for the company at one time or another. It was during the Christmas break from school in 1969 when the first production began and Kathy, Michele, Chris, and Mark were at their father's side.

Chris Miller is a Marine Corps veteran who holds a B.S. in Science and an M.A. in Reading. Eight years ago, Bob challenged Chris to leave his teaching career and come back to work in the family business. This time Chris worked his way up through the company, holding positions in Quality Assurance, Operations and Sales before ultimately becoming President and Chief Operating Officer in 1999. Since joining Better Baked Foods, Chris has helped his father double the size of the company.

In 2003 the Board of Directors named Chris to the position of Chief Executive Officer of the Better Baked Foods Family of Companies. His father couldn't be prouder and said about Chris, "He has skills that I don't have."

Bob also credits Chris for being a "quick study" and says, "He has the keen ability to identify and

attract other bright and successful people."
One of Chris', major goals is "to continue the
profitable growth of the businesses through
second generation leadership and provide value
to our family, our associates, our industries and
the communities we work and reside in." If Chris,
performance up to now is any indication, the
company will be exceeding expectations for many
years to come

Michele (Shel), Bob's daughter, works closely
with Chris as Administrative Assistant to the
Chairman. Shel graduated with honors from the
University of Kentucky with a B.S. in Nutrition.
She rejoined Better Baked Foods in 1999, when
she returned to the Erie area with her family.
Chris, Shel, and Bob work closely together as they
develop their short- and long-term plans for the
future.

This enormously successful business was built
with honesty and hard work. In 1969, $30,000 was
raised from friends and relatives to build their first
9,000-square-foot bakery in Sherman, New York.
When production started on December 23, 1969,
six employees manufactured 800 lbs. of pizza that
first day. Within four short years, the company
had outgrown its Sherman location. In 1973
Better Baked received an S.B.A. loan to renovate a
former dress factory into a new 37,000-square-foot
bakery in Westfield, New York.

Once again, the increasing popularity of their
products demanded more production capacity, so
in 1977 they leased 20,000 square feet of space
from North East Industrial Park to add a modern
pizza production line. Two years later Better
Baked acquired North East Industrial Park, which
added an unlimited amount of manufacturing and
freezer space for future growth. In 1985 millions
were invested in a state of the art pizza production line in North East. In 1996 groundbreaking
took place for an $11 million bakery expansion in
Westfield, NY.

**"Better Baked Foods has brought many jobs to our area.
Over 500 associates at three local facilities produce
and sell over 150 million pounds of frozen baked
goods and French Bread Pizza annually"**

Growth has always been the driving force of Better Baked Foods. In 1999 the bakery operations were expanded with the acquisition of Drayton Enterprises of Fargo, ND. This addition allowed Better Baked to dramatically diversify its product lines. Drayton's bakery products are manufactured with the latest frozen dough technology and include frozen self-rising breads, sweet goods, and pizza crusts. Their most exciting new product is the microwaveable cinnamon roll, which is able to be fully baked in the microwave in just over one minute, and has the appearance, taste and texture of a gourmet cinnamon roll.

Today, Better Baked Foods Inc. has three plants and 700 associates who produce and sell over 150 million pounds of frozen baked goods and French Bread Pizza annually. New products are constantly being developed by Better Baked's R & D

Better Baked Foods invented French Bread Pizza but they didn't stop there. Multiple flavors, brand names, and varieties are currently on the market.

Department. They are currently introducing a line of microwaveable breakfast products that rival the taste and convenience of others already on the market. Ongoing capital investments each year ensure the facilities remain state of the art, and Better Baked Foods remains a low-cost producer.

Manufacturing is not their only strength. **Zap-A-Snack®** was co-founded by Bob Miller in 1995 on the concept of providing a sensible, effective alternative to the fundraiser, and more value to the consumer. The founders recognized that the fundraising industry had a need for high quality, convenient and value-priced products.

Zap-A-Snack® promotes delicious meal, snack and dessert options that are frozen, single serve and microwaveable. The Zap-A-Snack® product line features French Bread Pizza and Cinn-A-Mazing' cinnamon rolls, self-rising cinnamon rolls that fully bake in your microwave in just over one minute. Completing the Zap-A-Snack® line are traditional and filled soft pretzels and pre-portioned cookie dough.

Zap-A-Snack® Fundraising has grown from its roots in Pennsylvania, New York and Ohio. They are recognized throughout the East Coast and Midwest as the premier fundraiser of choice and have set goals to achieve national distribution. While Zap-A-Snack® has continually added unique product items to their line, they have remained true to their core belief of high quality, value-priced and quick-to-serve frozen items.

Their mission statement is "To ensure the fundraiser's success over and over again". Zap-A-Snack's fundraising success is best endorsed by their satisfied customers. When asked why they chose to run a Zap-A-Snack® sale, they respond "I can take this to my next door neighbor and feel good about it."

This story is about a dream that came true because Bob Miller had the courage to stick to his principles. He believed that in this country of free enterprise any worthy and honest goal can be achieved with hard work and persistence. Better Baked Foods' continued growth and success is a testament to those beliefs.

The Better Baked Foods company motto is "To do better today what you did well yesterday." Their mission statement is "Better than the Best." The Erie community is proud to have the "the Best" at home.

**BETTER BAKED FOODS INC.**

56 SMEDLEY STREET
NORTH EAST, PENNSYLVANIA 16428
814 725-8778
www.betterbaked.com

# STARTING FROM *SCRATCH*

**by Bob Miller**

One Sunday morning, in March of 1964, I met Bruce Underwood. Bruce's father owned the Ellery General Store, which was at least five miles from everything. As we drank a soda together, we talked about the opportunity for someone to build a hot dog stand right there next door to the General Store.

The following Sunday, Bruce's father, who had heard our previous conversation, asked, "When are you guys going to build that hot dog stand?" As we looked at each other in surprise, his dad offered to lease us the land next to the General Store for $1 a year, for 99 years. What a deal! We couldn't turn it down. We could do this evenings and weekends. With a handshake, we each agreed to borrow $500 and become partners in this new beginning.

We started the very next day. Two of our friends bought an old building for salvage and sold us all the 2" x 4" and 2" x 8" wood we could tear out for $50.00. Neither of us had any building knowledge, so we were fortunate when the carpenter across the street kindly offered to instruct us as we attempted to build our 15' x 24', hot dog and pizza stand, called the B & B Drive-In (we decided to add pizza to the menu and it was my responsibility to come up with

the recipe and I did! It was square, thick and delicious.).

Finally, the building was built. It had doors and windows, but wasn't painted. We had no plumbing or electricity! No equipment, except for the oven we bought for $60, a used hot water tank from a friend, and a used sink. And guess what? We were broke. We needed $1,500 to complete and open the B & B Drive-In.

The North East, Pennsylvania Better Baked Foods, Inc. facility today.

THE ERIE BOOK

1970 – First bakery in Sherman, NY

Groundbreaking for the Westfield, NY bakery expansion in August, 1996

Bakery in Westfield, NY as it is today.

Bruce suggested that the bank might lend us $1,500; after all, we now had a piece of real estate. We went to the bank and they laughed at the two guys who were trying to build a drive-in restaurant five miles from everything.

We wouldn't give up. I wanted this more than anything. This is what I dreamed of all my life. Somehow, we had to open the drive-in so that we could earn the money to finish what we started.

We went to the local fire department and borrowed a couple of folding tables and two refrigerators. We ran a hose from the general store to the hot water tank and a hose from the hot water tank to the sink, supplying us with hot water. We ran an extension cord from the general store to a cup hook in the ceiling. We had one light bulb. Then, we called our suppliers and they agreed to deliver the food supplies we needed on credit. The day before we opened, I painted a 4' x 4' piece of plywood white and with the white paint still wet I painted the word "OPEN" in black.

On Friday, July 3, 1964, we opened the B & B Drive-In. We started selling pizzas before we realized that we forgot to order pizza boxes. Pizzas were ready to come out of the oven and there was nothing to put them in. I ran next door to the General Store and borrowed some brown grocery bags. In the beginning we borrowed the land, the money, the equipment, the food supplies, the electricity and the water. We even borrowed the brown paper bags to carry out the very first pizzas ever sold.

Today, 35 years later, our company is called Better Baked Foods. We are the creators of French Bread Pizza and the largest manufacturer of hand-held single-serve microwaveable French Bread Pizza in the world. Our core strength is still baking. Our motto is "To do better today what you did well yesterday."

BETTER BAKED FOODS INC.

56 SMEDLEY STREET
NORTH EAST, PENNSYLVANIA 16428
814 725-8778
www.betterbaked.com

155

Rob Ruby

**Kelly Conboy** (Sales Center Manager) and **Harold Moore** (Cold Drink Manager) stand among a heap of the world's most recognized brand.

## ERIE COCA-COLA BOTTLING CO.

In "The Best Day", country legend George Strait sings about an 8-year-old boy going on a camping trip with his dad and describing it as the best day of the boy's life. As he describes the few supplies they needed to make it perfect, "a cooler of Cokes" is clearly heard.

**The Erie Coca-Cola Bottling Co.** was founded in 1911 and has been fulfilling the total beverage needs and wishes of the communities they serve, while at the same time being an active philanthropic partner to those communities.

With a strong commitment to Erie, they have sponsored events including the **North East Cherry Festival** and the **Greek Festival**. Boasting over 100 employees, the business continues to grow, with plans to expand into areas such as Olean, New York.

COCA-COLA BOTTLING COMPANY
2209 WEST 50TH STREET
ERIE, PENNSYLVANIA 16506
814 833-0101

156

Rob Ruby

## INDUSTRIAL SALES
## AND MANUFACTURING INC.

**W**hat is the one thing that train locomotives, Cadillac cars and golf carts all have in common? They each have components that were manufactured right here in Erie, PA at **Industrial Sales & Manufacturing Incorporated**.

In 1967 **James J. Rutkowski, Sr.** started Industrial Sales & Manufacturing - a business that provides contract machining, fabricating and assembly services - out of a corner of his garage. But by 1974 he outgrew the garage and moved the business to a location at West 15th and Lowell Avenue. Today, his sons **Charlie** and **James, Jr.** help to run the family business, which has grown in size to over 100 employees and can now boast a brand new 85,000-square-foot addition to the facility.

There is one thing that has not changed over the years. That is their dedication to quality in the components they manufacture and supply to industrial and non-industrial businesses alike.

**INDUSTRIAL SALES AND MANUFACTURING, INC.**
**2209 WEST 12TH STREET**
**ERIE, PENNSYLVANIA 16506**
**814 833-9876**
**www.ismerie.com**

## THERMOCLAD

Fall of 2003 marks **Thermoclad Company's** 40th anniversary as a manufacturer of ecologically friendly powder for applied protective and decorative coatings.

The backbone of Thermoclad's 'niche' business has been vinyl resin-based powder coatings that are applied as 100% solids from powder formulations, assuring practically total utilization of raw material by the fluid bed or electrostatic coating methods. The coated end products offer significant latitude in usage due to the versatility of vinyl resin durability in corrosion-resistant outdoor as well as indoor end uses.

Few may realize when they slide out a tray of hot, steaming dishes from the dishwasher, or stack some linens on the closet wire shelving, what has been accomplished by the Company. Every major manufacturer of appliances in the United States and Canada uses the powder coating technology and vinyl powder products, pioneered by Thermoclad's founder, Alan Renkis.

Since opening the doors in Erie in the fall of 1963, the Company has continued to refine its process of coating wire and other heat-resistant products with pulverized plastic particles. The unique chemical process that binds plastic to metal is what makes dishwasher baskets resistant to heat and humidity. It can make fences able to stand up to Erie winters, and air conditioning wire guards during the hottest summers. The vinyl powder-applied coatings also serve in less demanding environments to make wire shelves in homes, dorms and laundry rooms durable and attractive.

But what Renkis, now the chief executive officer and chairman of the board of directors of the Company, considers most valuable are his employees. The people on staff are attentive, technically astute and loyal to their many customers, he said. Regarding the formula that has made his company globally successful for more than 40 years, Renkis gives away the secret without pause: "Quality is our main ingredient."

**THE THERMOCLAD COMPANY**
**361 WEST 11TH**
**ERIE, PENNSYLVANIA 16501**
**814 456-1243**
**www.thermoclad.com**

Rob Ruby

Company founder **ALAN RENKIS** sits among some of the Thermoclad team - left to right - Das Gujrati, Bob Clark, Terry Seyfert, Mick Gashgarian, and Mary Rizzo.

Paul Lorei

## McCARTY PRINTING

Since its founding in 1918, Erie's oldest and most established commercial printer has always put the customer first. After acquisition by the **Sieber** family in 1947, **McCarty Printing** quadrupled the number of its employees, to 75. A physical plant dedicated to the highest quality direct-to-plate, full color process, and digital printing also swelled with demand to the current 40,000 square feet. Through the years McCarty's commitment to its customers also grew. To serve a complete range of needs, McCarty created its **Walco Label** subsidiary, an Underwriters, Laboratory-authorized supplier of pressure sensitive labels. The company also added embossing and foil stamping to its capabilities, and created a fulfillment division to provide solutions to customers, need for warehousing, mailing, database surveys, and refund and rebate offer handling. Whether offering eye-popping printed materials, quality labels or fulfillment services, McCarty Printing promises competitive pricing, assured quality, and dependable on-time delivery. "Printing shouldn't be a problem," says company president **Donald Sieber**. "That's why at McCarty Printing we approach every print job with a fresh eye, always looking for a better, simpler, faster way to meet customers' specific needs. Just like our customers, no two jobs are the same, and each has its own unique needs."

**McCARTY PRINTING CORPORATION**
**246 EAST SEVENTH STREET**
**ERIE, PENNSYLVANIA 16503**
**814 454-6337**
**www.mccartyprinting.com**

**159**

# MATT CATRABONE

## Tell us about Nicotra, Catrabone, Catrabone & Associates...

Nicotra, Catrabone, Catrabone & Associates is a branch of American Express Financial Advisors. The principal members of the group are Robert Nicotra, my brother Mark Catrabone, and myself, Matt Catrabone. We have a staff onsite as well as offsite. There are a total of ten persons involved in servicing our clients.

It is important to understand the vision behind our business to know how we assist our clients. Our vision is the bedrock of our business. It guides all of the decisions about the business: where we are taking it; and how we are going to get there. The vision of the three of us is rooted in a philosophical belief that people need to be listened to.

## What makes you different?

We believe that we have to understand every client. It is not always about a product; it is about the client. This is a paradigm shift away from how most do business in the financial services industry.

## How does this apply?

We operate under the assumption that very few people get listened to regarding their financial

Matt Catrabone, Rob Nicotra, Mark Catrabone

needs. We focus very heavily on that side of the equation. Sure, we have a full complement of investments and services, and that in itself is what many are looking for but, what makes our philosophy different is our approach to listening and understanding the needs of our clients.

Once we truly know the unique needs of our clients, we can begin improving their financial health. The quality of the improvement is directly a result of our close connection with the client.

### So is it all in the client relationship?

In the future, we will hear many different people; and as time passes, life and events we cannot predict will change the way people are thinking so we will have to listen differently. We recognize that our experience is only one component of what will ultimately determine one's financial success. The rest will have to come from knowledge, and the quality of the client relationship.

### How do you get to know your clients?

The culture found within Nicotra, Catrabone and Catrabone is also unique from most traditional business relationships. We offer the actively engaged client many opportunities: from workshops to special events not only for themselves, but also their families. We are building a culture that caters to the client, something different from what one would experience in most business settings. These activities help build our client relationships outside of the office walls; this is important.

### What will one need to consider for the future?

The environment in the future and how one accumulates wealth will more than likely not look like it did over the past 20 years. Success is based on the knowledge that we possess. We need to be proactive and not reactive in our

Photos: Rob Ruby

*"The vision of the three of us is rooted in a philosophical belief that people need to be* **listened to."**

**Matt Catrabone**

approach because growing your bottom line won't be as simple as it was over the last 20 years of the 20th century. We recognize this, and are well suited to adjust for the changing times. Contrary to what many may hear, or read about in their favorite journals, investment principle and design has and will continue to change according to the times.

### How can you accomplish this?

Our abilities range from the most conservative time-tested ways to accomplish financial independence, to the most creative leading-edge wealth-building ideas and strategies.

We are continuing to build our business with those people who are looking for exactly what this is. Smart, sound advice, people who do what they say they are going to do, and people who operate according to a well-defined philosophy, through guiding principles.

**161**

NICOTRA, CATRABONE, CATRABONE, & ASSOCIATES

1310 PENINSULA DRIVE
ERIE, PENNSYLVANIA 16505
814 838-4853

Paul M. Lorei

**Seated, from left to right**: Dean Piccirillo, Chris Sorce, Greg Sorce, Jim Voss and Keith Mitchell. **Standing, from left to right:** Ashleigh Wehrle, Chris Zehner, Sara Kallner, Vicki Baum, Michael Forbes, Brittany Ordiway, Stephanie Kotoski, Lucia Salvia, Andrea Mientkiewicz, Judy Steele, Lisa Suchar and Jennifer Dorsch. **Back Row, from left to right:** Mike Nasca, Jason Alward, Joe Kloecker, Kyle Hinsdale, Geoff Claridge and Jamie Vincent. *Absent from picture*: Heather Drake, Melissa Ryan, Sue Giddings, Amanda Socash, Giulia Zeolla, Corey Frank, Jeanne Richter, Kevin Bannon, Nate Ward and Paul Taylor.

## HILL, BARTH & KING LLC
## HBK SORCE FINANCIAL

Every investment decision you make has tax ramifications, so it makes sense to have your financial advisor and CPA working together for your benefit today and tomorrow. That's the thinking behind the merger of the Sorce Financial Group and the financial services affiliate of the accounting firm Hill, Barth & King LLC.

Founded in Erie in 1995 by brothers Greg and Chris Sorce, the Sorce Financial Group was a registered independent investment advisory and personal financial planning firm servicing individual and corporate clients. Hill, Barth & King began in 1949 with one office in northeastern Ohio and has grown into one of the nation's top 50 accounting and business consulting firms.

With 17 offices in four states, Hill, Barth & King and HBK Sorce Financial have the ability to provide the multidisciplinary resources of a regional firm while offering clients personal attention through a local office. By combining the

strengths of two companies that pride themselves on delivering quality work, timely service, and real value to their clients, Hill, Barth and King and HBK Sorce Financial are uniquely positioned to offer comprehensive financial, estate and tax planning, asset management, auditing and consulting services, technology consulting, and independent investment advice.

HILL, BARTH & KING LLC
ZUCK ROAD OFFICE PARK
5121 ZUCK ROAD
ERIE, PENNSYLVANIA 16506
814 836-9968
www.hbkcpa.com

HBK SORCE FINANCIAL
WRIGHT HOUSE
235 WEST 6TH STREET
ERIE, PENNSYLVANIA 16507
814 459-1116
www.hbksorce.com

Photos: Rob Ruby

## THE ERIE FEDERAL CREDIT UNION

The **Erie Federal Credit Union** is now chartered to serve all of Erie County and each person who lives, works, worships, or attends school within its borders. A period of growth fueled by acquisition of new members and mergers with

smaller credit unions will culminate in Spring 2004 in a full-service financial institution with six branch offices, 24-hour telephone and online account access, a no-fee network of 15 automated teller machines, $200 million in assets, and 30,000 members.

The Erie Federal Credit Union's motto is "Financial Solutions from Local People You Trust" because of its commitment to its members, who have access to savings and checking accounts, money market accounts, no fee MasterCard, first mortgages, safe deposit boxes, and a full range of financial consulting services. "When you're a member of a credit union, you're an owner," chief executive officer **Norb Kaczmarek** says. "We operate to serve our owners. You'll enjoy higher interest rates on your savings, a lower rate on loans, and a vote in how the credit union is managed by its volunteer board of directors. Because the credit union operates as a not-for-profit cooperative without stockholders, we're able to return that savings to our members," Kaczmarek promises.

ERIE FEDERAL CREDIT UNION
1109 EAST 38TH STREET
ERIE, PENNSYLVANIA 16504
814 825-2436
www.eriefcu.org

## ERIE GENERAL ELECTRIC
## FEDERAL CREDIT UNION

From modest beginnings during the Great Depression, the **Erie General Electric Federal Credit Union** has grown steadily.

Almost the only thing that hasn't changed in 67 years, Chief Executive Officer **Gail Cook** says, is its underlying principle: Credit unions are member-owned and operated. Members come first.

"Through mergers and growth opportunities the Erie General Electric Federal Credit Union can provide great loan and savings products to nearly anyone who lives in Erie County," Cook says, "and continues to be the name you know and trust."

The credit union is no longer just for GE employees and relatives. In the last 20 years credit unions have been allowed to offer membership to other businesses and communities.

In November 2003 the credit union opened its fourth office at the corner of West 26th Street and Greengarden Boulevard with a "Celebrate Erie" theme.

It joins the home office at 2154 East Lake Road, built in 1958 across the street from GE Transportation Systems; a branch at the General Electric Co. plant in Grove City; and a third, "Wave of the Future" branch at 1623 East 38th Street, which opened in 2002.

"Today members can take advantage of a variety of services, and technology has made it possible to conduct business twenty-four hours a day, seven days a week with on-line access " Cook says.

The Erie General Electric Federal Credit Union began in 1936 when Alvin B. Corzilius and a handful of General Electric employees applied to start a federal credit union at the General Electric plant in Lawrence Park Township.

Like other credit unions, it began as a way for members to save so they could borrow from each other at a low cost. Since the time of the 10 founders, the Erie General Electric Federal Credit Union has grown to employ 50 people. With $90 million in assets, it is larger than some local community banks. Boasting more than 16,000 members, it ranked 42nd out of 732 credit unions statewide by the end of 2002.

"We continue to be committed to serving the needs of our community by providing the services and technology that will benefit our members' financial well-being for many years to come," Cook says.

**ERIE GENERAL ELECTRIC FEDERAL CREDIT UNION
2154 EAST LAKE ROAD
ERIE, PENNSYLVANIA 16511
814 456-6231
www.egefcu.org**

1623 East 38th

Photos: Rob Ruby

Rob Ruby

## INFINITY RESOURCES

Infinity Resources is Erie's premier staffing and employment resource. Begun by **Charles Farrell** over forty years ago, Infinity has expanded from their Erie base to serve the region through staffing centers in downtown Erie, Girard, North East, and Harborcreek, Pennsylvania; Dunkirk, New York; and Painesville, Ashtabula, and Conneaut, Ohio. Infinity Resources is a key component in providing employment opportunities in local industry and business, which is a lynch-pin service for a vibrant economy in our area.

**INFINITY RESOURCES
119 WEST NINTH STREET
ERIE, PENNSYLVANIA 16501
814 453-6571**

## THE BERT COMPANY

For more than 25 years, **The Bert Company** and **Renshaw Insurance** have been providing clients with life insurance and employee benefit services, as well as multiple lines of property and casualty insurance products.

Within the industry their experience provides access to multiple insurers and Third Party Administrators (TPAs), allowing them to analyze and develop funding arrangements to deliver cost-effective solutions to clients.

In December 1994 The Bert Company acquired the Life Insurance and Benefits Department from Acordia of Western Pennsylvania. The office and staff of Renshaw Insurance merged with The Bert Company in January 2002. This affiliation has greatly expanded the overall expertise available in all lines of insurance for the clients of both organizations.

Rob Ruby

**THE BERT COMPANY
3645 WEST LAKE ROAD
ERIE, PENNSYLVANIA 16505
814 838-0000**

## JANITORS SUPPLY COMPANY, INC.

**E**rie has many companies that are growing exponentially, and Janitors Supply is a great example. The story of this family-owned business started back in 1955 when **Ed Mascharka Sr.** had the vision to build a company which would supply custodial equipment. Eventually his son **Ed Masharka Jr.** took over the business and has been involved ever since. Third-generation brothers **Ed III** (President) and **Tom** (Vice President) took the helm in 1992. Breaking the stereotype of a lazy third generation, the Mascharka brothers have grown the company five-fold. They have done it by acquiring several other janitorial supply companies, maintaining the companies' clients, and gradually incorporating as younger brother Tom calls it, "a seamless transaction."

With a service area encompassing western and central Pennsylvania, West Virginia, Maryland, eastern Ohio, and southwestern New York, Janitors Supply is the largest company of its kind in the region.

"We grew up on small accounts. We will service any customer regardless of size," says Ed Mascharka. "We have by far the largest selection and a vast inventory to serve our customers."

Janitors Supply now employs over 70 people who contribute greatly to the vitality of our community and region. Future goals include the company's expansion into new markets. A fourth generation looks likely as both Ed and Tom have been blessed with many children.

**JANITORS SUPPLY COMPANY, INC.**
**540 EAST SECOND STREET**
**ERIE, PENNSYLVANIA 16507**
**814 459-4563**
**www.janitorsupply.com**

Photos: Rob Ruby

Tom and Ed Mascharka

Zurn and Erie Copy Products seem to be sticking to their mission statement which is, "exceeding the customers expectations."

As if one major Erie company isn't enough, Zurn is also the owner of Beco Interiors - Business Environment Centre - which sells high end office furniture. Any business person knows that in order to increase productivity, the physical workplace that surrounds you must be functional, attractive and effective. Zurn has years of experience in knowing how to solve these problems and how to create work environments that maximize potential. Beco's list of clients is a virtual "who's who" of Erie businesses, schools, hospitals, organizations, and industries. They go to Beco because they know that they will receive quality time after time. Because as with Erie Copy Products, BECO seems to be "exceeding expectations."

**ERIE COPY PRODUCTS, INC.**
**2820 WEST TWELFTH**
**ERIE, PENNSYLVANIA 16505**
**814 833-4200**
**www.eriecopyproducts.com**

**BUSINESS ENVIRONMENT CENTRE**
**2651 WEST EIGHTH STREET**
**ERIE, PENNSYLVANIA 16505**
**814 835-0996**
**www.becointeriors.com**

## ERIE COPY PRODUCTS

Technology seems to be advancing at such an unbelievable rate that sometimes it seems confusing to know just which gadget or machine to buy next. Perhaps nowhere is this more evident than in the field of office machines. After all, having the right machines in your workplace can make or break your business.

Luckily, for the Erie community, there is **Erie Copy Products** - a provider of digital document and network imaging solutions - output devices that connect to the computer network to produce hard copy. This includes all multi-functional products: copiers, printers, fax machines, and scanners.

"The life cycle of our technology is about twenty eight months. We go to trade shows and manufacturers have national sales meetings to keep us on top of the newest technologies available", says business owner and CEO, **Frederick H. Zurn**.

An Erie native, and graduate of Strong Vincent High School and Ashland University, Zurn learned his business in Cleveland. After being recruited back to the Erie area in 1980, he became Vice President and General Manager of Erie Copy Products. He liked it so much, he bought the company in 1985.

Photos: Rob Ruby

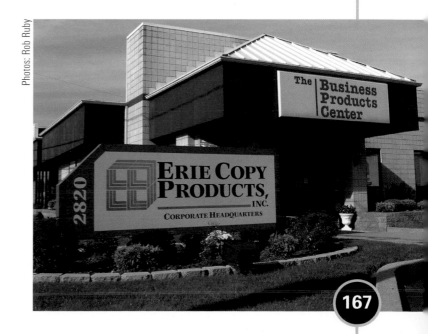

167

## SANNER OFFICE SUPPLY

**S**anner Office Supply has continued to build its customer base for over 65 years. The largest independently owned office supply company in Northwestern Pennsylvania began in 1938 when **Harry F. Sanner Sr.** realized his dream to start his own business. Since then, Sanner's has grown to include retail and commercial office supplies delivered in its own fleet of trucks. Sanner Office Supply has succeeded by providing excellent customer service and competitive pricing. As a locally based company, they are able to respond to each customer's individual needs and stay proactive in a changing marketplace.

Being a member of **Independent Stationers, Inc.**, a network of 11,000 independent office products dealers, gives Sanner's the ability to offer customers quality products at competitive prices along with excellent service.

In addition to office supplies, Sanner's offers an extensive line of office furniture through their **Office Furniture USA** showroom as well as their **Contract Furniture Division** specializing in Haworth furniture systems. Their experienced sales and design staff are capable of providing price-competitive quality solutions for any furniture environment need. No job is too large or small for their staff of certified installation and service technicians.

Since 1938, Sanner's has been helping customers maximize their time and resources by providing an extensive selection of the most current workplace products and services. From office supplies and furnishings to complete interior solutions, Sanner's works in close partnership with each customer to tailor programs that meet

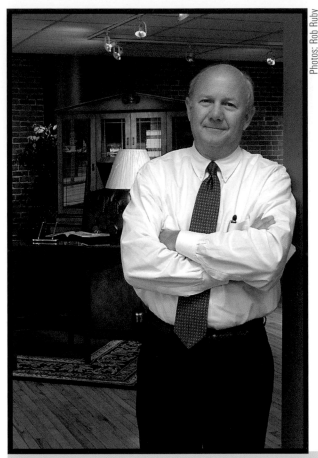

Photos: Rob Ruby

**Dave Sanner,** who is a third generation owner, is committed to serving in downtown Erie. His stores sell office supplies and office furniture.

specialized office requirements and changing business demands.

"We're community-oriented and we feel committed to being downtown," said President **David Sanner**. He continues to be committed to the policy of personal attention and excellent customer service on which Sanner Office Supply was founded.

SANNER OFFICE SUPPLY CO.
1225 STATE STREET
ERIE, PENNSYLVANIA 16512
814 454-6374
www.sanneros.com

Background photo: Rob Ruby

## HAGAN BUSINESS MACHINES

When **Hagan Business Machines** was founded in 1950, Royal typewriters and adding machines were the primary products sold and serviced. Office technology has changed drastically over the years, yet Hagan is still here to support its customers and community as "The Service Leader."

In 1960 **Frank Kneidinger** began his career with Hagan in the sales and service of Gestetner duplicators where he learned from **Paul Hagan**, the founder, the importance of providing the best service and support with honesty and integrity. Frank purchased Hagan Business Machines in 1977 and introduced copier sales and service. The company's growth skyrocketed.

Copiers are still the primary product for the company but today's copiers are also sold as the network printer, fax machine, and scanner, to best meet the ever-changing needs of today's modern office. Besides copiers, Hagan's also offers a full line of postage and mailing equipment, digital duplicators, paper shredders, and facsimile machines. "Because we're the #1 office machine dealer in the area, we can choose the best products from the best manufacturers. When you combine the best products with the best service, it is easy to stay number one," says **Kirk Kneidinger**, business manager.

Frank retired in 2002 after 42 years of outstanding service, but he left the company in good hands as five of his six children own and operate the business today. "It's not unusual for us to work with customers that our father worked with 30 or 40 years ago. It's a great feeling knowing that our customers are happy and well taken care of," says **Mike Kneidinger**, sales manager.

Nor is it unusual for a customer to deal directly with an owner. Besides Mike and Kirk, **Frank III** is service manager, **Kara** directs the office and billing, while **Julia** manages postage equipment and marketing. The equipment changes, locations change, customers change, ownership has changed, but one thing has remained the same, simply providing the best service and support to meet and exceed customer needs.

**HAGAN BUSINESS MACHINES INC.**
**1112 PEACH STREET**
**ERIE, PENNSYLVANIA 16501**
**814 456-7521**
**www.haganbusinessmachines.com**

**169**

Rob Ruby

**Jim Domino** is originally from Buffalo, but after graduating from Gannon, he built a strong career and countless friendships in Erie.

## DOMINO INSURANCE

Since founding the commercial insurance agency that bears his name, **James T. Domino** has watched his clients grow in both number and need. Part of the story of economic development in Northwestern Pennsylvania is the story of how Domino Insurance Agency Inc. has continued to be, as its founder said, "always there" since 1978. Long-term clients like Gary Miller Dealerships, Baldwin Brothers, Scott Enterprises, John V. Schultz Furniture and Perry Construction continue to add to Erie's landscape. But Domino Insurance, with six employees, is not planning on changing - much. "Our goal is to continue working very closely with our clients," Domino said. "We want them to feel like we are a part of their pertinent management team."

DOMINO INSURANCE AGENCY, INC.
3209 GREENGARDEN BLVD
ERIE, PENNSYLVANIA 16508
814 868-4851

Rob Ruby

## SILK SCREEN SPECIALTIES UNLIMITED

Want to advertise? Need promotional key chains to hand out at an exposition? How about T-shirts for the Little League team you might be sponsoring? Whatever your imagination can produce, the creative staff at **Silk Screen Specialties Unlimited** can turn it into reality.

Since 1974, Silk Screen Specialties Unlimited has been providing quality products to the Erie region, and the entire United States. Owner **Roy Glass** and his staff have even produced items for dignitaries including Richard Nixon and Henry Kissinger. More than just a silk screen shop, they can produce various items including buttons, stickers, hats, custom-embroidered patches, and coolie cups.

SILK SCREEN SPECIALTIES UNLIMITED
1702 WEST 8TH STREET
ERIE, PENNSYLVANIA 16505
814 453-4543

## CAREER CONCEPTS

The fact that **Career Concepts Staffing Services** has placed people in the upper ranks of **Fortune 500** companies isn't what makes its founder and president **Charles Campagne** most proud. What defines his business is its range. From placing people in high-profile positions to helping small, privately owned companies in Erie, Pennsylvania, get off the ground — Career Concepts is committed to doing whatever it takes to meet any client's needs.

Campagne, who opened the Peach Street office in 1983, has been in the staffing business for more than 35 years. He started out by recruiting top executives. Clients told him he should look into the booming temporary staffing business; it was good advice. Career Concepts now internally employs about 30 employees on a full-time basis and at any given time has 700 to 800 workers on various assignments throughout the tri-state area. In addition, the company Campagne started has welcomed a second generation. His son, **Paul Campagne**, is senior operations manager. His daughter, **Kimberly Campagne**, directs the office of human resources and another daughter, **Lisa Winschel**, works in the accounting department. Campagne also sees Career Concepts as part of a larger family, that of locally owned businesses working to keep dollars in the regional economy.

In addition to the Peach Street office, Career Concepts now has three other offices - in Girard, Meadville and Ashtabula, Ohio. Career Concepts has the ability to access job opportunities all over the country through a national network of independently owned staffing businesses. "These are people with many of the same philosophies we have," he said. And that is: keep the focus on the client, big or small, and always uphold quality. As the largest full-service and independently owned staffing service in the tri-state area, it seems that philosophy works.

Rob Ruby

**Charles Campagne,** the founder and President of Career Concepts believes that "keeping the focus on the client" is the key ingredient to success.

### CAREER CONCEPTS STAFFING SERVICES INC.

- **4504 PEACH STREET
  ERIE, PENNSYLVANIA 16509
  814 868-2333**
- **259 MAIN STREET EAST
  GIRARD, PENNSYLVANIA 16417
  774-0997**
- **MEADVILLE MALL - 920 WATER STREET
  MEADVILLE, PENNSYLVANIA 16335
  814-337-8670**
- **355 WEST PROSPECT AVENUE SUITE 116
  ASHTABULA, OHIO 44004
  440-992-2024**

**www.careerconceptsinc.com**

auctioneer for most of the annual charity auctions raising over one million dollars for local nonprofit organizations.

This past year has brought an exciting association with **Ace Auctioneers** and **Coldwell Banker Select Realtors**. Mark was asked to join the Coldwell Banker team so their agents could offer even more expert services to their customers. Locally, people have been selecting the auction method to sell real estate more frequently because the auction method offers so many advantages to the seller. Offering their customers more services is a hallmark of both companies.

This association allows Mark, who became a licensed real estate agent to facilitate the affiliation, to list and sell residential, commercial and industrial real estate under the standard MLS system. He can also auction real estate for any Coldwell Banker client or private party.

Whether you are concerned with the inside or outside of a home, Mark Tanenbaum of Ace Auctioneers & Liquidators, Inc. is the only person to call. Tanenbaum can sell and appraise the contents or auction and list the real estate.

MARK TANENBAUM
ACE AUCTIONEERS AND LIQUIDATORS, INC.
249 EAST 10TH
ERIE, PENNSYLVANIA 16503
814 434-0687

## MARK TANENBAUM
## ACE AUCTIONEERS & LIQUIDATORS, INC.

**M**ark Tanenbaum was born and raised in Erie. He and his wife **Ellie** have two daughters, **Abbe** and **Jenna** both at the Collegiate Academy. He started **Ace Auctioneers & Liquidators, Inc.** a quarter century ago. He has been selling and appraising antiques and collectables, as well as commercial and industrial equipment throughout his working life. Tanenbaum is frequently seen as

172

## LOCATION LOCATION LOCATION

Before 1970, as with most American cities, the primary shopping district in Erie was downtown. In Erie the major attraction was the legendary **Boston Store.** Another major downtown Erie business was, **The Koehler Brewing Company** which closed in 1978.

## MARX TOYS
## CHAS. MANNING REED

In early Erie history, the name **Reed** was synonymous with business. **Charles Manning Reed**, was reported to be the wealthiest man west of New York City at the time of his death in 1871.

## FUNNY MONEY

As early as 1816, Erie's shortage of cash flow forced the borough to begin producing its own money. When the local paper currency was declared unlawful by the state, Erie began producing equally counterfeit coins called **Pewternictum**. The start of local manufacturing businesses halted the "moonshine money" binge.

*unless noted, historical photos courtesy* **Erie County Historical Society & Museums**

SPORTS

Photo: Ed Bernik

*Denise Keim*

*Ed Bernik*

# SPORTS LEAGUES

Boys and Girls Baseball
City-Rec Fast Pitch Softball
Erie Admirals
Erie Lightning Soccer Club
Erie Runners Club
Erie Youth Soccer Association
Family First Sports Park
Flagship Niagara League
Glenwood League  men's baseball
Lake Erie Soccer Club
Millcreek Modified Softball
Millcreek Youth Athletic Association

**Field of Dreams**: Gannon Women's Soccer Team training on their new athletic field. Team sports are a huge activity for many school age Erieites.

**Bang!** Swimmers getting ready for another race at The Kahkwa Club pool.  Swimming lessons and races are not hard to find during the Erie summer.

*Denise Keim*

*Art Becker*

176

*Art Becker*

**Lake Erie, Presque Isle Bay and Lake Edinboro** all make good locations for outdoor swimming competitions.

## INDEPENDENT COMPETITIONS

There are many opportunities in Erie for athletes to train and test their abilities against each other (and themselves) in heated competitions. One of the larger organized competitions in the area is the **Quad Games,** which draw stellar athletes from Erie and the surrounding region. The Quad also serves a larger purpose: promoting wellness in the Erie community. Sponsored by **Highmark Blue Cross/Blue Shield** and the **YMCA** of Greater Erie, the Quad Games offer participants a regimen they can use to build year-round physical fitness.

Evenly spaced throughout the year, the games consist of a 5-mile cross-country ski race, a 100-yard swimming event, a 12-mile bicycle time trial, and a 5-mile run. Locals runners can also compete in the **Erie Marathon,** as well as quite a few 10k races, and for athletes looking to push their bodies even further, triathlon opportunities exist in both **Edinboro** and on **Presque Isle**. Throughout the warmer months, Presque Isle is a perfect site to host or watch a race.

177

Alan Chaffee

Jeff Aitken

**Presque Isle Bay**

## OUTDOOR SPORTS

Between **Lake Erie** and the numerous streams that feed it, there is not a lack of opportunities for fisherman looking to hook the big one. It's not uncommon to see cars parked roadside, near a stream or at the peninsula, with an angler nearby trying his luck. **The Pennsylvania Fish and Boat Commission** issues more than 25,000 standard, resident, fishing licenses each year in Erie County. Popular streams in Erie include **Elk Creek**, **Trout Run** and **Walnut Creek**. Also popular are the waters of **Lake Erie** and **Presque Isle Bay**. Record-sized fish are often pulled from the lake, including **Rock Bass**, **Smallmouth Bass**, **Yellow Perch**, **Chinook Salmon**, **Sheepshead**, **Sucker**, **Brown Trout**, **Lake Trout**, **Rainbow Trout**, **Steelhead Trout**, and **Walleye**. Hunting is also popular with outdoorsmen. Annually, the **Pennsylvania Game Commission** issues hunting licenses to about 10% of Erie County's population. Yearly harvest statistics put the number of **deer** killed at roughly 10,000. Also popular with Erie County hunters are **duck**, **pheasant**, **quail**, **turkey** and the occasional **bear**.

## BOATING

As a lakeside city, Erie is a city with a passion for boating. On the protected waters of Presque Isle Bay and the lake itself, you'll always find people taking advantage of watersports. In the summer, motorboating, sailing, waterskiing and jetskiing, abound. In winter, ice boaters take over the Bay. Boating enthusiasts can launch their crafts from several public and private marinas in the Erie area.

## YACHT CLUBS AND MARINAS

| | |
|---|---|
| Anchor Marine | Gem City Marina |
| Avonia Beach Boat Club | John Lampe Marina |
| Bay Harbor Marina | Jolly Roger Marina |
| Bayshore Marina | Lund Boat Works |
| Cherry Street Marina | North East Marina |
| Commodore Perry Yacht Club | Perry's Landing Marina |
| Erie - Angler | Presque Isle State Park |
| Erie Western Pennsylvania Port Authority Marinas | Presque Isle Yacht Club |
| | Walnut Street Marina |
| Erie Yacht Club | Wolverine Park |

**178**

179

Louis Colussi

## ERIE OTTERS

The **Erie Otters** arrived in Erie in 1996 and feature many of the finest young players in the world. These athletes are destined to become the National Hockey League stars of the future, and they are competing in Erie ... TODAY!

The Otters play in the **Ontario Hockey League**, which is operated under the sport governing guidelines of the Canadian Hockey League and conforms to the rules and regulations of the NHL. The OHL consists of 20 teams with the Otters, Plymouth Whalers and Saginaw Spirit the only members of the League based in the United States. The other 17 teams are located in Canada.

Approximately 65 to 70 percent of today's NHL players are graduates of the Canadian Hockey League. The list of graduates includes **Mario Lemieux, Joe Sakic, Mike Modano, Ed Jovanovski, Steve Yzerman, Ron Francis, Scott Stevens, Joe Thornton, Todd Bertuzzi** and many other NHL superstars.

Since the advent of the NHL Entry Draft in 1969, the Otters' franchise (which was previously located in Hamilton, Brantford, St. Catharines and Niagara Falls) has had 138 players selected by NHL teams (including at least one first-round selection in five straight NHL Entry Drafts from 1997-2001). It ranks as the second most of any junior team in the world.

In their first seven seasons in Erie the Otters have captured three Midwest Division titles (2000, 2001, 2002), an OHL Regular Season Championship (2001), a Western Conference Championship (2002), and an OHL Championship (2002).

The philosophy is simple. The Otters are a community-based team dedicated to representing the Erie community and providing affordable, action-packed family entertainment. Erie Otters Hockey - you "otter be there!"

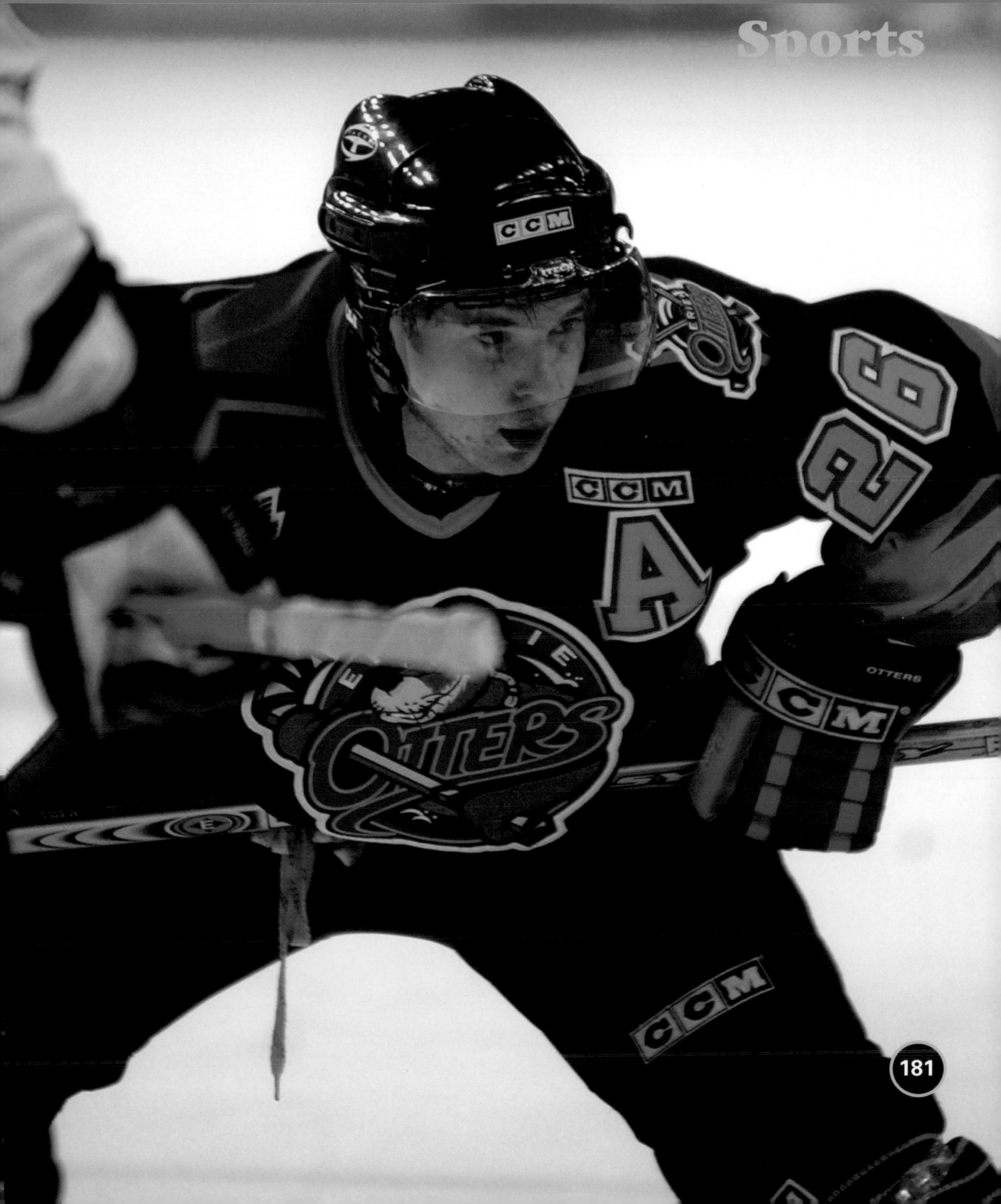
CCM
CCM
A
26
OTTERS
OTTERS
CCM
CCM

## GOLF COURSES

Beechwood
Brabender South Woods
Carter Heights
Country Meadows
Crab Apple Ridge
Cross Creek Resort
Culbertson Hills
Downing
Elk Valley
Erie Golf Club
Fox Run
Gospel Hill Golf Club
Green Acres
Green Meadows
Hailwood
Hemlock Springs
Highlander
Island Green
Joseph Martin
Kahkwa Country Club
Lake Pleasant
Lake Shore Country Club
Lakeside
Lake View Country Club
Lawrence Park
Maple Ridge
Mound Grove
Mt Hope
North Hills
Orchard Ponds
Oakland Beach
Over Lake
Peek n' Peak
Pleasure
Riverside
Scenic Heights
South Woods
Union City Country Club
Valley View
Venango Valley
Whispering Pines
Windy Hill

*Denise Keim*

## GOLF

**A**lthough the number of temperate months in Erie is limited, when the weather is fair you're sure to find people on the fairways. Golf is one of the most popular sports in the area, with local enthusiasts hitting the links during good (and sometimes bad) weather. The season is punctuated with a number of well-known local and regional events and tournaments, including many presented by local businesses as well as larger competitions organized by **The Erie District Golf Association** and **Erie District Women's Golf Association**. One large golf tournament of note in the Erie area is the **Lake Erie Golf Classic** which is held at the **Peek n' Peak** course.

*Doug Campbell*

*Denise Keim*

**It's not too early** to learn playing skills for these eastside youngsters who are enjoying a summer picnic.

## FOOTBALL

The autumn season wouldn't be complete in Erie without the presence of football. The city's almost equidistant location between Buffalo,

**A Prep Win**

Pittsburgh, and Cleveland splits professional allegiances three ways, with each fan giving reasons why the team he (or she) supports is the best. Besides the pro games, you'll find equal interest in the competitions taking place in vacant lots, high school fields and college stadiums throughout the city. The **Save-An-Eye** All-Star game is a well known sports event in Erie. The **Cathedral Prep** football team has perhaps one of the most fanatic followings, and with good reason, they won the state championship in 2000. Longtime Prep rival, **McDowell** also fields strong teams. College games at **Gannon**, **Mercyhurst** and **Edinboro** are popular events, particularly with the addition of Gannon's football stadium at its downtown campus. The popularity of football in Erie shows no signs of subsiding.

## LOCAL TEAMS AND MASCOTS

**PROFESSIONAL**
Erie Seawolves (baseball)
Erie Otters (hockey)

**COLLEGE**
Behrend- Lions
Edinboro - Fighting Scots
Gannon - Golden Knights
Mercyhurst - Lakers

**HIGH SCHOOL**
Cathedral Prep - Ramblers
Central - Falcons
Corry- Beavers
East - Warriors
Fairview - Tigers
Fort LeBoeuf - Bisons
General McLane - Lancers
Girard - Yellow Jackets
Harborcreek- Huskies

Iroquois - Braves
McDowell- Trojans
Mercyhurst - Lakers
North East - Grape Pickers
Northwestern- Wildcats
Seneca - Bobcats
Strong Vincent - Colonels
Union City- Bears
Villa - Victors

183

Bruce Baumgartner

Caryn Kadavy

## STAR ATHLETES

**E**rie County has produced a number of nationally and internationally recognized athletes. Among these hometown favorites is figure skater **Caryn Kadavy**, who was a member of the 1988 U.S. Olympic team and rose to the top of the figure skating world winning gold medals internationally. **Bruce Baumgartner**, well-known as the wrestling coach at Edinboro University, is also a four-time wrestling medalist. He brought home Olympic Gold medals for the United States in 1984 and 1992. He also had the honor of carrying the American Flag in the Olympic ceremonies. Actor and martial artist **Billy Blanks** is a native son. He was thrust into the national spotlight for creating the massively popular fitness workout, **Tae-Bo**. **Mark Stepnoski** won two Super bowl rings, had several Pro Bowl experiences, and is a member of the NFL's All-Decade team for the 1990's. American Bowling Congress member **Bob Learn Jr.** has won 4 Professional Bowler's Association titles. **Fred Biletnikoff** was voted the most valuable player of the 1977 Super Bowl. The playing field behind Central High School bears his name in recognition of his outstanding career in football. Erie is a city that loves sports and is proud of these and other athletes who have gone on to greatness.

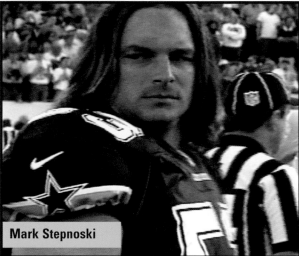
Mark Stepnoski

Bob Learn Jr.

### LAKE RACES

Prompted by a bitter rivalry between **White Star Lines** of Detroit and the **Cleveland Transit Co.**, the two undertook a steamboat race on June 4, 1901. The race, which drew interest from Detroit to Buffalo and all points in between, began in Cleveland and continued 94 miles northeast to the finish line in Erie. It was fitting that the **S.S. City of Erie** (Cleveland's boat) beat the **S.S. Tashmoo** (White Star's boat) in a neck and neck battle that saw firemen continuously feeding the intense fires powering the vessels. The top speed was 23 miles per hour, and interested parties were kept updated on the race by a carrier pigeon and signal kites.

### GOLF FOR CHARITY

The Erie Pro-Am golf tournament, the first incarnation of the Erie Charity Golf Classic, began play in 1970. The Classic, which has raised nearly $1 million for charity throughout the years, has attracted

Ed Bernik

many famous golfers, among them, Sam Snead, Arnold Palmer, Curtis Strange, Fred Couples, Ben Crenshaw, Davis Love III, Paul Azinger, Fred Funk, Jim Furyk, Chi Chi Rodriguez, and Fuzzy Zoeller. Lee Travino won the tournament twice in the 1980's and John Daly won in 1991.

John Horstman

### BUDNY SWIMS THE LAKE

On August 20, 1975, **Patrick Budny** became the first person to swim from Long Point, Canada to Presque Isle. Budny, who was only 17 years old at the time, swam across Lake Erie with another swimmer **Tim Hughes** who unfortunately had to be pulled from the water just 2 miles from the shore due to exhaustion. The distance between Long Point and Presque Isle is 23 miles, but because of strong lake currents Budny actually swam 31 miles. The swim took 26 hours. In honor of this incredible feat, what was formerly Beach 10 on Presque Isle was renamed **Budny Beach**.

### BREAKING BARRIERS

In 1950 **Sam Jethroe** became the oldest player to ever receive the Major League rookie of the year award, given every year by the Baseball Writers Association. Nicknamed "The Jet" because of his incredible speed, Jethroe joined the Negro League as a rookie in 1942. At age 32, Jethroe made his debut in the integrated Major Leagues and played there until 1954. One of the first black players to play Major League baseball, Jethroe finished his baseball career in the minor leagues in 1961. Jethroe established his home in Erie in 1942 and passed away in 2001.

unless noted, historical photos courtesy: **Erie County Historical Society & Museums**

HANDICAPPED
ENTRANCE
←

**LAW**

Photo: Denise Keim

The Erie County Courthouse is the oldest government building in continuous use in the county.

John Horstman

## ERIE COUNTY COURTHOUSE

The **Erie County Courthouse**, characterized by its distinctive Greek Revival architecture, is located just west of Perry Square on 6th Street. The west wing, built in 1855, is the oldest government building in continuous use in Erie County. The east wing and connecting structures were added in 1929. All licenses, permits, and certifications issued by the county are done through the courthouse (dog, fishing, and hunting licenses, marriage licenses, weapons permits, and weights & measures, just to name a few). The courthouse also maintains records for the county, including civil cases, court transcripts, estates and wills, marriage licenses, and realty records.

## ERIE FEDERAL COURTHOUSE

The **Erie Federal Courthouse**, located just off the east side of Perry Square at 617 State St., was constructed between 1937 and 1938. The courthouse is home to the Erie branch of the **United States District Court for the Western District of Pennsylvania**. The main courthouse for this district is in Pittsburgh, with a second satellite location in Johnstown. Collectively, this district court has jurisdiction over all federal civil and criminal matters arising in twenty-five counties of Western Pennsylvania.

## DISTRICT ATTORNEY

**A**s the chief law enforcement office for Erie County, District Attorney is a position that entails great responsibility. The district attorney is an elected position, responsible for signing all bills of indictment and conducting all criminal court and other prosecutions in the name of the Commonwealth. In addition to these duties, the district attorney also provides legal guidance in criminal matters for various police agencies and county departments. The County Detectives Bureau serves as the investigative arm of the District Attorney.

## PUBLIC DEFENDER

*John Horstman*

509 SASSAFRAS

**T**he role of public defender in Erie can be summed up in the statute that outlines their responsibilities: to represent individuals that are charged with criminal offenses where there is a possibility of jail provided they meet certain income guidelines. The public defender's office, located at 509 Sassafras, has 7 full-time and more than 10 part-time lawyers. In 2000, the office handled 2,684 adult criminal cases, 391 juvenile delinquency cases, and 421 mental health hearings. In addition, more than 100 juvenile dependency files were opened.

*Rob Ruby*

## RIDGE & McLAUGHLIN

**D**avid Ridge and **Matthew McLaughlin**, both graduates of Cathedral Prep High School, now practice law together next door to their alma mater. David Ridge and Matthew McLaughlin are lifelong Erie County residents. They both come from families who believe in hard work, dedication to the profession and involvement in the community.

David Ridge handles all areas of civil litigation and also concentrates on criminal defense, having handled some of the highest profile cases throughout the Commonwealth of Pennsylvania, in both state and federal court.

Matthew McLaughlin concentrates on automobile law and insurance coverage issues, workers' compensation, as well as medical malpractice.

Attorney Ridge has been a speaker at various seminars and has spoken on topics such as pre-trial preparation, ethics and trial procedure. Attorney McLaughlin is the solicitor for the Erie County Convention Center Authority and is also an assistance solicitor for the County of Erie. Ridge & McLaughlin also represents the Dr. Gertrude A. Barber Center, a nationally known institute serving special individuals throughout the Commonwealth of Pennsylvania.

**RIDGE & McLAUGHLIN**
**246 WEST 10TH STREET**
**ERIE, PENNSYLVANIA 16501**
**814 454-1010**

189

Buddy Stark is one of the area's few professionals with a CPA and law degree. He is the owner of The Stark Firm.

an interview with

# NORMAN "BUDDY" STARK
## *CPA & ESQUIRE*

**THE STARK FIRM**
100 STATE STREET
SUITE 210
ERIE, PENNSYLVANIA
814 454-9898
buddy@starkfirm.com

### Tell us about yourself and your firm
I practice law with a paralegal and a secretary in my own firm that I started four years ago. Before that I was with MacDonald Illig Jones and Britton where my father was a partner. I have eight children. That's ten people in one house! I do work hard but that is my nature and having a big family makes me work more efficiently.

### What was your first job?
I started my own painting company when I was a junior at Cathedral Prep. The first year I worked alone, the next year I hired two people, the next year five. We painted houses and boats - "Home Buddies" and "Boat Buddies" Painting Companies.

### Have you always lived in Erie?
Almost! I studied Accounting at Gannon University where I met my wife, Beata. I worked in Pittsburgh with Coopers & Lybrand, where I earned my CPA, and later with Price Waterhouse in Philadelphia. After marrying Beata in 1987, I attended Villanova Law School. In 1992, we were expecting our third child and decided to move back to Erie, where I joined MacDonald Illig.

### How many clients do you have?
I've acquired over five hundred clients in the last four years.

### What are your future career plans?
I have been approached by several large law firms to join them, but businesswise it made more sense to see my own firm grow. I have expanded my office - building three additional offices and a conference room which are leased to 2 attorneys. I am also talking with another business lawyer about coming in and working for me.

## How do you respond to the concerns of a new client?

Clients should not be shy about asking a lawyer to discuss fees. You should negotiate with your lawyer.

People should ask how long it will take to do the work and how much they may be billed. And that should be a firm commitment. Then there is an understanding with no surprises.

## What is your specialty?

My primary work is in business formation, restructuring, and transitioning. What I mean by transitioning is buying or selling or transferring to other owners or bringing a partner in.

## What about estate planning and business succession?

Planning is important if you want to make sure your business goes to your son or daughter, a key employee, or if you want the proceeds to go to your spouse or children or be held in trust until they get out of college. After a person dies, their lawyer has to take care of all the claims against the estate and distribute the balance to the beneficiaries. Another thing we take care of is real estate transactions.

## Why should a potential client choose you?

When they come to me, they receive excellent service with no surprises. They get a lawyer who understands their legal issues and takes care of them from the start.

I treat each and every person with respect and work hard to help them reach their goals whether it is a complex business transaction or a will and power of attorney. I want them to leave feeling that the problem has been fully analyzed and the problem will be resolved promptly at the lowest possible cost. I want them to leave feeling they have received good service. If you choose the right lawyer with the right skill, he or she will be able to quickly appreciate your problem and look at it from many angles and show you sides that you may never have considered. That might change your business decision.

## BAR ASSOCIATION

The **Erie County Bar Association** (ECBA), located at 302 W. 9th St., is an organization dedicated to promoting the legal and judicial system, protecting the rights and privileges of all individuals, assisting the courts, providing continuing legal and public education, as well as offering services and benefits to all its members. The ECBA has over

500 members, made up of attorneys and judges with residences or employment in Erie County. Benefits for the Erie community include a free legal referral service.

191

Rob Ruby

with shaping his practice which emphasizes personal injury, family law and criminal defense.

He employs two paralegals and embraces the efficiencies afforded by technology. A high-speed internet connection makes email convenient and provides instant access to appellate court opinions, statutes and other legal resources. PowerPoint has also been used successfully at trials.

"Our singular objective is to help people solve problems," he says. "We also carefully limit our caseload to ensure that our clients receive personal representation."

**J. TIMOTHY GEORGE**
**246 WEST 10TH**
**ERIE, PENNSYLVANIA 16501**
**814 455-5700**

Tim George embraces new technology to help clients solve problems.

## TIM GEORGE

In his office hangs photographs of his grandfather who taught mathematics at Gannon College for nearly 40 years and after whom Freeman Hall is named. His great-grandfather was a longshoreman in Erie.

"Erie is our home and has been the community where our families have worked for more than a century," says **Tim George** about his wife, **Kathy Scibetta**, also a lawyer, and their two children.

After graduating from St. Bonaventure University and receiving a law degree from the Dickinson School of Law, Mr. George returned home in 1992 to practice law. He credits the training provided by more experienced lawyers with whom he has worked, his time as a prosecutor, and his parents

John Horstman

## THE McDONALD GROUP

Paul M. Lorei

**A** law firm is only as good as its lawyers and supporting staff. In the case of **The McDonald Group**, its reputation for excellence is well deserved.

Providing legal services of the highest quality, and delivering those services in a manner which promotes client understanding and participation, are the hallmarks of The McDonald Group representation.

The firm was founded in 1986 by **James D. McDonald, Jr.** who brought with him more than 20 years experience as an Erie practitioner. The practice has grown to its present complement of six attorneys as **Gary Eiben**, **Thomas J. Buseck**, **Joseph P. Conti**, **Brian M. McGowan**, and **John J. Estok** joined the firm.

Teamwork among the staff promotes mutual respect and provides the opportunity for individual initiative, coupled with group synergy, all to the benefit of The McDonald Group's clients. The match between attorney and client is especially important. The background and experience of each attorney plays a significant role in the clients he represents. Each client matter is analyzed and assigned to the attorney best qualified to respond to the client's needs.

Areas of emphasis include personal injury and business litigation, business planning and tax representation, employment relations, real estate, estate planning and administration, and health care law, and creditors' rights.

Health care law is one of the fastest-growing areas of specialized practice for The McDonald Group. In its representation of professionals, the firm serves clients in the areas of malpractice defense, professional practice dissolution and realignment, licensure, and peer review problems. The McDonald Group is sensitive to the specialized problems faced by health care .

By working together as an effective team, the attorneys of The McDonald Group will continue to display great potential for accomplishment.

**THE McDONALD GROUP, L.L.P.**
**456 WEST SIXTH STREET, P.O. Box 1757**
**ERIE, PENNSYLVANIA 16507-0757**
**814 456-5318**
**www.tmgattys.com**

## THE ERIE JUDICIAL SYSTEM

When most people think of the court system in Erie County, they are probably thinking of the **Erie County Court of Common Pleas**, which is responsible for many of the civil and criminal

cases that make local headlines. The Court of Common Pleas is headed by a president judge who oversees two administrative divisions: the Trial Division, which encompasses all civil and criminal matters, and the Family Division, which includes all family matters, juvenile matters, and Orphans' Court. The work of each division is coordinated by an Administrative Judge who collaborates with the judges assigned to each division. In 2002, judges presided over 109 criminal jury and 20 non-jury trials, 23 civil jury and 20 non-jury trials, 1,700 family support hearings, 140 custody hearings, 242 indirect criminal concept hearings resulting from PFAs (protection from abuse), 205 Orphans' Court hearings, and 1,729 delinquency and dependency hearings. Additionally, the judges heard pleas, arguments, post-trial motions, conducted settlement conferences, revocations, bail hearings, and over 6,000 miscellaneous motions and petitions.

What many people don't realize, however, is that the Court of Common Pleas is only one part of a hierarchical structure known as Pennsylvania's Unified Judicial System. Subordinate to the Court of Common Pleas are a number of special courts: District Justices, Municipal Courts, and Traffic Courts. Presiding above the Court of Common Pleas are the Pennsylvania Superior Court, Commonwealth Court, and Supreme Court. All branches of the Pennsylvania Unified Judicial System serve different, specific purposes, yet work together as a whole to ensure that the state's judicial system provides justice to the people of Pennsylvania.

## STRUCTURE OF THE FEDERAL LEGAL SYSTEM

The Federal courthouse in Erie serves far more than the city or the county. Pennsylvania is divided into three federal court divisions (eastern, middle, and western), and Erie's federal courthouse represents the entire western area. That division encompasses Crawford, Elk, Erie, Forest, McKean, Venango, and Warren counties. The western division has one federal judge who is appointed by the president and serves his term for life. Additionally, there is one federal bankrupcy judge who serves a fourteen year term. The western division includes one full-time public defender, a U.S. Attorney, and two assistant prosecutors. On average, the western division of the Federal court annually hears 350 to 400 civil cases and 40 to 50 criminal cases.

*John Horstman*

## ELECTED OFFICIALS
### ERIE COUNTY JUDICIAL SYSTEM

| | |
|---|---|
| County Executive | Clerk of Records |
| Controller | Sheriff |
| Coroner | District Attorney |
| County Council Members | Judges |
| | District Judges |

*top left photo courtesy:* WSEE

## LAW ENFORCEMENT OFFICES IN ERIE COUNTY

**FEDERAL**
Federal Bureau of Investigation

**STATE**
Pennsylvania State Police
  Corry Station
  Erie-Troop E Station
  Girard Station

**ERIE COUNTY**
Erie County Sheriff
Erie County Police
  Cambridge Springs (Borough)
  City of Corry
  Edinborough (Borough)
  City of Erie
  Fairview Township
  Franklin Township
  Girard (Borough)
  Greene Township
  Harborcreek Township
  Lake City (Borough)
  Lawrence Park Township
  Millcreek Township
  North East (Borough)
  Spring Creek Township
  Union City (Borough)
  Venango Township
  Waterford (Borough)
  Waterford Township
  Wesleyville (Borough)

" *Law is order*
*and good law*
*is good order* "
*—Aristotle*

## CRIME AND PUNISHMENT

There are two major correctional facilities in Erie county, **the Albion State Correctional Institution** in the county's most southern borough, Albion, and the **Erie County Prison**, located at 1618 Ash Street. A pre-release center for prisoners also exists within the city of Erie. The Erie county Sheriff's office, which is responsible for serving subpoenas and guarding courthouses, also transfers inmates from the County Prison to the courthouse for trial. The average daily population in Erie County jails is 579 prisoners*.

| Major Crimes Per Year |
| --- |
| 5 murders |
| 54 forcible rapes |
| 219 robberies |
| 189 aggravated assaults |
| 694 burglaries |
| 2,453 larceny-thefts |
| 223 motor vehicle thefts |
| 51 arsons.** |

*Doug Campbell*

*PA Department of Corrections, Division of Planning, Research, Statistics and Grants, 1999 statistics.
** Uniform Crime Rates, 2000, issued by the FBI, United States Department of Justice

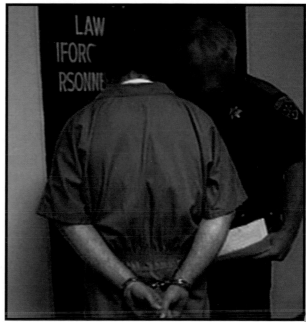

*photo courtesy:* WSEE

" *Men are never so likely*
*to settle a question rightly*
*as when they discuss it freely.* "

*—Macaulay*

## PROHIBITION

As early as 1829, temperance societies were so well organized in Erie that the city jailer, who was paid in proportion to the number of wrong doers, complained that the movement was ruining his business. During prohibition years, "Rum runners" transported alcohol across Lake Erie from Canada while **The Erie Brewing Co.** made **Brownie Root Beer**.

## EXECUTION

**Henry Fancisco** was the first man hanged in Erie County under civil law. He was executed on March 9, 1838, for the death of his lover, **Maria Robison**. Maria, who died in a suicide pact with Fancisco, was described as "one of the handsomest girls ever seen in Erie."

## EARLY COURTHOUSE

Before the grand **Erie County Courthouse** on West Sixth Street was built in 1855, a much humbler structure stood in west park.

## MAYOR FLATLEY

In October 1954, Erie was rocked by one of its worst political scandals. **Mayor Thomas W. Flatley** and a police inspector were exposed as part of a $20 million gambling empire. The case brought 360 charges, mostly of bribery and conspiracy, against fifty different defendants.

197

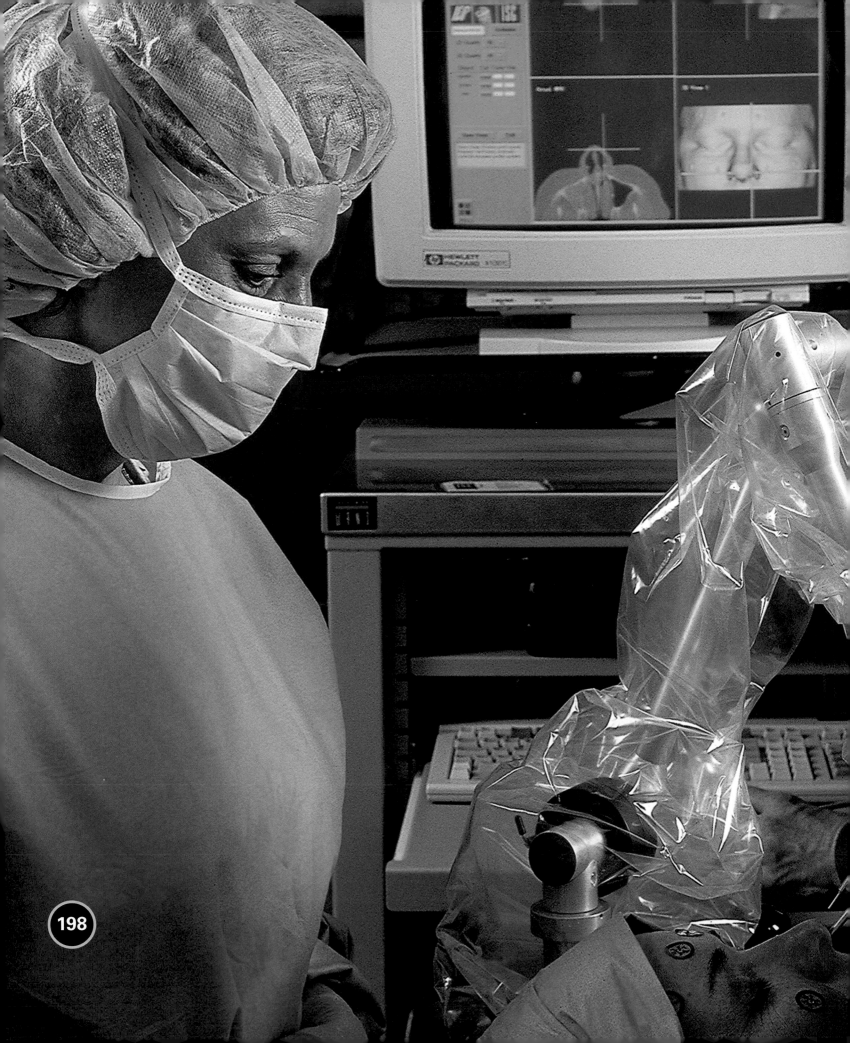

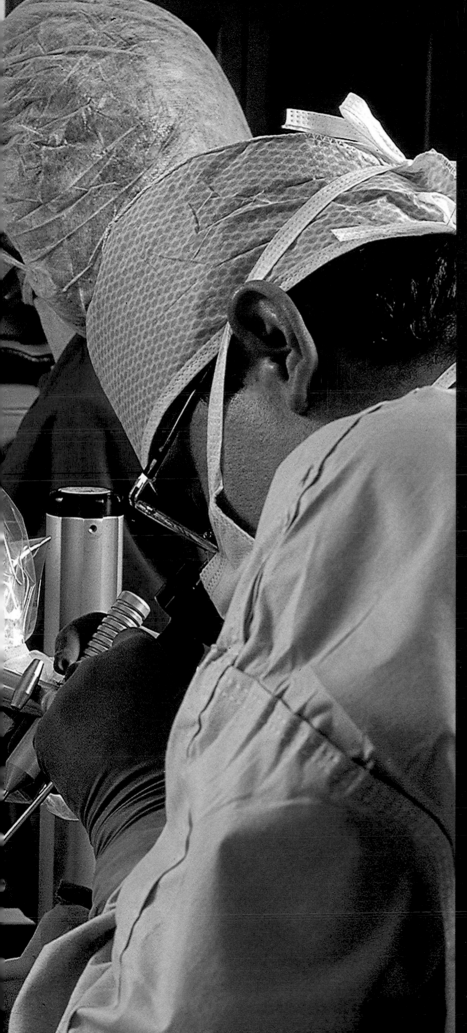

# HEALTH CARE

Photo: Ed Bernik

## SAINT VINCENT

For more than 128 years, **Saint Vincent Health System** has been dedicated to compassion and clinical excellence in health care services. Founded in 1875 by the Sisters of Saint Joseph of Northwestern Pennsylvania, Saint Vincent now stands as the region's most integrated network of sophisticated medical specialties.

Anchored by Saint Vincent Health Center, a 450-bed not-for-profit tertiary care facility located at 232 West 25th Street in Erie, Saint Vincent has earned its status as the region's top tertiary care provider. From northwestern Pennsylvania to northeastern Ohio and southwestern New York State, Saint Vincent associates and physicians ensure access to world-class, holistic health care for more than 1 million individuals, and bring leading-edge treatment and unparalleled compassion to more than 19,000 inpatients and 200,000 outpatients each year.

The health center's 14 distinct centers of excellence share a commitment to the same level of expertise and quality present in the Saint Vincent Heart Center, which stands as the number-one place in the entire state of Pennsylvania to receive heart care. In a recent rating, the center - also among the top 5 percent of heart hospitals nationwide - posted the best cardiac, surgical and procedural outcomes among the 56 Pennsylvania hospitals that perform open-heart surgery (HealthGrades, Inc., 2003).

Saint Vincent extends its reach into the region through 12 primary care medical practices, 11 specialty medical practices, and strategic affiliations with seven community hospitals and thousands of area physicians and medical providers. Through community collaborations, Saint Vincent has also championed advanced regional services that include laboratories, the blood bank, insurance programs, ambulance and helicopter transport, The Regional Cancer Center and Northwest Pennsylvania's first DMAT - Disaster Medical Assistance Team.

With 2,500 employees and an annual payroll of $60 million, Saint Vincent Health System is the 6th largest employer in the city of Erie and one of the largest in northwestern Pennsylvania. The health system has an annual operating budget of $231 million, and creates an additional $324 million in local economic activity every year. Saint Vincent contributes more than $14,461,000 every year to community service, charity and uncompensated care to improve the region's quality of life, and remains unconditionally focused on delivering the highest quality patient care and service to the community.

**SAINT VINCENT HEALTH SYSTEMS**
**232 WEST 25TH STREET**
**ERIE, PENNSYLVANIA 16544**
**(814) 452-5000**

Photos Courtesy: Saint Vincent

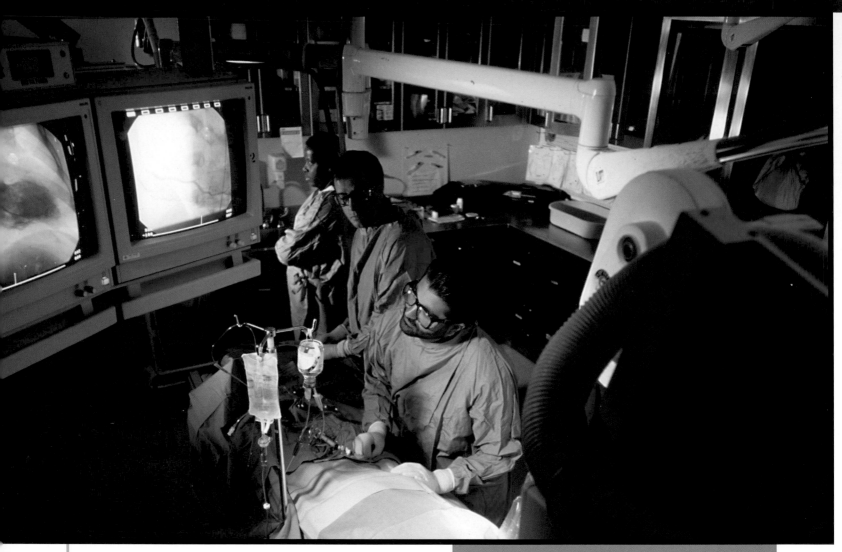

## CONSULTANTS IN CARDIOVASCULAR DISEASE INC.

Consultants in Cardiovascular Disease Inc. (CICDI) believe that a healthy heart is the result of a successful partnership among patients and their family members, primary care physicians, and the cardiologist or cardiac surgeon. Through this partnership, the continuum of care extends beyond diagnosis, treatment and rehabilitation into the patient's lifestyle to include proper diet, exercise and weight control.

The CICDI Cardiovascular Division provides patients with state-of-the-art surgical treatments for all types of diseases and disorders associated with the heart, lungs and blood vessels of the chest. Recognized for their experience and unwavering commitment to quality patient care, they have proudly entered a new age in cardiothoracic surgery.

CICDI experts are committed to improving patient care through clinical research, advanced training and leading-edge treatment alternatives. With 18 board-certified cardiovascular specialists and dedicated staff, Consultants in Cardiovascular Disease Inc. are proud to provide the finest heart care to the residents of Erie County and the surrounding region.

**CONSULTANTS IN CARDIOVASCULAR DISEASE INC.**
**311 WEST 24TH SUITE 401**
**ERIE, PENNSYLVANIA 16502**
**(814) 453-7767**

**GIVING BLOOD** is an easy way to make a major contribution to your community.

## COMMUNITY BLOOD BANK OF NORTHWEST PENNSYLVANIA

The **Community Blood Bank of Northwest Pennsylvania** has been the provider of blood to all the hospitals in the area since it was formed as a joint venture between **Hamot Medical Center** and **St. Vincent Health Center** in 1966. The Community Blood Bank, a non-profit corporation regulated by the FDA, facilitates the donation of blood from volunteer to patients in need at area hospitals. The Community Blood Bank (C.B.B.) is consistently ranked among the lowest-cost blood providers in the nation. By keeping costs down, the C.B.B. saves area hospitals hundreds of thousands of dollars every year, which helps keep healthcare costs down for the entire region. When someone is injured in an accident and rushed to the emergency room, no thought is given to the blood the victim will receive, the blood is there ready to help save a life.

Getting enough blood to the hospitals is a monumental task. In 2003, 30,000 units were transfused in Northwest Pennsylvania. About 2,500 donors are needed every month to maintain a safe blood supply. The number of eligible donors continues to decline as new diseases and regulations prevent people from donating. At the same time, use is up due to longer lifespans.

The Community Blood Bank has a fixed site at 26th & Peach Streets that receives donors six days a week. Walk-ins are welcome, and no appointment is needed.

Statistics show that 1 out of every 3 people will need blood during their lifetimes. By giving blood, you are making sure that your friends and neighbors and other members of the community have the blood they need when they need it. Keeping local blood local is good for the Community. Our Community. Please take the time to make a difference in someone's life, they'll be glad you did and so will you.

**COMMUNITY BLOOD BANK
OF NORTHWEST PENNSYLVANIA
2646 PEACH STREET
ERIE, PENNSYLVANIA 16508
(814) 456-4206
www.fourhearts.org**

## MILLCREEK COMMUNITY HOSPITAL

**M**illcreek Community Hospital has been a major trailblazer for the medical industry in the Erie community since 1948. They funded the region's first 9-1-1 system. They also established **Lake Erie College of Osteopathic Medicine** (LECOM), which is quickly on its way to becoming the largest medical school in the country. With more than 100 active and associate physicians providing inpatient and outpatient services and 24-hour care, the facility has 168 beds and operates additional neighborhood clinics and physician offices.

As a leader in osteopathic medicine, Millcreek Community Hospital serves as the primary teaching hospital for LECOM and provides student

externships, internships, and residency programs in family practice, internal medicine, orthopedic surgery, ENT, and podiatric medicine. The **Millcreek Health System** is a major economic force in northwestern Pensylvania with approximately 500 employees and well over $110 million in total assets.

> **Millcreek Community Hospital** is dedicated to osteopathic medicine which provides a holistic approach to health, treating both body and mind.

Left to right:
MCH orthopedic surgeon **Anthony J. Ferretti, D.O.**
LECOM President **John M. Ferretti, D.O.**
LECOM Provost **Silvia M. Ferretti, D.O.**
LECOM Student **Russell McElveen**
MCH OB/GYN **Paula A. Gunduz, M.D.**
MCH President **Mary L. Eckert**

**MILLCREEK COMMUNITY HOSPITAL**
**5515 PEACH STREET**
**ERIE, PENNSYLVANIA 16509**
**814 864-4031**

**www.millcreekcommunityhospital.com**

## CORRY MEMORIAL HOSPITAL

Corry Memorial Hospital has served Southern Erie County since 1894. The ties of community are strong in Corry. These strong ties are the basis for the philosophy of care at Corry Memorial Hospital. At CMH, accepting responsibility for a "healthier community" is addressed by offering a wide array of services and programs, providing free health educational programs open to the public, and investing in the future of healthcare by partnering with local school systems to provide job-shadowing experiences.

A diverse range of specialties gives our community the best that medicine can offer. The Corry Memorial Hospital family recognizes quality, service, courtesy, human dignity, integrity, and respect as our core values. These values are the foundation of the Hospital's ability to achieve excellence in meeting the needs of their customers.

**CORRY MEMORIAL HOSPITAL**
**612 WEST SMITH STREET**
**CORRY, PENNSYLVANIA 16407**
**814 664-4641**
**www.corryhospital.org**

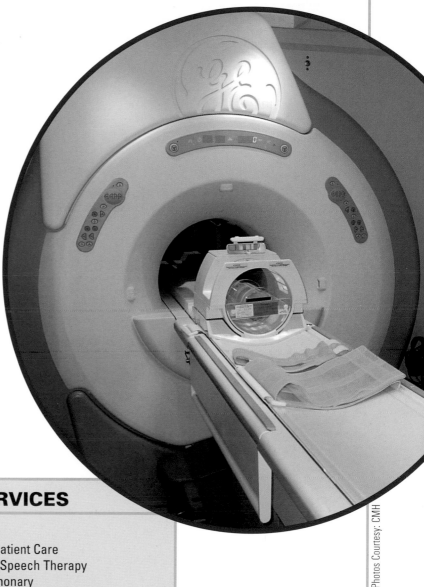

Photos Courtesy: CMH

## C.M.H. SPECIALTIES AND SERVICES

| HEALTH SPECIALTIES | SERVICES |
|---|---|
| Anesthesiology | Acute In-Patient Care |
| Audiology | Audiology/Speech Therapy |
| Emergency Medicine | Cardiopulmonary |
| Eyes, Ears, Nose and Throat | Childbirth Education |
| Family Practice | Diabetes Education |
| General Surgery | Home Health Care and Hospice |
| Geriatric Psychiatry | Intensive and Coronary Care Unit |
| Internal Medicine | Radiology including |
| Obstetrics/Gynecology | *Mammography, MRI, CT Scan,* |
| Ophthalmology | *Nuclear Medicine and Sonography* |
| Oral Surgery | Laboratory |
| Orthopaedics | Occupational/Employee Health |
| Pathology | Oncology/Chemotherapy |
| Podiatry | Rehabilitation Therapies |
| Radiology | Social Service |
| | Transitional Care Plus Program |

205

## HIGHMARK
## BLUE CROSS BLUE SHIELD

Highmark Blue Cross Blue Shield is a leader in providing an extraordinary sense of security for more than 23 million health insurance consumers in the state and across the nation – including 400,000 members in eleven northwestern Pennsylvania counties served by its downtown Erie office location since 1950.

Highmark and the "blue" names are synonymous with a philosophy of community commitment deeply rooted in a tradition of social mission programs to help people.

Highmark is one company with a singular mission to help Pennsylvanians receive access to affordable, quality health care to ensure they live longer, healthier lives.

**HIGHMARK, INC.**
**717 STATE STREET**
**ERIE, PENNSYLVANIA 16501**
**814 871-6772**
**www.highmark.org**

Rob Ruby

## VILLA MEDICAL SUPPLY

Villa Medical Supply, a division of the **Tansey Company**, doesn't make the same "rock-bottom" offers of mammoth department stores. What it offers instead is service. For more than 30 years, Villa Medical Supply has been helping Northwestern Pennsylvania families equip their homes with healthcare needs that improve their quality of life. "We service our clients and we service what we sell," said owner **Edward Tansey**, who acquired the business in 1989 with his wife **Bonnie** when they made the decision to come home to Erie.

What they found when they returned from California was not only an established, independent company, they also found an experienced and knowledgeable staff, several of whom are still doing what they've been doing since the 1970s - taking care of people.

**VILLA MEDICAL SUPPLY**
**1460 WEST 38TH**
**ERIE, PENNSYLVANIA 16508**
**(814) 866-1999**

Rob Ruby

## NASH CHIROPRACTIC OF ERIE

**N**ow in its third generation, **Nash Chiropractic of Erie** is a family tradition as well as an alternative approach to healthy living. Founded in 1946 by **Dr. William Nash**, a Graduate of Palmer 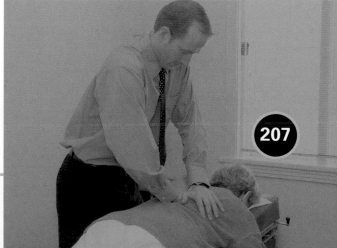 College of Chiropractic, this practice has been built on the philosophy of treatment without the use of drugs or surgery. Today, his son and grandson continue to provide relief to people suffering from a variety of problems. Through spinal manipulation, biomechanics, and nutritional therapy, the body's inherent recuperative powers are stimulated and supported.

**Dr. John T. Nash**, also a Palmer College Graduate, has been practicing in Erie since 1963. For the past 40 years he has strived to provide the most up to date and comprehensive care to his patients. "Our commitment to educating the Erie community about the benefits of Chiropractic care remains a primary goal of Nash Chiropractic," says **Dr. Trevor Nash**, Palmer College Graduate, Mercyhurst College Adjunct Faculty Member, and Consultant for the Olympic Training Center. "Back pain and sports injuries are regularly treated with success, and people are aware of this,

Photos: Rob Ruby

but so may other health problems can be resolved through a total health approach," Nash informs.

Dr. Trevor Nash has been practicing with his father since 1998 on Peach Street, just a few doors down from the original office.

**NASH CHIROPRACTIC HEALTH CARE**
**3201 PEACH STREET**
**ERIE, PENNSYLVANIA 16508**
**(814) 456-1600**

**Dr. John T. Nash** and **Dr. Trevor Nash** solve numerous physical ailments without the use of drugs or surgery.

*Above* - Manchester Village
*Left* - A symbol of Presbyterian homes, the butterfly, symbolizes change and beauty.

## PRESBYTERIAN HOMES

In 1946 young Americans - Tom Brokaw called them "The Greatest Generation" - turned their attention from the responsibility of fighting a World War to a more domestic endeavor that would arguably leave just as great an impact on the future of America. In short, they began to have babies.

Fifty-five years later, the AARP began automatically sending the requisite free membership cards to these Baby Boomers as they commenced turning 55 at a rate of 1 every 18 seconds. Yet along with the Senior Citizens discount that this milestone brings, many members of this much-heralded generation are facing the increasing pressures of caring for their own aging parents. For many, it is one of the most difficult and confusing challenges they've ever faced.

Fortunately, families in northwestern Pennsylvania have been able to rely on the **Presbyterian Homes** to provide a caring, comfortable, and safe living environment for their aging loved ones. The fact is that Presbyterian Homes first began

providing living space for senior citizens in 1943 - a full two years before the Greatest Generation stormed the beaches of Normandy. In the 60 years since, one thing has remained consistent: Presbyterian Homes' mission is to minister to the physical, intellectual, emotional, and spiritual needs of the elderly in the dignified manner to which they are entitled.

Of course much has changed over that 60 years, too. In September of 1943, the fledgling mission started with a single house at 239 North Main Street in Cambridge Springs and a mere $10,000 capital. The need was immediate, and the home was quickly filled to a capacity of 25 men and women. Today, by contrast, the network of Presbyterian Homes includes 5 facilities spread throughout the Presbytery of Lake Erie capable of servicing a population of more than 400 seniors.

**Yvonne Atkinson**, President of Presbyterian Homes also points out that the options available to

**Yvonne Atkinson**

today's seniors are much broader. "Sixty years ago, when older folks got sick, they went to the hospital and often didn't return. Today, there are so many more options that help to keep people out of the hospital and in the community." Presbyterian Homes prides itself in offering an array of services ranging from simple personal care to skilled nursing. Their newest offering, **Manchester Village**, even includes resident-owned condominiums that further integrate the seniors into their community.

Commitment to excellent service is a hallmark of

the work that Presbyterian Homes has done over the years. In the early years they relied on a small team of committed individuals to provide a comforting environment to their residents. Today, the non-profit organization employs more than 400 full and part-time staff, including doctors, nurses, physical therapists, recreational therapists, and an impressive array of specialists. Their network of care includes 5 homes in northwestern Pennsylvania.

One thing that hasn't changed at all, though, is that Presbyterian Homes has always welcomed people regardless of their religious affiliation or financial capabilities. With the expertise gained from 60 years of operating as the region's premier provider of long-term care and assisted living, Presbyterian Homes continues to help families access dignified housing for their aging loved-ones.

Battles Village, a 42 apartment independent retirement community for low income seniors in Girard, PA.

**PRESBYTERIAN HOMES OFFICES**
**2816 ELMWOOD AVENUE**
**ERIE, PENNSYLVANIA 16508**
**814 868-4891**

Portraits - Ed Bernik; others courtesy: Presbyterian Homes

**Diana Ziemniak,** *Director of Development*
**Yvonne Atkinson,** *President*
**Theresa Martin,** *Marketing Director*

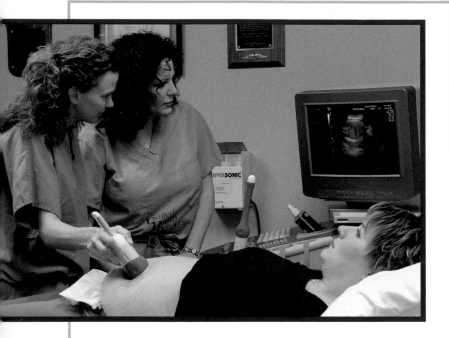

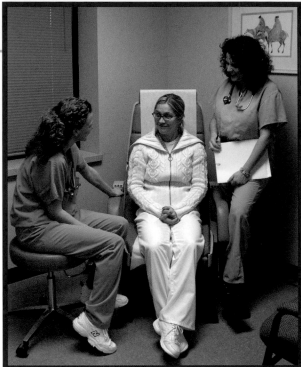

Photos: Rob Ruby

## WOMAN TO WOMAN PC

The office practice was founded in 1966 by **Gerald E. Beck, MD.** Dr. Beck worked as an independent physician for 34 years, caring for thousands of Erie women. In 2000 he was joined

Mark Fainstein

**DR. MOREY AND DR. POLON**

by his daughter, **Dr. Pamela Beck Morey**, and her close friend, **Dr. Michele Polon**. They took a new name, **Woman to Woman PC**, and the doctors settled into their current roles. Drs. Morey and Polon provide complete primary medical care in addition to obstetrics and gynecology. Dr. Beck specializes in sonography, surgery, and infertility. They pride themselves on prompt, flexible appointments, physician-only care, and a friendly staff who welcomes you.

Every woman has unique healthcare needs when she comes to the office - from first exams to pregnancy to menopause and everything in between. The doctors at Woman to Woman PC offer individualized, personal healthcare. As Dr. Morey says, "The time we spend talking and getting to know one another is time well spent. It helps us become at ease, and our doctors feel that is something every woman needs - a comfortable, genuine relationship with her physician."

Dr. Polon encourages, "When you come in for your appointment, bring your questions - especially the ones you don't feel you can ask anyone else. We will always listen and give you accurate information along with all the support we can offer. We hear all the time from our patients how much they appreciate the extra attention they get from Woman to Woman PC. We wouldn't have it any other way."

That's an approach to healthcare that improves results, and it's the kind of care women deserve.

**WOMAN TO WOMAN PC**
**510 CRANBERRY SUITE 200**
**ERIE, PENNSYLVANIA 16507**
**(814) 459-3141**

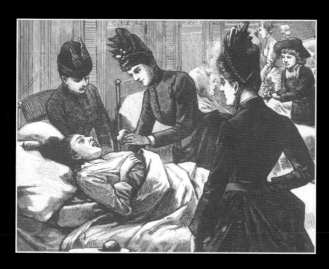

## INFLUENZA OUTBREAK

In 1918 the "War to End All Wars" was raging overseas. Many American troops had become infected with Influenza Type A, then known as the Spanish Flu. Returning soldiers brought the disease to our shores in September. On October 2nd the first Erie case was reported. All gatherings from saloons to Sunday schools were closed in a statewide quarantine from Oct. 5th to Nov. 10th. As crowds gathered and celebrated the end of the quarantine, the disease spread rampant with 287 new cases reported on Nov. 19th. By mid-December the epidemic was in its final stages after claiming over 500 lives in Erie.

## PRESBYTERIAN HOMES

One of the tougher decisions one has to make in life is where to live in your golden years. Lucky  for Erie, there is Presbyterian Homes - although the original Presbyterian Home was built in Cambridge Springs for $10,000 and opened in 1943.

## SAINT VINCENT HEALTH CENTER

The sisters of St. Joseph ran a home for orphans in Erie. One day in 1872, a man broke his leg in front of the orphanage and went inside for care. Before long, others came to the charitable sisters and next thing they knew, St. Vincent Hospital was born.

211

**ART**

Photo: Erie Art Museum

## ERIE ART MUSEUM

The Erie Art Museum, located at 411 State St., is a nonprofit member-supported community organization that boasts a year-round programming

John Vanco

schedule: art exhibitions, classes, workshops, concerts, group tours, art in the schools, children's programs, lectures, artists' services, traveling exhibits, publications and more. All of this is made possible by a dedicated and creative staff including longtime Director, **John Vanco.** The building that houses the museum was originally the **Bank of the United States**, built in 1839. This original purpose explains the building's distinctive Greek Revival architecture. Today, the museum's provocative look supports its role as the centerpiece of **Discovery Square**, a cultural and educational center in downtown Erie. Besides the museum itself, Discovery Square is home to a full-service framing gallery and the **Erie County Historical Society and Museums**.

## ART CLASSES

Where can you take art classes in Erie? Just to name a few options, kids have great opportunities - outside of school - at places like **The Neighboorhood Art House** (see next page), while both kids and adults alike can learn a wide variety of creative skills through **The Erie Art Museum,** which has directed classes both on-site and at **1505 State Street**. Ceramics enthusiasts are encouraged to mold their talents at **Claytopia,** and stained glass artisans can let their skills shine at **The Glass Stop.**

Dev Jana

**201 EAST 10th**

## NEIGHBORHOOD ART HOUSE

The inner-city Neighboorhood Art House, located at 201 East 10th St., provides free lessons in the literary, performing, and visual arts to over 800 inner city children each year. Most programs take place after school, on Saturdays and throughout the summer. In addition to its art classes, the Neighborhood Art House also offers tutoring and one-on-one reading programs. **The Benedictine Sisters** of Erie, who started the program, believe the need for the arts in the lives of the poor is as real as their need for bread.

## ARTISTS' GROUPS

Many professional artists in the Erie area, such as **Fran Schanz**, belong to the **NPAA** (Northwest Pennsylvania Artists Association) or the **PIAA** (Presque Isle Artists Association). The **Arts Council of Erie** is a vital catalyst for countless regional endeavors and the nonprofit group **Artists Incorporated,** has created numerous important and successful projects around town.

## 1505 ARTWORKS

If there's such a thing as an artists' community in Erie, it would have to be **1505 Artworks**, located, by no coincidence, at 1505 State Street. The

photo courtesy: Erie Art Museum

building itself had a rich history before it became studio space for local artists. It was built by the **Mayer Brothers Construction Company** in 1899 as a headquarters for their business. Later, however, it served numerous light industry uses: a spice mill, a makeshift hospital, an electric company, and a furniture company to name just a few. Then in 1988, **Dave McGeary** and his father purchased the building. "A bank owned it at that point," remembers McGeary, "and it was in pretty bad shape. They wanted to get it off their hands, so we got it at a decent price." McGeary didn't have plans for it right away, but when artists kept asking if studio space was available, the idea for Artworks was born. McGeary, who had had construction experience, made the interior into 35 separate units, including 14 painting studios, two photography studios with darkrooms, and 4 darkrooms for renting to the public. The idea worked. Despite the cliche of the starving artist, artworks retains a 90 to 95% occupancy rate throughout the year. McGeary is often forced to turn away artists away because of its popularity. The variety of the artists in the building is just as unusual as the idea. Just a few of Artworks' many tenants include the **Schanz Gallery**, a hot spot for local and national artists, **John Totleben**, a professional comic book illustrator who has been featured in Marvel Comics, and **Brad Lethaby**, who has the distinction of selling numerous paintings through New York galleries.

## RALPH MILLER GALLERY

**E**nter the gallery of **Ralph Miller Jewelers** and you might discover, on a typical day, an 11-foot-tall statue of Lady Justice from a Pennsylvania courthouse, made in fiberglass by one of the in-house artists at Miller Jewelers.

Look left and you might see African wood carvings. To the right, Tibetan prayer wheels or Brazilian crystal balls. Over here, Roman and Egyptian artifacts. Over there, the largest cut stone in the tri-state area, a quartz weighing 3,000-plus carats. On the walls hang original oil and watercolor paintings. In the display cases, estate jewelry, pearls, and their unique designer jewelry.

In short, a visitor is liable to find some object of natural or man made beauty, ancient or modern, from every inhabited continent.

**Jan** and **Dan Niebauer**, the wife-and-husband co-owners of **Ralph Miller Jewelers**, converted the former Christian Science Reading Room next door to their store into a gallery.

What is the common denominator of such varied objects? "Different," McKenzie answers in a word. "We try to have things that are off the beaten path. Where else do you go in Erie to buy a 400-million-year-old (fossil) scorpion or a seashell from the coast of Australia?"

**RALPH MILLER JEWELERS AND GALLERY**
**28 WEST EIGHTH STREET**
**ERIE, PENNSYLVANIA 16501**
**814 452-3336**

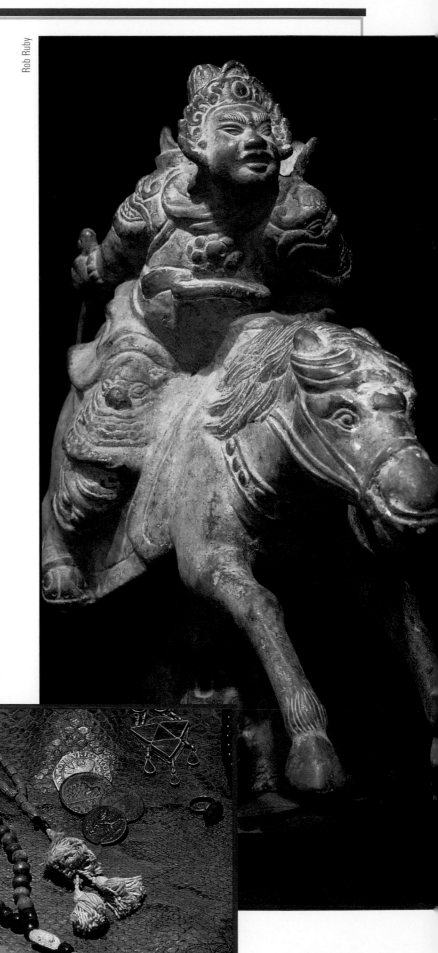

Rob Ruby

### Rare & Spectacular Objects de Art
Asian bronze and
Middle Eastern jewelry

216

## GALLERIES

**E**rie walls are not bare. With dozens of small art galleries around town (too many to mention all of them here), patrons are sure to find work in a variety of media: painting, sculpture, photography, furniture, and jewelry just to name a few. Show openings, and sometimes closings, draw nice crowds when promoted well. Rooms such as **Glass Growers Gallery**, **The Kada Gallery and Frame Shop** and **A La Carte**, have gained local reputations for consistently presenting diverse and beautiful objects. Spaces such as **The Schanz Gallery**, **Urraro Gallery** and **Erie Art Museum Frame Shop** are known around town for displaying an eclectic mix of shows which tend to lean towards the cutting edge. While the focus of **U Frame It** (page 295) is you guessed it, framing, art objects are not foreign to its walls. **The Bayfront Gallery** is a co-op of local artists who collectively pack the walls with their work in a renovated space tucked into Dobbins Landing. Local pen and ink artist,

**Schanz Gallery**

*Denise Keim*

**James E. Sabol,** makes his work of regional landmarks available in his westside gallery. Newcomers such as **Indulge**, **The Auer Gallery** and **Boone's Art and Frame** are making a mark. In Lawrence Park, folks can stop in **Harger's Landmark Studio** for creative gifts. The girls of **Relish** have built a great reputation for making unique jewelry out of beach glass. Clearly, there are many more galleries around Erie, both small and large, and listing them all is difficult, but if you would like to support the arts, most galleries advertise themselves in the yellow pages or you can look for show openings and reviews listed in the **Showcase,** which is a supplement to the **Erie Times** published every Thursday.

*photo courtesy: Urraro Gallery*

**Urraro Gallery**

*photo courtesy: Glass Growers Gallery*

**Glass Growers**

**Bayfront Gallery**

*John Horstman*

218

Louis Colussi

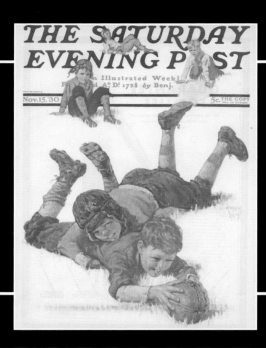

## DRAWING ATTENTION

Erie has been home to a number of well-known artists. Erie illustrator **Eugene Iverd** produced covers for the Saturday Evening Post in the 1930's. Erie native **Richard Anuszkiewicz** was a pioneer of an artistic movement called "Op Art," which was characterized by the optical illusions it created. **Joseph Plavcan** was a well known portrait and landscape painter, many Erie artists credit as being a teacher and major influence.

*courtesy:* **Erie County Historical Society & Museums**

## A MUSEUM IN THE MAKING

The **Art Club of Erie** was founded in January of 1898. The objective of the group was to promote art education and appreciation in the public schools. For fifty years they presented exhibits at the Erie Public Library. In 1956, the group became, **The Erie Art Center** and established their home at 338 west sixth street. In 1968, to further the organization's development, The Erie Art Center hired **John Vanco** as it's first Executive Director. Below left, Vanco with **John Silk Deckard**, who was the sculptor of **Eternal Vigilance**, a bronze figure placed in front of the Erie Art Museum on State Street.

*Vanco/Deckard photo courtesy:* **Kathy Merski**

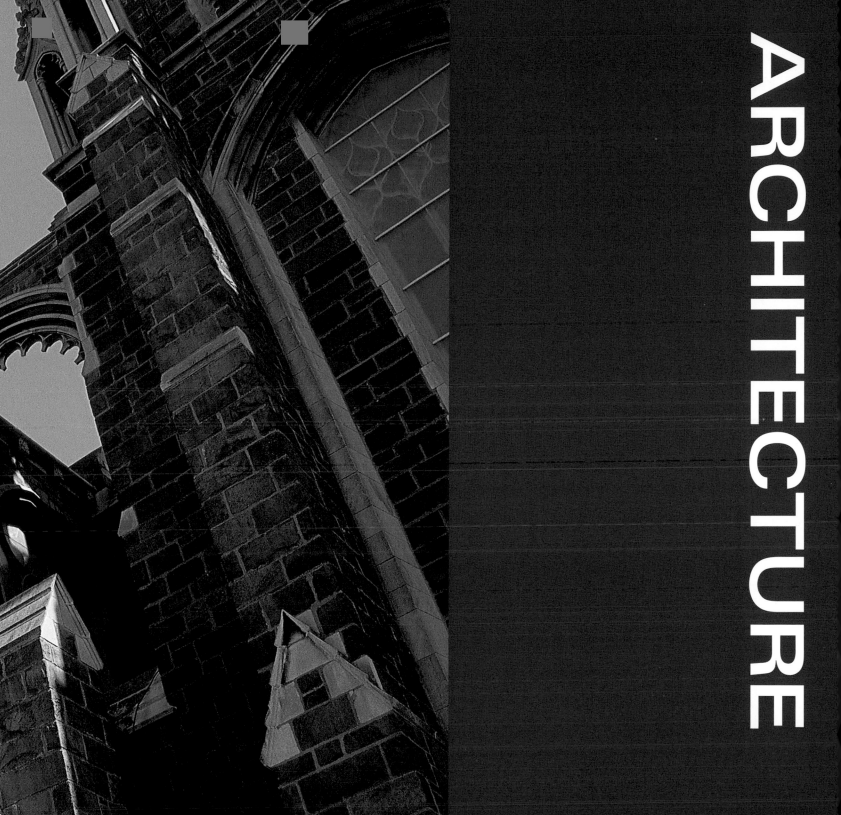

# ARCHITECTURE

Photo: Bob Hagle

**Saint Peter Cathedral,** an Erie landmark on 10th and Sassafras streets that's tough to miss, went through a major face lift in 1993. On the left is the pre-renovated cathedral and on the right is the church as it appears today.

## DIVINE ARCHITECTURE

**E**rie is noted for the beautiful architecture of its churches. While the list is too extensive to name them all, the **First Presbyterian Church of the Covenant** is one worth mentioning. Located on the 200 block of West 6th St. the First Presbyterian Church of the Covenant was built between 1929 and 1930 at a cost of more than $1 million. The 20th century Gothic structure has a base of limestone, while the remainder of the exterior is seam granite. Other notable features of this church include its numerous, interior stained glass windows and exquisite carved woodwork.

Another well-known Erie church is **The Church of the Nativity of Christ**. It is impossible to miss its onion-shaped dome at 247 East Front Street. Better known to the public as the **Russian Orthodox Church**, it was built in 1987 after the previous structure was destroyed by a fire in 1986. It is well known for the icons, or religious images of Jesus and the saints, that line its inside walls.

**St Peter Cathedral**, located at 230 W. 10th St., is another Erie landmark. The 108-year-old cathedral, with its imposing tower, is a fixture of the Erie skyline. The church, a Victorian interpretation of 13th century French Gothic style architecture, serves as the "mother church" of the Erie Catholic Diocese. In April of 1993 $2 million worth of renovations were completed, restoring the cathedral to a brand new splendor.

Also, noteworthy is one of the older churches in Erie, **Saint Patrick**, located at 130 E. 4th Street. Saint Patrick's congregation, which dates back to 1837, built two other churches before completing the current structure between 1903 and 1906 at a price of $180,000. The stations of the cross, or life-size statuary depicting Christ's march to Calvary, are among its best known features. The pieces were the work of master German wood-carvers who spent more than three years creating them.

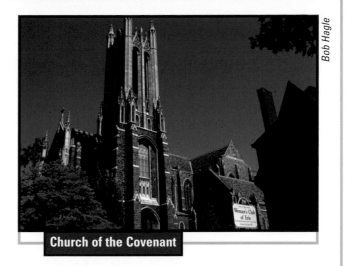

**Church of the Covenant**

Bob Hagle

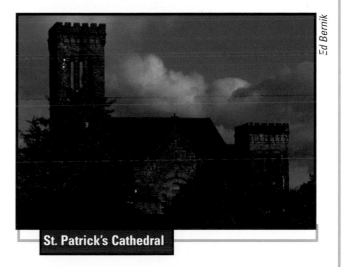

**St. Patrick's Cathedral**

Ed Bernik

**Church of the Nativity of Christ**

Art Becker

**225**

## HISTORICAL LANDMARKS

**E**rie is a city rich in architectural history with a number of structures to provide insights into its colorful past. As Erie's oldest structure, the **Dickson Tavern**, located at W. 2nd St. and French St., is a prime example of historical architecture. It was built in 1815 by John Dickson and served as a tavern under a succession of innkeepers until 1841. In that year it was converted to a home and in 1924 the city rescued the structure from pending demolition. The **Watson-Curtze Mansion** is another of the city's architectural treasures. The Richardson Romanesque building was constructed in 1891 and contains stained glass windows, mosaics, friezes, marble fireplaces, and decorative woodwork. Erie has two historic lighthouses. The **Presque Isle Lighthouse** on the peninsula and **The Land Lighthouse** located at the foot of Lighthouse Street on the Erie's eastside. Other well-known historical buildings include the home of **Erie Art Museum** (see page 134) and the building adjacent to it, the **Cashier's House**.

Erie's other lighthouse: **The Land Lighthouse**

Many of Erie's historic buildings are under the care of the **Erie County Historical Society and Museums**, an excellent resource for more information about Erie's rich past.

**The Watson Curtze Mansion** is prime example of some of the incredible homes along West 6th Street's "Millionaire's Row".

226

## URBAN RENEWAL

Between 1955 and 1978, Erie began an initiative known as "Urban Renewal." The project's purpose

was to improve run down neighborhoods, but the effort also marked the destruction of a number of historic buildings. The look of Erie today, in large part, is due to the Urban Renewal project.

## FORT PRESQUE ISLE

The first known structure in the area, built by white men, was the French **Fort de la Presque' Ile**. The fort stood from 1753-1759, and was eventually burned by a collective effort of the British and the Indians. The British rebuilt their own **Fort Presque Isle** on the site in 1760. The replica of the British, log structure, shown above, can be seen at **The Erie County Historical Society**.

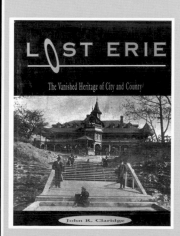

### Further Reading
In 1991, The Erie County Historical Society published the book **Lost Erie**. Written by local historian, **John Claridge**, the book tells the story of many of Erie's landmark buildings which no longer exist. If you are interested in historic architecture in the region, this is an excellent resource.

## LAWRENCE HOTEL

The Lawrence Hotel, built in 1913, was at that time Erie's largest and finest hotel. It was torn down in the 1970's to make way for downtown development.

227

# HOMES

Photo: John Horstman

In the late 1800s, West Sixth Street was the prestigious place in Erie to build a home. It's where you'll find many of the grand old mansions of yesterday. At the corner of Sixth and Peach is the Strong Mansion, now used as the Administration Building for Gannon University.

It was built as a wedding gift for Anna Wainwright and Charles Hamot Strong. Across the street is the Reed Mansion built by General Charles Manning Reed and currently home to the Erie Club. A few blocks west is the Watson-Curtze Home, built by H.F. Watson and later purchased by Felix L. Curtze. It currently serves as the Erie Historical Museum.

Now, more than a century later, new home construction is taking place throughout all of Erie County, with some of the largest concentrations occurring in subdivisions of Southwest Millcreek, as well as Summit and Harborcreek Townships. There you'll find homes constructed by builders such as Laughlin, Paterniti, Renaud-Peck, Pastore and Paul Luciano, to name a few.

There's been a strong demand for new construction and renovation in the past three years due to the economy. "We're at a 30-year low for interest rates," explains Dan Adamus, Executive Vice President of the Builders Association of Northwest Pennsylvania. "And with the uncertainty of the stock market, people want to invest in their house which has always been considered to be a solid asset."

A big trend for newer homes today, according to Susan Wendel, owner of Interiors of Erie, is toward very appointed details - crown molding, wide trims, multiple roofs, and arched windows. "In the 70s and 80s the new homes were relatively free of detail. But now the details have come to be expected," says Wendel.

"There's an emphasis on kitchens and baths, especially master baths, with walk-in showers and Jacuzzi tubs being the minimum amenities," Wendel notes. And in the living room, homeowners want what Wendel describes as elegant comfort. "These are not the formal living rooms of our parents' houses," she says. "The fabrics are soft and comfortable yet very elegant." Gail Panella, who assists customers through the building process with Renaud-Peck, finds that buyers today want a more open style floor plan. "They're getting away from the formal closed-in rooms. They want a great room," says Panella. She also notes that master suites are getting larger and incorporating sitting areas, while spare bedrooms and children's rooms are getting smaller to allow more space for the living areas.

Another important feature of new homes, according to Panella, is an office. They have become a must, since everyone has a computer these days. And attached two - or even three - car garages are in demand. But she notes that lot sizes are getting smaller, because people don't want all the work of a large yard. "That's why planned communities with green space are becoming very popular," Panella explains.

In addition to new homes, condos are in big demand, as are patio homes, or freestanding condominiums. Dan Adamus attributes this trend to empty nesters and snowbirds (people who spend part of the year in a warmer climate). "They still want all the amenities without the upkeep and maintenance of a bigger home." What do you know? Turns out you can have it all.

## INTERIORS OF ERIE

If **Susan Wendel** had to describe **Interiors of Erie Inc.** in one word, she'd choose "professional." It's a point of pride at her company that you'll rarely talk to a machine, and if you do, your call will be returned the same day. Your interior design consultation will be booked within a week, and you'll have a written estimate 48 hours later. If Wendel could pick a second adjective, it'd be "diverse." Interiors of Erie is more than an interior design and decoration service; it also specializes in space planning, color coordination, furniture and accessories, materials specification, and supply and installation of wall and floor coverings and window treatments. In fact, Interiors of Erie is the region's largest supplier of window blinds, particularly the high-volume blind installations needed by businesses, hospitals, schools, and apartment buildings. (**Ultra Clean**, an Interiors of Erie subsidiary, cleans and repairs blinds and washes windows in homes and offices.) "We're busy because people know that they can rely on us," Wendel says. "We stress quality and workmanship, and keep a professional schedule. We follow through. You'll never wait three days for a call from us."

INTERIORS OF ERIE INC.
3831 WEST RIDGE ROAD
ERIE, PENNSYLVANIA 16506
814 833-8110
beautify@adelphia.net

**Creativity & Professionalism**
are traits that have kept
Susan Wendell and son, Eric
at the forefront of the
homeowner's mind.

Rob Ruby

Ed Bernik

## DESIGNER GLASS

**D**eborah Trocki of Designer Glass is confident that Erie will embrace decorative stained glass

overlays just as warmly as they've been received everywhere from the casinos of Las Vegas to the cathedrals of Europe. "What attracted me to this product is the versatility of design," says Trocki, who in 2002 signed on as an independent franchisee of Stained Glass Overlay Inc., a California company that's been creating custom looks for restaurants, houses of worship, and private homes for 22 years. "You have the impact of a unique stained glass creation, but it's sturdy, because you're not working with tiny pieces of glass soldered together. That's what makes it so versatile. It's great for kitchens, baths, entryways, dens - anywhere you want a conversation starter." The look of a Stained Glass Overlay is limited only by a client's imagination, and the actual process of bonding mylar film and lead strips to glass works with any type of new or existing window. And does it look like real stained glass? "People argue with me all the time," Trocki says with a laugh, "It looks like stained glass and it looks gorgeous."

**DESIGNER GLASS**
**2232 W. 23rd St.**
**ERIE, PENNSYLVANIA 16506**
**814 455-4336**
**www.stainedglassoverlay.com**

**233**

Rob Ruby

# Home Values

an interview with

## MARSHA MARSH

*Marsha Marsh is a successful Coldwell Banker realtor. She works out of their West 8th Street office.*

**MARSH AT COLDWELL BANKER**
**2100 WEST 8TH STREET**
**ERIE, PENNSYLVANIA 16505**
**814 440-8181**
**www.ladanmarsh.com**

**234**

**What kind of real estate do you sell?**

I sell all kinds of real estate. I enjoy single family resale probably the best but I am enjoying more the new builds. As the rates come down, I have enjoyed helping clients have their dream home built and be able to afford it. I have sold commercial, residential, investment, land and well, just about everything. I am a Senior Housing Specialist, Previews Property Specialist with Coldwell Banker for their luxury properties, and a Relocation Specialist. I am also an Accredited Buyers Representative so I enjoy all aspects of the buying and selling process with clients.

**When did you start?**

I started in 1997 with classes at Gannon University and received my license to sell in February 1998. I worked with Holland Metro at the time. My mother sold real estate in Corry for many years and I learned a lot from her experience years earlier.

**Do you have any other family in the business?**

As I said before my mother sold real estate in Corry beginning with Merle Dodd in the 1960's. In 1999 my mother took her license out of escrow and worked with me at Holland Metro. Mother found it much more difficult after 30 years when it went from a 1-page contract to 20 pages with many hours in between. After working a while she placed her license back in escrow but continues to give me advice and encouragement. My son Levi has had his license since 2001 with Coldwell Banker. Levi was 20 years old when he was licensed and had 1 million dollars in sales his first year. My son Laban, 24, received his license in May 2003 and has been working with us at Coldwell Banker also. Hopefully my daughter-in-law who is studying for her license will be joining us soon. As a family we enjoy all aspects of the real estate business. My husband and other sons, although not directly involved in the business, help out tremendously as "support" staff and handy persons when we need extra help.

**What's special about Coldwell Banker?**

They are the oldest and most recognized name in real estate. I have personally met Alex Perillo, our CEO, and he is a wonderful person with very high integrity and character. The company at its highest level is superb, and at our local level I have a great deal of respect and admiration for our owner/broker Toby Froehlich. Toby and his dad Ted were in business together for many years before Ted retired. Toby and now his wife Jacky, who is in the mortgage business, continue to do everything possible to help the Coldwell Banker agents be successful in the Erie market, and I think our numbers speak for themselves in the market place.

**What made you want to start selling real estate?**

Watching my mom through the years. As our 4 boys were older and leaving home for college, the empty nest syndrome set in and I wanted a little more freedom with my time and finances. Herb Logan, a local builder, encouraged me, as did my Pastor, Rick Crocker, to pursue the challenge of going to school, taking the state board and getting licensed. I am a people person and enjoy the personal satisfaction of serving others as I did through my church and community for years previous, and could now make my own income according to my work ethic. The race was on with my family's encouragement.

**What are your favorite neighborhoods in Erie?**

I don't have a favorite because all are special in their own way for each buyer and seller. I will say I enjoy going into a neighborhood, seeing the lawns well groomed and flowers blooming and

John Horstman

235

◄ **"From our house to your house"**
General Manager Eric Zimmerman shown with
parents and owners Karen and Dave Zimmerman.

The goal for his family's store, he said, remains being the best in its niche.

The Zimmermans and nine others on staff know volumes about quality furniture at reasonable prices, and they want to share that knowledge with the community. In that sense, growth, according to Eric Zimmerman, means staying a familiar, trusted local business that offers products designed to last, like his family's business, for generations.

ASBURY HOUSE, LTD. FURNITURE
5613 WEST RIDGE ROAD
ERIE, PENNSYLVANIA 16506
814 833-0620

## ASBURY HOUSE

From our house to yours." That's the message from family owned and operated **Asbury House Ltd. Furniture** on West 26th Street in Erie. Too often, people make major furniture purchases without being able to feel and touch what they're buying, said General Manager Eric Zimmerman. Asbury House offers a homey middle - to upper-scale furniture store and showroom - where people can see what they're buying - with personal service from certified and experienced interior designers. It's the designers on staff, including **Les Fobes**, **John Carrick**, **Cindy Grassi** and **Arlene Ivarone**, who can make complicated decisions seem easy. **Dave Zimmerman**, president of Asbury House Ltd., opened the store in 1986. His son, Eric, grew up there - mowing the lawn during high school and making deliveries. Throughout the years, he learned the ropes of the business inside and out, eventually earning the promotion to General Manager.

*(continued from pg 235)*

know the people enjoy living there...it just looks "happy" and it is fun to sell these neighborhoods the most.

### What makes a house a home?

Of course the people in them. I really enjoy meeting people and we build such a great relationship that when the settlement comes I hate to not see them as much. I try to keep in touch and it is great when they send me info on a new baby or marriage and sad when I know someone has passed away. The people definitely make a house a home. Watching the home change when a new buyer moves in is so gratifying. When a seller is moving who has lived in the home over 40 years, and it is sad to have to sell...bringing in that "perfect" buyer makes you feel wonderful.

### Do you have any advice for new families who have just moved into Erie looking for a house?

I enjoy relocating buyers because Erie has been very good to my family and I can truly say it is a great place to live and raise a family. I tell them to drive through the neighborhoods and get a feel for the area. Know what their interests are and try to find a home that fits your "needs" and "wants." Home is a haven after a long day at school or work and you want to enjoy coming home. Our area is very affordable. I attend Coldwell Banker conferences throughout the country and correspond with many agents who cannot believe how affordable Erie is...we need to appreciate that.

### How can families looking to sell their homes improve their value?

Keep the homes up to date! So many homes do not keep up with the market trends in decorating and landscaping. When I take buyers into a home that is move-in condition both in decorating and cleanliness, the value goes up immediately... buyers' sight and smell are the senses that most come into play when making a decision to purchase. •

## GENERAL EXTERMINATING

The pests are gone, but **General Exterminating** is in Erie to stay. The third-genration business started by **Jim Reese's** grandfather in 1932 has been in the hands of partners **Donna** and Jim Reese since 1990. "We pride ourselves on still being the little guy," Donna Reese says. Name a pest; General Exterminating has been getting rid of it in commercial and residential settings for decades. The Peach Street location was added in the 1940s, when the busy thoroughfare was little more than a dirt road. The neighborhood changed, but the foundation of General Exterminating hasn't - the Reeses still offer a valuable local service to customers.

GENERAL EXTERMINATING COMPANY
5526 PEACH STREET
ERIE, PENNSYLVANIA 16509
814 864-4984

Rob Ruby

**Matt and John Schultz** stand in their Summit Towne Centre location.

238

## JOHN V. SCHULTZ FURNITURE

Little of the historic commercial boom on upper Peach Street includes independently owned businesses. Ever fewer are family owned and in the hands of third-generation leadership. **John V. Schultz Furniture and Mattresses** is the single exception. The expansion of what **John V.** and **Audrey Schultz** began in 1940 now includes a huge, sprawling store in the booming **Summit Towne Centre** as well as a busy outlet store on the West 12th Street corridor of Erie. The Company's success from the early days is considerable.

John V. Schultz circa 1940

When John and Audrey envisioned a furniture store that sold quality products from name brand manufacturers at prices set low enough that people didn't have to haggle, the couple had only a few hundred dollars in the bank. But the President of Security People's Bank in Erie believed in their vision and lent them $20,000 to make it reality. The couple worked long hours together, building their Company into a profitable leader in the community until John, 54, died of a heart attack in 1962. Audrey Schultz continued to lead the growing Company, turning it over to her son, **John V. (Jack)** and his wife, **Carol**, in 1968. Now Jack, Carol and Audrey's grandchildren - **John III**, **Heidi** and **Matthew** - are at the helm with more than 100 employees.

The Company outgrew the West Eighth Street location, moving into three times the amount of space on upper Peach Street and I-90 in 2001. The new location, designed by a preeminent store architect, is one of the largest furniture stores in the country. In addition, interior designers are on hand as a complimentary service to help turn your "house into a home."

The third generation still prides itself on their grandparents' founding principals – cater to a broad spectrum of customers with product to fit any budget. From the highest quality to closeout values, John V. Schultz is staffed by professionals willing to listen and serve. And best of all you can buy with complete assurance because their motto is, "If we can't beat a price anywhere in the country, your furniture or mattress is free."

**JOHN V. SCHULTZ FURNITURE**
**SUMMIT TOWNE CENTRE**
**7200 PEACH STREET**
**ERIE, PENNSYLVANIA 16509**
**814 868-7125**
**www.johnv.com**

**FURNITURE & MATTRESS OUTLET**
**2147 WEST 12TH**
**ERIE, PENNSYLVANIA 16505**

Photos Courtesy: JVS

Rob Ruby

239

## GEORGE WINSTON COMPANY

**O**n a plumbing job one day at the Erie Club, **Richard G. Winston** discovered a basin installed and initialed by his grandfather, the co-founder and namesake of the plumbing, heating and air conditioning company which Winston now owns.

"There have been many changes over the years, from the heavy cast iron pipe my granddad used to the plastic pipe we use today," Winston says. One thing has stayed constant: George Winston Company has served homes, businesses and industries for 92 years. For the past five decades the company's home has been the corner of West 12th and Plum Streets, making the Winstons Erie's "Plumbers on Plum."

"We go all over the county," Winston says. **George Winston** started the business with a partner in 1911. He was succeeded by his son, **Richard L. Winston**, in 1956, who was succeeded in turn by his son, Richard G. (below), the current owner, in 1976.

Today, the third-generation owner and his nine employees sell, install, service and repair brand-name lines such as Lennox, ITT Bell & Gossett, Moen and Weil-McLain. "Our goal is to continue to serve the community for another hundred years, with the best-quality service and best products we can provide," Winston says.

**When a business is around for nearly 100 years,** they must be doing something right. Such is the case with George Winston who's no-nonsense work ethic keeps him on top.

**GEORGE WINSTON COMPANY**
**832 WEST 12TH**
**ERIE, PENNSYLVANIA 16501**
**814 454-0752**

## HOME SWEET PENINSULA

One of the most unusual abodes in Erie is the Presque Isle Lighthouse. Built in 1872, the lighthouse was constructed solely with materials shipped by boat to its current location. Many different lighthouse keepers over the years have toiled to make sure the light is always on. Although times have changed, the Presque Isle Lighthouse is still used today. Another creative neighborhood on the peninsula is the houseboats. Russian immigrants, mainly fishermen, formed this community in the 1800s as a convenient, yet functional place to live and work.

## ETHNIC NEIGHBORHOODS

Birds of a feather flock together. Not surprisingly, Erie,s ethnic groups built homes in neighborhoods where others from their homeland lived. Because there were so many Germans living in south Erie, in the early days most of the road signs were both German and English. In the same time frame an Irish community was formed between Cherry and Myrtle near the Erie Cemetery and African-Americans built homes on Erie's lower west side in a neighborhood known as Jerusalem.

## MILLIONAIRES ROW

West 6th Street in Erie was known as Millionaires Row for obvious reasons. Many of the industrialists and civic leaders of the time built along a stretch from State Street to Poplar Street homes that would be considered grand by any community. From the mid 1800s through the early 20th century, the neighborhood was filled with tenants such as the Reeds, the Scotts, and the Strongs.

ENTERTAINMENT

Photo: Art Becker

Rick Klein

**The Erie Playhouse,** known for colorful musicals, is the third oldest community theater still running America.

## ERIE PLAYHOUSE

The Erie Playhouse, located at 13 West 10th Street, is a hot spot for local theater. Most often, the Playhouse offers musicals but rounds

out its repertoire with a fair share of comedy and drama. Season ticket holders and casual show-goers can choose from over 20 productions a year, including more than a few Broadway favorites. Most of the shows star a solid cast of local thespians and often fill the 520-seat theater. People interested in joining the fun are welcome to try out at one of the open auditions. While the casts and crews are made up entirely of volunteers, the nonprofit Playhouse employs nine full-time staff members who keep the theater running. The Erie Playhouse Youtheatre also offers kids an opportunity to "get in on the act". Young people from the ages of five to eighteen years old have the opportunity to participate in classes, productions and even a traveling dance troupe.

Photo Courtesy: Matthew's Trattoria

## ENTERTAINMENT DISTRICT

With most cities, there are one or two neighboorhoods that seem to be the place to go on a Friday or Saturday night. You know, New York City has Soho, Miami has South Beach and Erie has the **Entertainment District**. The area around State Street from 12th to 14th Street has a slew of clubs. Names like **Calamari's** and **papermoon** are nightly hot spots. Just to the west is **The Metropolitan** and 2 blocks east is the upscale martini lounge area of **Matthew Trattoria's** (shown at left) where folks can listen to big city jazz with small city parking.

Rick Klein

**Amanda Post**

## ROADHOUSE THEATER

The 264 seat Roadhouse Theater is Erie's premiere venue for alternative theater geared toward adults. The nonprofit theater, founded by local actors **Scott** and **Kim McClelland** in 1988, is located at 145 West 11th Street in a renovated church. While there is no such thing as a "typical" Roadhouse Theater production, memorable shows have included stage productions of **Reservoir Dogs**, **Night of the Living Dead**, a slew of works by **Tennessee Williams**, and the periodic musical including the **Rocky Horror Show**. During intermissions and post-show gatherings, patrons can hang out in the back of the theater in the popular coffeehouse cabaret. One of the Roadhouse's biggest successes to date was the production of **"Always...Patsy Klein,"** starring **Amanda Post**. So popular was this production that it was later played at the 2,500 seat Warner Theatre for an unprecedented six performances.

## VENUES

**W**here are the big shows? In Erie, try the Bayfront and Downtown. It's hard to escape the **Erie Civic Center Complex**. The **Warner Theatre**, **Louis J. Tullio Arena**, and outdoor **Jerry Uht Park** are all parts of the Civic Center. All are wonderful spots to catch sporting events and national performers. Erie's hockey team, the **Erie Otters**, has a comfortable den in the Tullio Arena and the **Seawolves** baseball team calls Jerry Uht Park home. You can catch some of the area's best artists and performers at the **Port Authority's Liberty Park Amphitheater**. Located on the Erie bayfront, Liberty Park is home to many popular events including the **Erie Summer Festival of the Arts**.

## LARGE VENUES

D'ANGELO PERFORMING ARTS
LOUIS J. TULLIO ARENA
ERIE PLAYHOUSE
JERRY UHT STADIUM
LIBERTY PARK AMPHITHEATER
MARITIME MUSEUM AUDITORIUM
ROADHOUSE THEATER
SCHUSTER THEATER
WARNER THEATER

245

Photo Courtesy: Chamber

should be commended for supporting local talent, particularly younger groups. Another club in Erie which deserves notice is **Forward Hall** (24th and Peach), one of the few rooms in Erie which has given those under 21 (and over) a place to see live music. Space restraints prevent the listing of every club in Erie that features live music. If you are interested in finding out more about who's gigging where, your best bet is to pick up a copy of Erie Times News **Showcase Magazine** which lists concerts, reviews, and schedules in a special section called **Music Muse** or go to online resources like **Doerie.com** or **Playerie.com**. Mention and congratulations should be given to Erie musician **Pat Monahan** who recently wrote the song "Drops of Jupiter" (in Erie) which went on to win a **Grammy** (Rock Song of the Year) for his band **Train** in 2002.

## LOCAL MUSIC

There are always several bands performing around town on any given Thursday, Friday, or Saturday night. Giving folks a place to catch live music are certain nightclubs who have supported the local music scene faithfully over the years. Many clubs are located on State Street including **Docksider Tavern** (10th and State) and **Sherlock's** (5th and State) who both feature rock, blues, and ethnic music, and **State Street Tavern** (10th and State) which typically presents music with a harder edge. An occasional national act can be seen in any of these rooms. **Calamari's** (13th and State) frequently features acoustic performers on their patio in the summertime. For listeners whose tastes run more towards jazz, **Scotty's** (3rd and German) and **Matthew's Trattoria** (East 13th Street) are the places to go. Just west of downtown Erie are **The Beer Mug** (10th and Liberty) and **Goofie's** (12th and Raspberry). Both of these rooms

## CLASSICAL MUSIC

What is a classical music lover to do in Erie? Check out the **Erie Philharmonic** and the **Erie Chamber Orchestra**. The Erie Philharmonic has been entertaining Erie with grandiose performances since 1913. Currently the orchestra regularly performs at the **Warner Theatre** with occasional stints at **Jerry Uht Park** for the popular "Pops in the Park" performances. "The Phil", as it is affectionately known, has a proud tradition of bringing the world's most prominent musicians to participate in performances. **Itzhak Perlman**, **Duke Ellington**, **Andres Segovia**, and **Dudley Moore** are among the guest musicians who have performed with the Erie Philharmonic.

Founded in 1978, the Erie Chamber Orchestra concentrates on bringing the classical music experience to the masses by presenting "free

Ed Bernik

**THE ERIE PHILHARMONIC** and **THE WARNER THEATRE** are an inseparable team providing classy entertainment in Erie.

admission" concerts. The Chamber Orchestra benefits from having residency at **Gannon University** as one of the University's cultural services to the Erie area. The University also serves as a major sponsor for the Chamber Orchestra and promotes the idea that anyone can enjoy classical music if given the opportunity to experience it. Another presenter of interesting music productions (both classical and other) in the region is the **Erie Civic Music Association**.

## HONEYBEAR RECORDING STUDIO

When it comes to recording and processing sound **Walt Slivinski** has all the toys. As the owner of **Honeybear Recording Studios**, 2510 Raspberry Street, he can call on a veritable storehouse of equipment ranging from state-of-the-art digital workstations to warm vintage analog recorders that would have been right at home in the Beatles' rehearsal studio. You name it, he's got it. No slave to technology, though, Walt is

Rob Ruby

**HONEYBEAR RECORDING STUDIO** is a small studio that pumps out big studio quality.

quick to point out, "It's not so much the equipment as how you use it." It's not surprising that songwriters, polished bands, forensic police, savvy advertisers, churches, and community groups have relied on Walt's expertise since 1982.

With a resume, as long as a Miles Davis jam-session - he gigged for 3 years at the Peppermint Lounge in NYC, opened for Sinatra in Vegas, wrote the theme-song for Don Knotts, classic flick "The Love God", and learned recording under the tutelage of legendary producer Don Costa - Slivinski consistently delivers top quality product. His award winning services include production work for songwriters, audio restoration, and full-service recording including artwork.

**HONEYBEAR RECORDING STUDIO**
**2510 RASPBERRY**
**ERIE, PENNSYLVANIA 16502**
**814 459-2327**

# *Live*

## *from*
## THE HISTORIC
## BOSTON
## STORE

I t's really amazing how many Erieites have awoken with Richard Rambaldo. Even more unbelievable, it's done 24/7 on State Street in downtown Erie!

Don't jump to any conclusions. "Rick" is Vice President and partner in NextMedia, the visionary national broadcasting company that owns and operates six Erie radio stations. Rambaldo's a virtual one man nuclear power plant, radiating a seemingly endless supply of energy. Born to sell, Rick broke all the sales records at legendary WMMS/Cleveland. Bored at the top in the city of the Rock and Roll Hall of Fame, Rambaldo made a gutsy move to the world of ownership in Erie when he launched Rocket 101 in 1989.

Cleveland's loss would be Erie's gain. Catch him - if you can - on any given day and you'll find Rick expertly juggling the responsibilities of running all six radio properties...STAR 104, ROCKET 101, FROGGY 94.7, US 93.9, SPORTS RADIO 1330 AM and JET 1400 AM. Of course with so many balls in the air, Rambaldo doesn't personally wake up tens of thousands of Erie listeners. For that trick, Rick relies on his, um,

250

RICK RAMBALDO

MULTIPLE personalities.

"I've been incredibly fortunate to assemble a team of radio personalities that are from Erie, or in the cases where they've moved here from out of town, all have completely woven themselves into the fabric of the community they serve. Our talent loves Erie, and it comes through. They reflect the community because they are part of it."

A result of this morphing is a rare longevity among the NextMedia "air" force. Star 104's Craig Warvel is an icon. He has been waking up Erie for more than twenty years. Captain Dan of Froggy 94.7 was born here and has been a fixture on the dial for 33 years! Mojo McKay, Natalie Massing and Ron Kline have been working together on the Rocket since 1990. Rambaldo gratefully acknowledges, "This kind of tenure is unheard of in radio. Disc Jockeys come and go, but these people have formed a real bond with their audiences. They are personalities, friends and family."

Community, it turns out, is a big word in the NextMedia lexicon. More than just a credo, radio-as-community is repeatedly put into action. In fact, when Rambaldo became a partner in NextMedia in 2000, his first order of business was to move all six radio stations to the

THE NEXTMEDIA ON-AIR FAMILY

historic Boston Store in downtown Erie. Just being in the center of the city wasn't enough for Rick, though; he solidified a dream to put his radio stations in the windows of the much loved old department store. It was a brilliant move that put NextMedia Radio Erie on the pulse of the town.

"One can walk down State Street and SEE Mojo, Nat and Ron doing their Rocket morning show. In the studio you might see them talking with comedian David Brenner or enjoying the live music of rock legend George Thoroughgood. As you continue your walk, the WJET 1400 studio may be interviewing the mayor or the county executive. Pass the STAR studio window and Warvel and Curry may have

## VEHICLES

Rocket 101 Hummer
Froggy 94.7 Diner
Star 104 Boom Box
Star 104 Street Jeep
Star 104  Live Truck
Rocket 101 Live Truck
Rocket 101 Rider Truck
Froggy 94.7 Rider Truck
Station vans for all 6 stations

a dog in the studio for "Adopt-A-Pet" Wednesday.   All the while, you're just blocks from the Courthouse, City Hall, Gannon University and the Warner Theater. It's a vibrant community, indeed, and Rambaldo is clearly thrilled to be a part of it.

That community, by the way, includes a big helping of sports. Sports are on the AM dial everyday, whether it be ESPN RADIO, or live game broadcast of the Pittsburgh Steelers, Cleveland Cavaliers, local high school football or Erie Otters. Sports Radio 1330 THE FAN is the home of all of these broadcasts along with

a live local daily talk show hosted by local sports legend Jim LeCorchick.

Travel away from the Boston Store and the fleet of NextMedia vehicles are everywhere. After all, they've got a platoon of 14 tricked out rigs ranging from Hummers and Jeeps to live broadcast vans and even a diner on wheels. Witness the All-American Country US 93.9 van broadcast live from a local blood drive; the entire Rocket road crew and a local band entertaining tens of thousands at Discover Presque Isle; Craig Warvel pumping up the sold out crowd at a home Erie Otters hockey game; Captain Dan at a Toys for Tots fundraiser; or The FAN broadcasting a Prep football game live from Veteran Stadium. If there is a community event going on, Rick Rambaldo's radio stations - and wheels - are there.

The fact is that, in spite of the big display windows of the historic Boston Store, there is no separation between the radio stations of NextMedia and the community of Erie.  They are one and the same.

"Broadcasting from the Boston Store is a **Entertainment** tremendous benefit for our morning show

The building itself is a historic reminder of

Erie's wonderful past and serves as a symbol to its future growth...

Plus we have a BIG WINDOW."

Captain Dan
Star 104's Craig Warvel
and Rocket's Mojo, Nat and Ron

John Horstman

## FAIRS AND FESTIVALS

Erie's event calendar is filled largely by the many fairs and festivals that have often become local favorites and annual traditions. Naturally, the majority of these events fall within the summer months, when locals are eager to take advantage of the temperate weather. There are, however, several festivals that celebrate Erie's snowy winter season, including a winter carnival on the Bayfront. One of the most popular summer events is the **Erie Art Museum Blues and Jazz Festival** held annually at Frontier Park. The event is a free, 2-day concert which always bills top notch talent. **Celebrate Erie** (a transformed version of the "We Love Erie Days" festival created by well loved former Erie mayor **Lou Tullio**), got off to a big start in 2002, and Erie's best kept secret is **Amerimasala**, the city's hippest festival dedicated to the celebration of diversity.

John Horstman

## FAIRS AND FESTIVALS

Amerimasala
Autumn Fest at Asbury Woods
Bay City Summer Festival
Celebrate Erie
Dan Rice Days
Discover Presque Isle
Erie Air Show
Erie Area Summer Festival of the Arts
Erie Art Museum Blues and Jazz Festival
Erie County Fair
Erie Festival of the Dance
Erie Irish Festival
FallFest at Peek 'n Peak
German Heritage Festival
Harborfest
Irish Festival
Jazz Walk
Lawrence Park Days
Liberty Park 8 Great Tuesdays
New Year's Eve's First Night Erie
North East Fireman's Cherry Festival
North East National Rib Fest
Panegyri Greek Festival
Saint Paul's Italian Festival
Strawberry Festival
Waterford Heritage Days
Wild Rib Cookoff and Music Festival
Wine Country Harvest Festival
Zabawa Polish Summerfest
Zoo Boo
Zoo B-Que

Art Becker

# 25 THINGS TO DO IN ERIE COUNTY

**1. Go to a Play-** Support local theater at The Erie Playhouse, Roadhouse Theater, Director's Circle, or Gannon's Schuster Theater. You may be caught off guard by the talent.

**2. Go to the Top of the Bicentennial Tower-** If you think you've seen it all in Erie, try a different angle. Visit the top of the Bicentennial Tower (free on Tuesday) for a bird's eye view that is sure to offer you a new perspective on Erieland and Presque Isle.

**3. Attend a Dance Recital-** Erie has quite a few dance companies and most of them list performances in Showcase Magazine. Though not always supported, dance is simultaneously beautiful, primitive, and exciting. Erie dancers are worth watching.

**LET A LOCAL THESPIAN BRING OUT YOUR EMOTIONS**

Rick Klein

**4. Check Out a Local Band-** Support Erie's local music scene at one of the many clubs offering live music like Docksider, Sherlock's, or Forward Hall. Showcase Magazine lists schedules and cover charges are usually low.

**5. Go to an Ethnic Festival-** Erie is a melting pot, but you'll still find the pure flavor of its many original immigrants. Try the Polish, Italian, Greek, Russian, or Irish festivals to get a little world culture and tasty cuisine.

**6. Visit the Erie Art Museum and Frame Shop-** Both are located on the 400 block of State Street and feature always changing shows.

**7. Go Fishing-** Whether on the water during warm weather, or through the ice when it's freezing outside, Lake Erie and its tributaries offer some of the best fishing in the region. In fact, Erie used to be thought of as the "fresh water fishing capital of the world"! You might even get dinner out of it.

**8. Visit a Historical Landmark-** Erie's history still lives in the city's landscape. Why not visit the Brig Niagara at the Blasco Library, or the Dickson Tavern, the oldest structure in town, at West 2nd and French. There are enough landmarks to make a day's adventure of it. Contact the Erie County Historical Society for a complete list of historical landmarks in the city.

**9. Go to a Classical Concert-** For a world class cultural experience in a local venue, attend a concert of Erie's excellent Philharmonic or Chamber Orchestra. Both will blow you away. Performances showcase some of the greatest works of Western classical music, as well as featuring frequent guest artists.

**10. Visit the Planetarium-** For a trip into the outer limits without leaving the city limits, check out the Erie Planetarium at 6th and Chestnut.

**11. Go Hiking-** If you'd like to get away from it all for a few hours, why not take a hike on one of Erie's scenic woodland trails: Wintergreen Gorge, Presque Isle, or Asbury Woods. All of them present an everchanging array of colors year round.

**12. Catch a Sunset-** There's an urban myth that Erie was cited in National Geographic for one of the top ten sunsets in the world. While you might have a hard time proving it, many locals would agree. Sunset Beach at Presque Isle is one of many beautiful spots to watch the sun set across the lake.

**13. Picnic at One of Erie's More than Three Dozen Parks-** You might think that there are only a handful of parks in Erie, but you'd be wrong (see page 75 for a list). Why not vist one of the less frequented parks for a picnic with family or friends?

**14. Attend a High School or College Sporting Event-** Between local universities and high schools, there are frequent opportunities to attend basketball, football, baseball, or hockey games. Local TV stations and The Times News keeps folks updated on schedules. Your old science teacher will love to see you there.

**15. Visit a College Art Gallery-** Check out the talent of student artists at one the local university galleries: the Schuster Gallery at Gannon University, Cummings Gallery at Mercyhurst College, or the Bates Gallery and Bruce Galleries at Edinboro University. Springtime usually brings student group shows. Buy something and you'll make a starving artist happy.

Art Becker

**STICK YOUR NECK OUT AND VISIT THE ZOO**

**16. Research Your Genealogy at the Erie County Historical Society-** Get in touch with your roots at the Erie County Historical Society. The organization offers vast amounts of genealogical research and can put you in touch with other individuals or organizations devoted to discovering people's ancestry. Who knows what you might find out about Grandma.

**17. Take the Kids to the expERIEence Children's Museum-** For a museum experience custom tailored for children, visit the expERIEence Children's museum at 5th and French. The place does a good job of disguising learning as fun.

**18. Go to an Amusement Park -** Take the family to Waldameer or Water World for the day. The Pirate's Cove and Comet Rollercoaster will bring you back to being a kid. Family First also features fun activities.

**19. Visit a Local Retailer-** Before you jump in your car and drive you-know-where, don't forget about the inner city's one-of-a-kind specialty shops. Most times, you'll find that you actually saved money and support-ed your neighbor's livelihood at the same time.

**20. Catch a Professional Sporting Event-** You don't have to travel to another city to catch a professional sporting event. Professional sports are a business and no fans equals no teams. Plus your kids are more apt to catch a fly ball and get it autographed.

**21. Take a Boat Tour of the Lake-** You've looked out on the lake innumerable times, but how many times have you seen the city from the lake? Boat tours of the lake leave from Dobbins Landing, and, during warm weather at Presque Isle State Park, you can explore the lagoons on a rented canoe or on a guided pontoon boat tour.

**22. Visit Local Wineries-** If you've ever driven north along the lake, you're sure to have seen the fields of grapes. Consider a tour of one of the wineries in this area. Most offer free tours and tasting.

**23. Go to the Zoo-** Part of Glenwood Park, the Erie Zoo is filled with animals from around the earth and regulaly features special events during the holidays where the grounds get decorated and comes alive at night time.

**24. Visit Edinboro Lake-** If you are looking for a new beach to take the kids or place to launch the boat, don't forget about the other lake that is just a few minutes south.

**25. Visit the Marx Toy Museum-** Marx Toys was a big employer in Erie and one of the largest toy manufac-tures in the world. Discover their story at 50 East Bloomfield Parkway. You might remember something from your past.

## STILL STANDING

Where did early Erie settlers go for a pint of ale? Beginning in the early 1800s, **John Dickson's Tavern** was one of the area's only gathering places. Providing accommodations for stabling for pioneers and their horses, the tavern quickly became a hub for trade and business. Now under the care of The Erie Historical Society, you won't get a pint of beer there but periodically can get a tour. The tavern still stands in the shadow of **Hamot Hospital** at 2nd and French.

## WE KNEW 'EM WHEN

Circus owner and famous clown **Dan Rice**, who owned a home and farm in Girard in the mid 1800s, was the inspiration for the **"Uncle Sam"** character. Rice was one of the highest paid entertainers in the world at the time. **Anne B. Davis**, Strong Vincent Class of 1944 and Erie Playhouse veteran, became a piece of

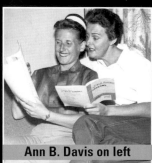

Ann B. Davis on left

American pop culture as "Alice" on the television sitcom **The Brady Bunch**. **Harry Burleigh**, born in Erie, was a renowned composer and songwriter who penned the classic "Nobody Knows the Trouble I've Seen" and the great American spiritual "Swing Low Sweet Chariot".

## EIJI OUE

In 1990, Oue picked up the **Erie Philharmonic** conductor's baton and became one of the city's best loved entertainers. Aside from being an exciting and diverse music leader, he also earned his way into the hearts of Erieites with his colorful personality. Oue stayed in Erie a short six years before moving to Minnesota and in honor of his service the city named a street after him, **Eiji Oue Way**.

## PARK OPERA HOUSE

**The Park Opera House** hosted some of the best actors and actresses of the late 19th and early 20th centuries. All types of shows surfaced at the Opera House, including drama, recitals, concerts, lectures, minstrel shows, and, of course, opera. The Park Opera House survived two fires at its location on **North Park Row** between State and Peach Streets. It was torn down in 1939.

## STEP RIGHT UP

Turn of the century folks knew **Waldameer** as a charming lakeside spot for picnics and gatherings. A carousel was added in 1905, and roller coasters, a theater, dodgem bumper cars, and the **Hofbrau German Beer Garden** were added over the next few years. The Beer Garden was closed in 1919 due to prohibition, but the park kept growing. People loved the addition of **Rainbow Gardens**, The Comet in the 1950's, **The Wacky Shack** in the 1970's, **Ruth Express Train** in 1978, the renovation of Rainbow Gardens in 1977, the **Skyride** in 1978, **WaterWorld** in the 1980's, and **Thunder River** in the 1990's.

## THE GOOD OLD DAYS

Where did Erieites go to see the big shows until 1983? The **Erie County Fieldhouse**. Originally built for the **Erie Lions** hockey team, the Fieldhouse saw its share of sporting events. The Fieldhouse hosted local boxer **Lou Bizzarro's** bout with **Roberto Duran** for the World Light-Weight title in a nationally tele-vised match in 1976. Music acts from KISS and AC/DC to old-school crooner Barry Manilow also found their way to the Fieldhouse.

259

# Tourism

Tourism has been a major economic force in the Erie area for many years. The leading magnet for visitors is Presque Isle State Park, and though Presque Isle has always beckoned tourists to its beautiful beaches, the development of Erie's Bayfront without a doubt has made the area far more attractive to visitors than ever before. Only since the mid-1990s has it become possible for out-of-town visitors to come view the Peninsula in its entirety from atop the Bicentennial Tower - or to enjoy a sunset cruise and dinner on the Victorian Princess, tour the U.S. Brig Niagara moored at the Maritime Museum, see a live comedy act at Junior's Last Laugh, catch a baseball game at Jerry Uht Park, or hear a concert at the Liberty Park Pepsi Amphitheater.

Wally Knox, owner of the Boothby Inn on West 6th Street says, "Many of our guests who have been to Erie before are very surprised to see how Erie has developed in what is available to tourists, including the attractions, restaurants, and downtown festivals. And many guests who are first time visitors to Erie say how beautiful the waterfront is and that they would definitely return for a visit."

But improvements in Erie's tourism extend beyond the Bayfront. When Waldameer Park & Water World opened its outdoor water park in the mid-1980s, they began to see a steady increase in the number of people coming from eastern Ohio and the Pittsburgh area.

Waldameer's general manager Steve Gorman says, "It definitely brought more people from out of town. They're coming from farther away, and they're staying at the park for a longer time."

Lest you think Erie attracts tourists only in the summertime, there are lots of reasons for visitors to come during even the coldest of months. Probably number one among those reasons now is Splash Lagoon, a one-acre indoor water park with tropical temperatures all year long. Lisa Anderson-Titcombe, Director of Sales and Marketing for Scott Enterprises, estimates that nearly 70% of their customers are from outside of the Erie area, coming from a 200 mile radius, including Pittsburgh, Cleveland and Buffalo. "But we've even had people coming from as far as New Jersey, Washington and New York City," she says.

With all of what's new in tourism for Erie, perhaps another change should be in its motto. Too bad "Welcome to Paradise" is already taken.

Photos: Beata Stark

261

**Kerry Schwab stands ready to greet his guests at Erie's finest hotel.**

# Bel-Aire Clarion

**A**ny Erie insider knows that one of the town's most popular and elegant spots is the Bel-Aire Clarion. Located on West 8th Street, near Peninsula Drive, the Bel-Aire Clarion is a hotel, conference center, restaurant and bar. Many locals have celebrated weddings and other key events in their lives at the Bel-Aire Clarion and regularly enjoy its fine casual dining facilities.

A fixture in Erie's business landscape since 1961, the Bel-Aire recently teamed up with Clarion Hotels. Executive VP and Managing Director Kerry Schwab says that combination offers his clients the best of both worlds: "We (The Schwab family) still

◀ **Presque Isle is seconds away from the Bel-Aire Clarion.**

Photo:John Horstman

262

own the hotel, we are still a family business. You'll get that personal touch as you attend functions...for the international market, the Clarion portion is very important." Clarion is part of Choice Hotels International, which franchises thousands of hotels in 48 countries. Schwab says the Bel-Aire's affiliation with Clarion offers customers airline miles, points for free hotel nights and other awards, among other benefits.

The Bel-Aire Clarion's restaurant, Maximilian's, offers an excellent menu accompanied by one of the best wine selections in the area. Customers can choose wines from around the globe to accent the wide variety of choice found on Maximilian's menu. The restaurant offers anything from soup and salad to lobster, and its experienced chefs are prepared for special requests. Not only is variety to be found in the food: visitors can dine on the terrace of The Bel-Aire Clarion's Mediterranean-style pool, cozy up to the elegant fireplace, or enjoy their meal in a tastefully decorated dining room. Maximilian's also offers Happy Hour, live entertainment, and a host of specials. One of the most popular is the Executive Express Lunch, a buffet of favorite hot and cold entrees, which changes daily. The price is right, the service is speedy, and the satisfaction is guaranteed!

The Bel-Aire Clarion offers business travelers rooms that provide a number of amenities and services specially tailored for getting the job done: two-line speaker phones, a larger work desk with data ports, executive high-back desk chairs, free in-room coffee, and brighter lighting - just to name a few. Guests can also start their day with a complimentary hot breakfast buffet. The hotel offers a

**The Bel-Aire Clarion has been consistently rated in Lodging and Hospitality Magazine as one of the top 100 suburban hotels in the country. If you haven't already, come and find out why!**

gorgeous indoor swimming pool, sauna, Jacuzzi, and a fully equipped exercise room.

For locals, the Bel-Aire Clarion has always been a favorite place to celebrate the bigger events in life; and it is famous for its elegant wedding receptions. The staff prides itself on its attention to detail and personalized service to make your event

263

a most memorable one. Featured on the Bel-Aire Clarion's website, www.clarionhotel-erie.com, Sherry Vetter credits the Bel-Aire Clarion with making her wedding day a wonderful one: "The service here was impeccable, the food was unbelievable. I still hear comments from people at my wedding how beautiful the atmosphere was and how wonderful the food was." Remember the Bel-Aire Clarion for your bridal showers, rehearsal dinners, and post-wedding brunches, too!

For conventions, meetings, seminars, exhibits and other special events, the Bel-Aire Hotel and Conference Center can accommodate a gathering of up to 600 people. Let their professional meeting planners help make your next meeting a success with their full conference and convention planning service.

The seasoned management team at the Bel-Aire Clarion has a combined total of 115 years of experience and is behind the hotel and conference center's unparalleled service. It is a third-generation family business. Kerry Schwab, whose son has now joined the team, says that being independent has a lot of great attributes - like the ability to cater to special requests and to be flexible.

Photos Courtesy: Bel-Aire

**The Bel-Aire Banquette Room is a spectacular room to host an event.**

**2800 West 8th Street • Erie, Pennsylvania 16505 • 814-833-1116**

One of over 800 Hampton Inns is Erie's Hampton Inn North. This Hampton Inn has a spectacular location. It is just a few minutes from Erie International Airport and Presque Isle State Park. Travelers are well-acquainted with the wide variety of services and amenities offered by this AAA-rated hotel. The comforts of home are here along with everything you need to conduct business from a remote location. Rooms are appointed with coffeemakers, irons, and ironing boards. Phone, facsimile, and copying are available and make the Hampton Inn North your extended office.

In the summer months, guests can lounge around the beautifully landscaped, heated pool. Enjoy their complimentary continental breakfast buffet and in-room movies. Non-smoking and handicapped accessible rooms are available and children under 18 stay free.

**3041 West 12th Street • Erie, Pennsylvania 16505 • 814-835-4200 • www.hamptoninn.com.**

LAKE ERIE
ICE WINE
VIDAL BLANC

266

2002

MAZZA

Bob Mazza admires one of the best natural resources that the region has to offer.

# Mazza Vineyards

There are few things in Erie County more romantic than a drive out into the plateau country of North East in the autumn when countless acres of grapes are ripening on the vine. To truly experience the glory of the harvest, though, folks in the know insist on a visit to Mazza Vineyards, the crown jewel of area wineries.

The vineyard is a place where Old World ambiance meets with cutting-edge technology to make some of Pennsylvania's most beloved wines. Visitors can sample the White Riesling that won the Gold Medal at the 2003 Pennsylvania Farm Show, taste the native fruit of Niagara (the best selling homegrown wine in the state), or sip any one of a vast array of Mazza offerings.

Proprietor Robert Mazza, who operates the winery with his wife Kathie and their two children, Mario and Vanessa, knows wine. After all, he was born on the hillsides of Calabria, Italy. It was in North East, Pennsylvania, in 1973, though, that Robert found the ideal location for the winery and began the process of producing wines that would bear his name. In the intervening 30 years, Mazza has been a pioneer and innovator in Pennsylvania winemaking.

Mazza Wines are available throughout the Pennsylvania State Store system, at their specialty shop at 2006 West 8th Street, or at the winery.

11815 East Lake Road • North East, Pennsylvania • 814-725-8695
• www.mazzawines.com.

# Penn Shore

**N**othing prepares the true wine lover for a visit to Penn Shore Winery and Vineyards. It's one of Pennsylvania's oldest wineries. Penn Shore began production of wine in September of 1969 with one of the first two limited winery licenses issued by the state. Since that time, they have been producing award-winning wines.

Visitors to the winery are treated to a close-up look at the wine-making process with a guided tour of the facility. From the selection of the grapes to the corking and aging of the finished wine, they will explore all the facets of the art and science of wine making.

And oh, what wine! At the 2003 Pennsylvania Farm Show, Penn Shore wines earned eight medals of distinction. With a full palate of varietals and blends from European and native fruits, Penn Shore has the perfect libation for any occasion.

Penn Shore Winery and Vineyards offers free guided tours seven days a week. The winery is located at 10225 East Lake Road (Route 5) in North East, PA. For additional information contact Penn Shore at 814-725-8688 or visit them online at www.pennshore.com

Photos: Rob Ruby

## ERIE BREWING COMPANY

**E**rie Brewing Company was penned into creation in 1992, during the challenging, waning days of the microbrewery craze. A small, gutsy group of entrepreneurs tipped their collective hats to Erie county's extensive and colorful brewing history (after a nearly 20 year dormancy).

John Horstman

After the opening at downtown's **Union Station** location in conjunction with **Hoppers Brewpub**, Erie's local brewing drought was over.

By 1999, **ERIE BREWING COMPANY** moved from the very profitable retail market into stand alone manufacturing, packaging, and ultimately distribution. Moving into the current location facing West 12th Street (1213 Veshecco Dr.) saw a massive expansion, in the scope of 200% increased fermentation volume.

The brands currently consist of: the award winning **Railbender Ale**, the venerable **Mad Anthony's Ale**, and - the pinnacle measure of any brewery, a pilsner - their **Presque Isle Pilsner**, available in bottles and draft; and available in specialty seasonal draft; Golden Fleece Maibock, Red Ryder Big Beer, Erie Special Beer, Sunshine Wit, Heritage Alt, and German Wheat beers just to name a few. Further information can be found at eriebrewingco.com. Cheers!

268

Perhaps nothing provides the true "flavor" of a city and its people more so than the food and drink for which they are known.

Erie's traditional favorites are certainly a reflection of our rich cultural heritage. For example, it was the Italian immigrants of Erie's Little Italy who brought us what is now known as pepperoni balls and are still a favorite in shops like Pio's and Barbato's. Another Italian immigrant by the name of Romolo brought us sponge candy when he accidentally added too much of a certain ingredient while making a batch of taffy, according to his grandson Tony. Customers still flock to Romolo's Chocolates for their famous melt-in-your mouth candy.

The cultural diversity in Erie and its impact on our tastes can be seen at the many local festivals. Sample gyros and baklava at the Panegyri Greek Festival, enjoy shepherd's pie and corned beef at Erie's Irish Festival, or try the Latin and African American dishes at Amerimasala. Or, experience it all at Celebrate Erie, which offers a "Taste of Erie."

Climate is another factor that has had a strong influence over the tastes of this region. A drive out Route 5 along the Lake Erie shoreline gives a scenic view of the vineyards, providing us with the delicious wines of our area's wineries, such as Mazza and Penn Shore, as well as grape juices and jellies from Welch Foods. By the end of each summer, local farm stands like Mason Farms give us the pleasure of enjoying Erie County corn, the sweetest corn on the cob you'll find anywhere. For fresh and inexpensive produce, plus a real adventure, Erie County Farms is an Erie tradition.

The beautiful summer months in Erie also give rise to other culinary delights. What ball-game at "The Uht" would be complete without a Smith's hot dog - anyone who's ever had one knows that no other hot dog will do. Every backyard barbecue is sure to include a bag of locally produced Troyer Farm's potato chips. And for kids and grownups alike, it's always a treat on a hot summer day to get an ice cream cone from Connie's, Brewster's or Sara's, or if you prefer an Italian ice from Rita's.

Wash it all down with a local beer from the Erie Brewing Company which serves up its brews with names that are representative of the Erie area, including Mad Anthony's Ale and Presque Isle Pilsner. It may bring back memories of another beer which was "Known by the Collar it Keeps." Koehler's Beer was brewed at the Koehler Brewery building on State Street from 1889 until the company's closing in 1976.

As important as Erie's food is to its history, a locally manufactured cookware gained its own fame. In the 1880s, shortly after the end of the Civil War, The Griswold Company opened in Erie and began casting skillets, pans, griddles and other items. By the 1950s, the company discontinued its operations in Erie, but the old Griswold items, which can be identified by their Griswold or Erie, PA stamping are now considered to be the most collectible cast iron cookware there is. Though many of the items can still be purchased at flea markets, antique stores or auctions for a relatively low price, there are some pieces that, if in good condition, can be worth up to thousands of dollars.

Now if all that doesn't whet your appetite, take a look at the pages ahead to see the best of Erie's cuisine today.

Rob Ruby

John Horstman

## An Interview with
# Todd Czerwinski
# of Erie Estate Buyers

### What does Erie Estate Buyers do?

We buy and sell quality furniture, estate jewelry, anything in the higher end, oriental rugs, art, pottery, glassware, silver, watches, and clocks. "I have a 20,000 plus square foot showroom on three floors located at 1215 Parade Street. The first floor is the main retail area with 20 showcases of estate jewelry, higher-end furniture, glassware, smalls, and several large pieces of furniture including architectual pieces such as mantels, leaded windows and light fixtures," says owner Todd Czerwinski.

### How did you get started in this business?

It all started back when I was 19 years old. When I moved out of the house with my brother I bought an apartment building and to furnish it I started buying to fill up the empty rooms. Then I started selling because I had bought so much that I couldn't possibly keep everything. I realized I enjoyed what I was doing and there was a profit in it. When I first started I thought it was just going to be a hobby but it soon grew into a full-time job. From the time I was 19 until I was 23 I was in the apprenticeship program at G.E., and when I graduated jobs were few and far between. I decided instead of pursuing what I was trained to do, I would go into this field, buying and selling antiques full time. I figured I would give it a shot and if, after six months, I couldn't make it I would look for a job in another area.

## What is the most challenging aspect of your business?

To sell retail in Erie is very challenging. It's a very hard market to sell in but my business has grown to where a lot of Erie people have supported me. Having so much space in my store, I am able to provide a huge variety of items to the general public and I think that because of that I am able to survive in the Erie market. When I first bought this building they were tearing down the buildings across the street. It was hard to find a property downtown. My building was originally The Lincoln Market from the 1920s to 1970 and later Duggan's Appliance Store, which was located here for twenty five years.

## What are your favorite types of items to deal with?

Architectural items. If it's a part of the past, whether it's a leaded window or a fabulous fireplace mantel - it's something you can add into a home and it will add a lot of character. For the most part, if you can add architectural detail to a room, you can make a new house have a wonderful "old feel" about it.

## Are there any items you personally collect?

I collect from The Arts and Crafts Era which would date from around 1902 until 1910. Anything from that period is appealing to me; whether it's art, furniture, lighting, or pottery from back around the turn of the century.

## Do you refinish the furniture yourself?

Not personally, but I do have someone who refinishes furniture for me full-time. I also send furniture out to subcontractors.

## What does it take to staff a business like this?

I have two women who work full-time and run the retail part of the business selling furniture, glassware, art, and jewelry. They are also responsible for phone appointments and scheduling. I also employ a restorer from Latvia who is one of the top woodworkers in the area. He also repairs clocks and anything with fine detail. He works on my best furniture and clocks.

John Horstman

**Carrie Herrmann and Carrie Breski working in the front of house.**

## What advice would you give someone getting interested in antiques?

Start with one area and then expand your knowledge into other areas. Come over to the store and see what we have to offer. If you have an interest in something, our three floors have such a variety of items that you'll probably find something that fits your needs. If not, I'll try to find it for you.

**1215 Parade Street • Erie, Pennsylvania 16503 • 814-459-0277**

360 million years have passed since <u>Protolimulus eriensis,</u> a horseshoe crab, lived here. Erie was sunken beneath a saltwater ocean. Shellfish called Brachiopods and glass sponges are found here as well as giant armored fish that once patrolled the deeper water. Below are one-of-a-kind designs by Jan and Dan Niebauer.

Photos: Rob Ruby

**Jan and Dan Niebauer create their one-of-a-kind jewelry.**

# Ralph Miller
# Jewelers & Gallery

Few places romance the stone, or the precious metal it's set in, like Ralph Miller Jewelers and Gallery at 28 West 8th Street in downtown Erie. "What you see here, you will not see anywhere else," says Dan Niebauer, co-owner of the business along with his wife, Jan Niebauer. With their slogan "We'll design what you have in mind," the jewelers at Ralph Miller's make custom design jewelry in gold, silver, and platinum and even have an original diamond cut called appropriately "the RMJ Custom Cut" featured in their store.

"What makes us different - one of the most important things - is that we make most of the things you see in the jewelry cases," says Scott McKenzie, a member of the Miller Jewelers' staff. "We make one piece at a time, one of a kind."

On staff are master jewelers and goldsmiths. Both Niebauers hold master's degrees in jewelry from Edinboro University of Pennsylvania. Dan Niebauer says all jewelers on staff hold bachelor's or master's degrees in the

Photos : Rob Ruby

jewelry fine arts. "Our people are not just certified bench jewelers. They are real artists," he says.

Artists in the store's restoration division repair statuary and unusual large art objects, ranging from towering Lady Justice statues to knee-high ivory chess pieces, to the Warner Theatre's chandeliers.

In addition, the jewelers repair pieces sent to them by other Erie-area jewelry stores.

"We are the jewelers to the jewelers," Niebauer says. "What they can't repair, we can."

Ralph Miller Jewelers is a 104-year-old Erie landmark, now under its fourth owner. It was mainly a silver store when it opened under the name "Beyers." For eight years the Sommerhof family ran the store, then sold it to Ralph Miller, a noted Erie jeweler. The Niebauers, who were friends and business associates of Miller, took over the business in 1995. They have enlarged the store to include workshops and an art gallery. Employees include (photo above left to right) Marge Barney, Darlene Churchley, Liza Magee,

Carrie Magee, Don Bower, Evan Carrier, (back row) Jan Niebauer, Russ Banks, Dan Niebauer, and Scott McKenzie. McKenzie teaches geology at Mercyhurst College and oversees the jewelry store's fossil collection. One of the collection's proudest pieces is a horseshoe crab fossil, one of the oldest of its kind anywhere, found in Erie County in the 1800s and named after Erie.

Among the artists from Erie and surrounding areas whose works have been on exhibit in the Ralph Miller Jewelers Gallery are Karen Savakis Bournais, Diane Wenzel Pierce, Martha Hapeman, Kevin Bednar, Gerald Sundean, Ron Cocke, Liza Magee, James Bove', Jean Stull, Lori Lang, and Don Bower.

Throughout the store the Niebauers have surrounded their original jewelry designs with paintings, sculpture, cultural objects, antiquities, and natural rock.

"There are things shaped by nature, things we shape, and things from nature that we shape," McKenzie says.

28 and 30 West 8th Street • Erie, Pennsylvania 16501 • 814-452-3336
www.created-uniques.com

Festive, fun and functional describe what you'll find at a la Carte. Located in the Colony Plaza on West 8th Street, this unique store offers a delightfully eclectic mix of gifts and accessories. From the individual tables devoted to each bridal registry, to the personalized stationery, Vera Bradley purses, and Department 56 items, you're sure to find something truly special.

a la Carte was opened in 1971 by Nancy Walker, with a focus on exceptional service and selection. Her four daughters, Mimi Sherwin, Kit Kershaw, Challis Wright and Lisa Kline, now carry on that tradition even as the store has evolved with the times. "We've dropped lines and added others as the lifestyles of our customers change and entertaining becomes less formal and more spontaneous," says Kershaw.

Though you'll always find something new and unusual at a la Carte, what will never change is their devotion to offering the extraordinary.

**2624 West Eighth Street
Erie, Pennsylvania 16505
814 838-6749**

Rob Ruby

# a la Carte

Rob Ruby

# The Boothby Inn

**F**ully restored to its circa-1888 Victorian splendor by owners Wally and Gloria Knox, The Boothby Inn, LLC, opened in 2001 and boasts the most luxurious accommodations in Downtown Erie. Situated on the historic street that was once known as "Millionaires' Row," the Inn is close to many of the amenities in Erie's Bayfront and Downtown Entertainment Districts. Guest rooms, each uniquely decorated to showcase the travels of the Inn's owners, allow guests to experience exotic places such as Scotland and Africa.

The Inn carries a 3-diamond AAA approval and was voted Inn of the Year - 2003 by the readers of Pamela Lanier's Complete Guide to Bed & Breakfasts, Inns and Guesthouses International. In 2002, the Boothby Inn, LLC was also named by Travel and Leisure Magazine as "One of 30 Great US Inns."

Imagine your stresses melting away with leisurely breakfasts on a garden patio; strolls through the perennial garden and relaxing evenings on the front porch with a glass of lemonade.

But wait, the Inn is not just for the vacationer, the rooms are also equipped with desks, phones and data ports to serve the business traveler.

**311 West Sixth Street
Erie, Pennsylvania 16507
814 456-1888**

Colao's Ristorante invites you to taste authentic dishes from Venice, Rome and Southern Calabria. Erie has a strong Italian-American community and the Calao family knows just how to serve their taste buds. Patriarch Santo and matriarch Assunta Colao make their pastas, soups and sauces from scratch using top quality, fresh ingredients and hormone and steroid free meats from local vendors. This is no national franchise Italian cuisine either. This is authentic Italian from "the neighborhood" - so real you'll think that you are on vacation in Rome. Originally opened in 1933 as Nissin's Grill, the Colao Family reopened the restaurant as Colao's Ristorante in 1998. Dedicated to keeping the Old Italian Tradition alive, owners Joe and Saverio Colao run the restaurant with their wives Laurie and Ellen. Youngest brother Santino runs the "front of the house". Filet Mignon A Bosco and Shrimp Santo are featured on a menu of Old World specialties to tantalize. Open for dinner at 5:30 p.m. Tuesday through Saturday; gift certificates, carry out, and deliveries are available. Reservations appreciated.

Rob Ruby

# Colao's Ristorante

**2826 Plum Street**
**Erie, Pennsylvania 16508**
**814 866-9621**

John Horstman

# Calamari's

Who says you can't be everything to everyone? Lunchtime hot spot, sports bar, live music, indoor dining, outdoor dining, pool tables, great prices, catering, free delivery, stellar jukebox - man, is there anything that this place doesn't offer?  True, in daylight hours Calamari's Squid Row is the place to be for a casual sandwich or lunch meeting. Customers can select from over 60 tempting items from the menu, including fresh salads, sandwiches and juicy burgers. Best of all, for those on the run, the service is always fast and friendly.

But make way by nightfall. Owners J. and Marci Honard know how to host a party and know how to keep folks coming back. From the rocking good fun and live entertainment on Saturday nights, to low-key Sunday nights when wings and drafts are enjoyed at the bar, Calamari's is where the action is. Always. But this is no corner bar where you won't have room to move - "Cali's" has enough space for everyone to bring a friend - and most do. In fact, there's even a room to host your own private event or party.

Catch your favorite sports teams from Calamari's multiple televisions or simply relax on the outdoor deck during the summer months. It's just like they say - Good Mood! Good Food! (see page 142)

**1317 State Street**
**Erie, Pennsylvania 16501**
**814 459-4276**

Family owned and operated since 1955, the Colony Pub and Grille is located in the Colony Plaza in Millcreek. The restaurant is a west-side staple in Erie. Whether you are looking for a special place to "wine and dine" a business prospect or the perfect room to bring the family for a meal after church, The Colony Pub and Grille is the best choice. Elaborate fireplaces and three dining areas welcome you to a cozy atmosphere where you are sure to be comfort-able. As you peruse the menu you will find unique dishes such as Marsala Mussels Filet Asiago, and Dijon Shrimp. The Camp family serves mouth-watering hand-cut steaks and prime rib, fresh seafood and fresh veal, along with specialty salads, gourmet sandwiches, chicken, pasta and a healthy side menu such as fresh grilled vegetables. Being 1 mile from Presque Isle, The Colony is also a great place to come in and enjoy a sandwich after a day at the beach. The walls are decorated with his-toric local photographs and artwork from Erie artist Mary Baldwin, and the sound of live music is heard two to three times a week.

If your parents are from Erie, odds are they ate at The Colony and you should too. Open for lunch at 11:30 a.m. daily, and dinner from 4 p.m. and Sunday noon to 9:00 p.m., the Colony Pub and Grille is available for business meet-ings, rehearsal dinners, showers, weddings, luncheons, or formal brunches, for 25 to 125 and banquet seating from 75 to 225. Reservations appreciated and all major credit cards accepted.

**2670 West Eighth Street**
**Erie, Pennsylvania 16505**
**814 838-2162**

Rob Rut

# Colony Pub & Grille

Rob Ruby

# Competitive Gear

**W**hether you are a mountain bike trailblazer, a rip-it-up road racer, or a leisurely cyclist, Competitive Gear is the one spot in Erie that's sure to have the reliable service and expert advice you need. That's because the staff is made up of avid bikers who are totally dedicated to the sport. In fact, as owner Peter McMaster puts it, "It's just in our blood!"

McMaster opened Competitive Gear in 1983 with the promise of providing equipment and service to riders who competed in local races such as Erie's Quad Games. What he didn't know was how quickly it would become one of Erie's foremost bicycle shops, not only for competitive riders, but for casual riders and kids as well.

If you are looking for a new bike, odds are you will find just the right one among Competitive Gear's large selection. But if your dream bike simply doesn't exist - it's not a problem. Peter and his staff have been known to build custom bikes from the ground up! Now that's service.

**3501 West 12th Street**
**Erie, Pennsylvania 16505**
**814 833-8274**

The Millcreek Ice Cream Company, Incorporated was founded by long time Erieites Constance and Gerard McDonald in 1986. But of course, locals know them much better as Connie's Ice Cream. The business is a family affair with a brood of sons , Michael, Patrick, Russell, Sean, Christopher, and daughter Stacie conducting the business as well.

The ice cream that Connie's makes is done daily on location. The ice cream is a super pre-mium product with a high butterfat content and loaded with the finest of inclusions, flavoring and ingredients. Connie's most popular flavor, Turtle, is a tasty blend of chocolate, caramel-fudge and buttered pecans. The business is known to mix up their menu frequently, having featured over a hundred flavors from time to time. Restaurant owners as well as independent dipping locations have gotten to know Millcreek Ice Cream well throughout the years. Connie's Ice Cream also supports the Erie arts community by bringing their tasty treats to many local festivals and events throughout the summer.

**6032 Peach Street**
**Erie, PA 16509**
**814 866 1700**

John Horstm

# Connie's Ice Cream

Rob Ruby

Back when Jim and Donna Reese were customers of The Cookie Mug & Creations, they had two kinds of cookies to choose from: oatmeal raisin and chocolate chip. But they liked the business. So much so that they bought the company. Now that Jim and Donna own the Peach Street business, five full-time employees are baking from scratch six kinds of cookies every day. And they're not just creating cookies. Packed gift baskets include the ever-popular "Erie Pride" with all locally made products. Another creative gift is long-stem cookie roses - even the guys will like that one. The Reeses also specialize in unique corporate gifts complete with a customized logo mug advertising the sweet giver. The Cookie Mug is the perfect choice when you are looking for that special gift for almost any occasion - business or personal. Birthdays to graduations - housewarmings to holidays, having a package sent from The Cookie Mug lets them know that you care. They'll even customize a basket to perfectly fit the receiver.

# Cookie Mug
# & Creations

**5526 Peach Street**
**Erie, Pennsylvania 16509**
**814 866-6847**

As Plato said, "music and rhythm find their way into the secret places of the soul." Let Custom Audio set your soul on fire, let them elevate your musical experience; transport you to a jazz club or concert hall. Close your eyes and feel Miles Davis, John Coltrane, Led Zeppelin or your favorite musicians materialize themselves in your room. Founded in 1983, Custom Audio has always been Erie's choice for quality and value oriented car and home audio and video equipment. Staffed by music lovers not sales people. Custom Audio will educate you about the latest in audio/video technology or take you back to the beauty and romance of Vacuum tubes and turntables. Their goal is to get your foot tapping, so you can discover those secret places of your soul.

**4453 West 26th**
**Erie, PA 16506**
**814 833-8383**

Rob Rub

# Custom Audio

Rob Ruby

# The Erie Book Store

Aged wood, exposed brick, stone and antiques combine to form a warm and inviting ambiance at The Erie Book Store, Erie's only full-service independent bookstore. Established in 1921, this Erie Tradition has had three downtown locations and three owners (Albert Nash, Glenn Cantrell and Kathleen Cantrell).

At its new location in the historic 1880's Lovell Manufacturing building at 137 East 13th Street, The Erie Book Store continues to provide a wide array of current titles and best-sellers while specializing in regional history and local authors. With a cozy children's department second-to-none, it is also renowned for its exceptional collection of used and rare books.

A knowledgeable staff, dedicated to truly personalized service and backed by extensive research facilities, will help you locate hard-to-find titles, whether old or new, out of print, or simply a well-loved book from childhood.

The Erie Book Store includes an in-store café, plus a lounge for hosting special events and autograph parties, or just for nestling in front of the fireplace with a good latte and delectable pastry, surrounded by fine books.

**137 East 13TH Street**
**Erie, Pennsylvania 16503**
**814 480-5671**

E very community has its legends and Erie is no exception. Joe Root was a colorful Erie "character" who spent most of his time on Presque Isle. He built a number of shacks throughout the peninsula and sustained himself by hunting and fishing. Perhaps enough amusing and charming stories about Joe Root could fill their own book but one thing is for sure, his namesake went on to be connected with good times on Preque Isle.

In business since 1999, Joe Root's is open year round with lunch available from May through September. Fresh preparation is the signature at Joe Root's Grill. All sauces and most dressings are made from scratch. The scents of Marinated Black Diamond Steak, St Louis Ribs, and the freshest seafood (voted Top Seafood Restaurant by the Times-News) greet you with a full-service oak bar.

Owner Elmer Keisel offers the only full-service dining, great prices, selection, and awesome food at the entrance to Presque Isle State Park. After catching an awesome sunset on the beach or swinging down Peninsula Drive for a weekday lunch, Joe Root's is the place to leave your cares behind for a moment. You can taste the difference at Joe Root's Grill.

# Joe Root's Grill

**35 Peninsula Drive**
**Erie, Pennsylvania 16505**
**814 836-7668**

Rob Ruby

# Matthew's Trattoria
## and Martini Lounge

One of the unsung heroes of the restaurant scene, Erie native Chef Matthew Sarbak, who has a plethora of awards, accomplishes his goals by preparing every dish to order from scratch using only the absolute freshest ingredients available. Featuring authentic Italian and contemporary American cuisine in a upscale atmosphere, Matthew's Trattoria and Martini Lounge was quoted as "arguably the finest restaurant in Erie" by the Times-News on July 31, 1999.

It's all served up in an atmosphere right out of downtown Manhattan. Walk in the door and stroll across beautiful Italian mosaic tile to the theatre-style cooking area where you see Chef Matthew himself display his crafts across a black granite countertop. Listen to smooth sounds of cosmopolitan jazz complemented with the percussion of clinking martini glasses. And by the way, those martinis were voted best in the city, along with the lounge, and the chef himself. When you finally decide to peruse the menu, decisions aren't easy. From U.S.D.A. prime steaks to jet-fresh seafood, home style pasta and veal dishes, they are all works of art: Chicken Romano, Beef tenderloin, Chilean Sea Bass, and New Zealand Escolar. After a memorable meal, walk over to the lounge for a cocktail and some lively conversation in an over-stuffed chair.

Come alone or come with a group. Matthew's can serve up to 600 of your best friends. And if you just can't leave your place, Matthew brings the show to you with fully catered events.

Tuesday through Saturday, dinner served 5 to 10 p.m. with reservations recommended. Appetizers served until 11, and hand rolled sushi on the weekend 5 to 11p.m.

**153 East 13TH Street**
**Erie, Pennsylvania 16503**
**814 459-6458**
**www.matthewstrattoria.com**

Unforgettable. Located in the Bel-Aire Clarion Hotel and Conference Center, Maximilian's provides a comfortable yet elegant atmosphere for all to enjoy. The perfect choice for a casual meal or for an important business dinner, Maximilian's delicious dinners, attentive servers, and relaxing environment guarantee a wonderful experience. Only the freshest ingredients are used to prepare the wide array of appetizers, entrees, and desserts offered at this fine establishment. Some of the made-to-order specialties include Authentic Louisiana Gumbo, Filet Oscar, Shellfish Provencale, and Coconut Shrimp The Magnificent Seven Chocolate Cake, Strawberries Grand Marnier, and Bananas Foster are sure to more than satisfy any sweet desires. Owner Kerry Schwab Jr. also offers a unique poolside setting in an area of the restaurant for the more casual diners. Open 7 days from 11:30 a.m., Maximilian's is sure to please and, together with the Clarion Hotel, offers all-inclusive weekend getaways.

**2800 West Eighth Street**
**Erie, Pennsylvania 16505**
**814 838-9270**

# Maximilian's

Rob Ruby

# papermoon
## restaurant, gallery & jazz club

An illuminating experience in the arts and international cuisine, papermoon was unveiled on March 23, 2001, by Donald McCain, Ginny Rogers, and Edward Lee. The restaurant is nestled along Erie's emerging State Street entertainment district, just off the corner of 14th and State Street. Sit at the bar and enjoy live jazz performed by the finest regional musicians. Look in any direction and find original work from selected local artists. It is no doubt a 'hip' environment, but the main act is the food. Chef Edward Lee works his culinary magic creating unique dishes inspired by every region of the world. Chef Rick Raybuck also serves dishes that satisfy the eye as well as the palate. papermoon's fresh seafood is unmatched in Erie; the Chefs' flair for maximizing flavors shines through in their Thai and Malaysian specialties. The menu is also packed with American classics like Filet Mignon, Atlantic Salmon, and Rack of Lamb. Complement your meal with a wide variety of fine wines from a full -service bar. A private drawing room is available for parties of up to 40 guests. Gift certificates and carry-out are offered for your convenience. Erieites know that this is a hot spot ,and tourists are quickly discovering this fact as well. Dinner served Monday thru Thursday, 5 to 10 pm; Friday and Saturday, 5 to 11 pm; Sunday 4 to 8 pm. Live Jazz Monday through Saturday evenings. Major Credit Cards accepted.

**1325 State Street**
**Erie, Pennsylvania 16501**
**814 455-7766**

While other restaurants may come and go, a funky cafe at a most unsuspecting corner of Erie has more than proven its staying power. Pie in the Sky Cafe at West 8th and Walnut Streets was opened in 1991 by husband and wife team Mike and Carmen Opperman. The name comes from their original focus on desserts, with Carmen's specialty being pies. But their menu quickly evolved to include breakfast, lunch and dinner.

The atmosphere is casual and comfortable, the food uncomplicated and honest. Breakfast has a loyal following of early risers. Hearty oatmeal and cream, French-style omelettes, crepes with fresh seasonal fruit and "Pie's" own buttermilk waffles with local maple syrup help start their day. Lunchtime guests enjoy fresh soups, salads and specialty sandwiches.

On Friday and Saturday nights, diners can choose from a variety of bistro style entrees including braised lamb shank, roasted chicken, pasta dishes, sole in almond crust, and sautéed trout. In a recent feature in the Showcase section of the Erie Times, "Best of Erie" critics chose Pie in the Sky Cafe for the "Best Fresh Seafood in Erie."

Lucky for us, Carmen still makes her delightful seasonal pies, in addition to tempting treats like bread pudding, crème brulee, cheesecakes and huge cream puffs. They're worth the trip all on their own.

Rob Rub

# Pie in the Sky

**463 West 8TH Street
Erie, Pennsylvania 16502
814 459-8638**

Mark Fainstein

# Porters Restaurant & Tap Room

All aboard for fine dining! Union Station has played a significant role in the lives of many arriving and departing to and from the city of Erie. With the goal of recreating "the way food service was at the height of train travel", two restaurants and formal banquet and meeting facilities are now operating in this historic landmark.

Porters, so named in honor of those dedicated train stewards, features a white tablecloth fine dining restaurant showcasing exquisite French and Mediterranean cuisine, and an incredible international wine list. Whether you choose Classic Lobster Bisque, or Canard a la Madeira as an appetizer, or Roquefort Chicken, Steak au Poivre, or Rack of Lamb as an entree, you have the assurance of meticulous attention to detail.

For more casual gatherings, you can enjoy the sophisticated cuisine of the less formal Tap Room. The 22 ounce Porters Porterhouse Steak, the Pepper Cream Shrimp, and the Veal a la Porter are real whistleblowers. The Tap Room is a great place to conduct business, engineer a friendly get-together or just get on board for some great food and fun.

Porters boasts some of the most elegantly appointed meeting rooms around and the Grand Concourse Ballroom is perfect for weddings and special events.

If you have a special occasion or special guests to entertain, you'll have to travel far to beat Porters.

**123 West 14th Street**
**Erie, Pennsylvania 16501**
**814 452-2787**

nviting, innovative, impressive. Located in the former Engine Company #1 which was built in 1908, Pufferbelly was the nickname given to the steam pumpers and fire engines in the late 1800s. Pufferbelly Restaurant - Erie's French Street Firehouse, is filled with antique fire-fighting artifacts that pay homage to the brave men of the Erie Fire Department. Open for lunch and dinner at 11:30 a.m. daily and Sunday brunch (an Erie favorite) at 11 a.m., owners Mary Ellen and Bruce Hemme offer fine dining in a casual atmosphere and an expansive, full-service bar. Menu selections include Horseradish Encrusted Salmon and Steak Madagascar, along with daily dinner creations by the chef. Signature desserts like Peanut Butter Pie, Bread Pudding, and Chocolate Snowball finish a remarkable dining experience at Pufferbelly Restaurant.

**414 French Street**
**Erie, Pennsylvania 16507**
**814 454-1557**

Rob Rub

# Pufferbelly

Rob Ruby

# Relish

Combing the shores of Lake Erie, sisters Jennifer Reed and Terri Reed-Boyer are in constant pursuit of beach glass - the remains of castaway bottles and jars confronted by nature's fury. But why do these two sibling-owners of Relish, Inc. seek broken pieces of clear and tinted glass? The answer is stunning.

Over time, when glass fragments are relentlessly pounded and polished by surf and sand, they undergo an amazing transformation. For Relish, Inc. the best result is a dazzling translucent gem, perfectly suited for handcrafting into beautiful jewelry.

Since 1996, Jennifer and Terri have combined their love of beach glass with their skills in jewelry-making to create an imaginative collection of rings, necklaces, pendants, earrings and bracelets. Even at a glance, each unique piece expresses an elegant work of art in colorful harmony with nature.

One stop at this funky westside gallery, where artists work their wonders, you will discover the allure of the treasures found along the beaches. But you'll find much more - original framed art, handcrafted woodwork, stained glass, regional books - they are all at Relish on West 12th Street, one block west of Powell Avenue. You can even gaze through a window in the store to watch as artists create their next masterpieces while you enjoy a complimentary cup of their signature blend of "Daughters of a Beach" coffee.

**3835 West 12th Street**
**Erie, Pennsylvania 16505**
**814 836-1827**
**www.relishinc.com**

**V**ery few sunsets in the world can compare to the beauty of our Presque Isle views at dusk. Nina Revetta and Debby Younkin decided on the name Sunset Optics because of the visual pleasure they enjoy from a Presque Isle sunset.

Dedicated to giving their customers the best eye-care and selection of custom eye-care products, Sunset Optics has been serving the Erie Community for the past 20 years.

The Erie community loves businesses that are not chain stores. Sunset Optics is an independently owned and operated business. Nina, Debby, and their staff consider the comfort and satisfaction of their clients first, by means of state of the art technology, choice frame selection, and continued education. After 20 years, they are still excited and are at the cutting edge of the Optical business in the region.

Sunset Optics is the home of LiteLines Eyewear, the ultimate in Rimless eyewear technology. Nina and Debby have developed keen craftsmanship in producing the popular rimless eyewear in their in-store lab for 20 years and they have the largest selection of this timeless eyewear in Erie.

There is so much more to know about Sunset Optics. Come and see...

Rob Rub

# Sunset Optics

**850 Millcreek Mall
Erie, Pennsylvania 16509
814 868-5455
www.sunsetoptics.com**

ob Ruby

# Tom Karle & Son Traditional Clothiers

K now what your customers want and provide it." Simply phrased, it's the longtime creed for success, of well-known Erie clothier, Tom Karle.

Tom knows his customers and he knows his clothes. In fact, knowing his customers is exactly what has given Tom a long and prosperous career as a clothier. Tom started at age 16, modestly, working as a stock boy at a popular local men's store. Embracing a commitment to superior service, he became the proprietor of Tom Karle's Varsity Shop in 1959 and specialized in clothing for young men. Since then, Tom has owned or partnered in several menswear establishments, all of which have been synonymous with much more than quality clothes and tailoring. Each was founded on his personal devotion to customers and their needs. Erie men know that Tom Karle's is the place to buy a new suit or tie and it has been for a long time. One thing is for sure - you will have enjoyed the experience.

Today, a visit to Tom Karle and Son still means experiencing uncommon care and satisfaction. And for Tom, that may be the most important measure of success. Stop in and pay Karle a visit.

**3424 Peach Street
Erie, Pennsylvania 16508
814-864-0525**

Few businesses can stake a claim to the same successful corner location for almost 3 decades. U Frame It was founded in 1975 by Michael and Ginger Mashyna at the corner of West 8th Street and Liberty. Originally a do-it-yourself shop through the 70s and early 80s, the shop now specializes in unique custom framing and expert preservation techniques. In 1988, Phyllis Mashyna and her husband, Matthew Lebowitz, came back to Erie to run the business undertaking a major renovation in 1998, doubling their display space to create room for The Poster Annex, a unique big city poster shop.

Matt Lebowitz is Erie's only Certified Picture Framer, a designation he earned in 1991. Says Lebowitz, "This distinction was created by the Professional Picture Framers Association and is the only proof in this business that any framer knows how to do things properly. Like the doctor's Hippocratic oath, the framer's creed is also 'do no harm', which is sometimes a challenge given the variety of mediums we see each day." U Frame It & The Poster Annex has framed everything from antique photos to antique christening gowns, signed sports jerseys and T-shirts, and all types of artwork.

The co-owners travel back to NYC once a year for a Framing & Art trade show that keeps the couple up-to-date with new materials and techniques, because at U Frame It and The Poster Annex, they know that you either keep moving forward or you get left behind. Innovation happens in framing as in life.

# U Frame It and the Poster Annex

**731 West Eighth**
**Erie, Pennsylvania 16502**
**814 456-1313**

# Walnut Creek Grill

Few buildings in Erie County can boast a history dating back to the 1700s. The Walnut Creek Grill in Fairview is such a place. Originally, the property served as the site of a local tavern. During the American Prohibition of the 1920s, bootleggers used the building for their risky endeavors; eventually the establishment served food in the 1930s. In 1965, The Skyway Tavern continued the tradition until 1995, when Scott Simonsen bought the tavern and dubbed it Walnut Creek Grill, a fine dining restaurant. Nowadays the aromas of fresh herbs and delicacies fill the air. Simonsen, executive chef, offers fresh seafood, pastas, chicken, ribs, and veal. Jack Daniels Salmon, their most popular dish, and certified Black Angus Steaks are served alongside luscious salads and sides. Join a tremendously long list of Erie County residents who have visited this special place to gather with friends, relax and enjoy a fulfilling meal. Open for dinners at 5 p.m. Tuesday through Saturday, Walnut Creek Grill is available for your parties, luncheons, and rehearsal dinners. Reservations are highly recommended for this popular and intimate setting.

**6590 West Lake Road**
**Fairview, Pennsylvania 16415**
**814 474-3304**

Rob Rub

# The Waterfront

John Leonard, owner of the Waterfront Seafood & Steakhouse, watched the bayfront of Erie build up around him. The Bicentennial Tower opened, changing the shape of the dock. His neighbors became the main branch of the Erie County Library and the Maritime Museum. But Leonard didn't just watch this expansion. He's kept up with it by doing some building-up of his own.

Already successful as a fine-dining establishment since 1993, the Waterfront in 2001 added the Miami Grill and the Outrigger Patio Bar to the foot of State Street, making prime real estate accessible to those with more casual tastes. The community responded by making it one of Erie's most popular locations. In addition, there's Waterfront Place, a full-service banquet hall with spectacular views, seating up to 180 people. The continued popularity of all of Leonard's establishments can't be completely attributed to the setting. The menus - heavy on fresh seafood and prime cuts of beef - and the consistently good service keep bringing people back. At the Waterfront Seafood & Steakhouse, patrons seated in style can choose everything from cherrystone clams to Lake Erie Perch to South African Lobster Tails or the finest steak in town.

Watch for future expansions as there is always something new at The Waterfront.

**4 State Street**
**Erie, Pennsylvania 16507**
**814 459-0606**

# Bibliography and Index

## MORE GREAT BOOKS ABOUT ERIE, PENNSYLVANIA....

**Birds of Erie County Pennsylvania Including Presque Isle**
Jean Stull, James A. Stull, Gerald McWilliams.
*Allegheny Press*

**Lore and Legend of the Blue Pike**
editor Alf H. Walle
*Ruth Jageman*

**Erie: A History**
Herbert Reynolds Spencer.

**Erie: Chronicle of a Great Lakes City**
Edward Wellejus.
*Windsor Publications Inc.*

**Erie: Link to the Great Lakes**
Carl B. Lechner.
*Erie County Historical Society Publications*

**Erie History: The Women's Story**
Sabina Shields Freeman, Margaret L. Tenpas.
*Benet Press*

**Erie Reflections**
*Times Publishing Company*

**Go Fish! The Offishial Tale**
Vanessa Weibler Paris.
*Erie Art Museum*

**Great Natural Areas in Western Pennsylvania**
Stephen J. Ostrander.
*Stackpole Books*

**Highlights of Erie Politics**
John G. Carney.
*Manhardt Printing*

**History of Erie County**
John Elmer Reed.
*Topeka: Historical Publishing Co.*

**Home Port Erie: Voices of Silent Images**
Robert J. McDonald and David Frew.
*Erie County Historical Society Publications*

**Images of America: Erie County Pennsylvania**
*Arcadia Publishing*

**Journey From Jerusalem**
Sarah S. Thompson.
*Erie County Historical Society Publications*

**The Lake Erie Quadrangle: Waters of Repose**
Dave Stone and David Frew.
*Erie County Historical Society Publications*

**Lightkeeper's Legacy**
Loretta Brandon.
*Erie County Historical Society Publications*

**Lost Erie: The Vanished Heritage of City and County**
John R. Claridge.
*Erie County Historical Society Publications*

**Presque Isle State Park:
A Scenic Tour of the Peninsula**
Matthew Walkor.
*Matthew D. Walker Publishing*

**Ramblers: The History of Cathedral Prep Football**
Dan Brabender, Jr.
*Meridian Creative Group*

**James E. Sabol**
James E. Sabol.
*Morgenstern & Reilly, Inc.*

**Tales of Old Erie**
John G. Carney.
*Advance Printing and Litho Company*

**A Town at Presque Isle**
Mary Mueller.
*Erie County Historical Society Publications*

*magazine/ newsprint publications*

**The Journal of Erie Studies**
*a product of Erie County Historical Society*

**The Erie Story** *(out of print)*

**Erie Times News**
*a product of Times Publishing Company*

*in production*
**Historic Erie County Illustrated**
Ed Wellejus.
*Historical Publishing Network*

photo illustration from Beata Stark photograph

302

305

Paul M. Lorei